في ذكرى

مارك لينز

Iran's Constitutional Revolution of 1906

Narratives of the Enlightenment

Edited by Ali M Ansari

GINGKO
LIBRARY

First published in Great Britain in 2016 by
Gingko Library
70 Cadogan Place
London SW1X 9AH

ISBN 9781909942-91-2
eISBN 9781909942-94-3

Typeset in Times by MacGuru Ltd

A CIP catalogue record for this book is available from the British Library.

Printed and bound in Spain by Liberdúplex.

www.gingkolibrary.com
@gingkolibrary.com

Contents

Introduction 1
Ali M Ansari

1. **Iran's Dialectic of the Enlightenment: Notes on Constitutional Experience and Conflicting Narratives of Modernity** 15
Ali Gheissari

2. **From Narrating History to Constructing Memory: The Role of Photography in the Iranian Constitutional Revolution** 48
Elahe Helbig

3. **The Enlightenment and Historical Difference: The Case of Iran's Constitutional Revolution** 76
Kamran Matin

4. **Shrinking Borders and Expanding Vocabularies: Translation and the Iranian Constitutional Revolution of 1906** 98
Milad Odabaei

5. **The Iranian Constitutional Revolution and the influence of Mirza Aqa Khan Kermani's Political Thought** 116
Pejman Abdolmohammadi

6. **Realism, Nationalism and Criticism: Iranian Enlightenment and the Philosophy of Literature in Mirza Fatali Akhundzade's Works** 129
Salour Evaz Malayeri

7. "To mean or not to mean?" as the underlying question of Western-inspired counter-Enlightenment discourse in Iran 149
Urs Goesken

8. In Search of the Secret Center in Constitutional Tabriz 170
Evan Siegel

9. Early Translations of Modern European Philosophy. On the Significance of an Under-Researched Phenomenon for the Study of Modern Iranian Intellectual History 200
Roman Seidel

10. Looking Back at Mashrutih: Late Pahlavi Narratives on the Constitutional Revolution 223
Siavush Randjbar-Daemi

Contributors 239
Index 243

Introduction: Developing Iranian Intellectual History

Ali M Ansari

Perhaps the most influential writer on the Constitutional Revolution of Iran was the British Orientalist Edward G. Browne. His 'Persian Revolution', published in 1909 effectively established the narratives that would dominate the historiography of the constitutional movement and the revolution it generated, for decades to come.[1] Browne effectively narrated it as an Iranian awakening – drawing explicit comparisons with the Italian Risorgimento[2] – that had its roots in the Tobacco Boycott of 1891/2, and which, perhaps more interestingly, was emphatically influenced by the intellectual leadership of Jamal al Din Al Afghani, the political iconoclast whom Browne cast as a 'pan-Islamist'. This was another characterisation that would help shape our understanding of both the constitutional movement to say nothing of Afghani himself.[3] Browne's deep affection for the country ensured that when the time came he would seek to not only explain, but in many ways promote, the constitutional movement that had emerged. His engagement with Iranian activists assured him a steady supply of information and some critics, especially in the Foreign Office, wondered aloud whether Browne was associating with undesirable revolutions and, rather than objectively assessing the situation, was allowing his judgment of the events to be unduly swayed. His enthusiasm

1 See: Amanat, A., 'Memory and Amnesia in the Historiography of the Constitutional Revolution', in Atabaki, T. (ed.), *Iran in the Twentieth Century*, London, 2009, p. 24.

2 Browne, E. G., *The Persian Revolution 1905–1909*, Washington DC, 1995, (first published by Cambridge University Press in 1910), p. 2.

3 Browne, *The Persian Revolution*, pp. 1–30.

nonetheless won him many Iranian admirers (an admiration that has barely subsided to this day) and has probably encouraged a less critical reading of a narrative that is, at once, history and political advocacy.[4]

Moreover, as a 'liberal' supporter of the constitutional movement, Browne's account has tended to confound the dominant narratives on imperialism and 'Orientalism' (as redefined by Edward Said in 1978), such that some interpretations have gone further and read into Browne's text a reading that owes more to current social scientific models, and political leanings, rather than the context of Browne's own intellectual milieu. Some of these draw on Browne's text explicitly, others implicitly, to make points about the popularity, nationalist, democratic, and occasionally Islamic nature of the movement. To take the latter example, Browne's emphasis on Al Afghani as a pan-Islamist, suggests to some an acute awareness of the constitutional movement as fundamentally determined by a popular Islamic impulse. But Browne himself qualified what he understands by the term 'pan-Islamic', and makes quite clear at the outset that in seeking to rehabilitate the term and help situate Iran's constitutional revolution within broader developments his domestic audience might better appreciate. At the same time he sought to reassure a readership that that tended to view any such transnational movements with fear and disdain. For Browne, pan-Islamic movements, should not necessarily be seen as any more, or less, fanatical to other movements, and can be a means by which 'national' movements can be energised (a view that probably owed much to Afghani). But even this was influenced by his own appreciation of Islam, which drawn from his own particular intellectual heritage, was arguably more romanticised and indebted to the Enlightenment than many might acknowledge.[5]

It is this 'liberal' Enlightenment context that has at times been both ignored and misunderstood. Browne, and those intellectuals – Iranian and European – with which he engaged, operated within an intellectual environment framed and informed by the ideas of Enlightenment. It is thus important to understand and

4 For an excellent account of Browne's influence see: Bonakdarian, M. 'Edward G Browne and the Iranian Constitutional Struggle: From Academic Orientalism to Political Activism' in *Iranian Studies*, vol. 26, no. 1/2, 1993, pp. 7–31.

5 Ridgeon, L., 'Ahmad Kasravi's Criticisms of Edward Granville Browne', in *Iran* vol, 42, 2004, p 224. Browne's 'mystical' (arguably romantic) reading of Islam, as Deist and Pantheist, implicitly drew a favourable comparison with orthodox Christianity and owed more to Enlightenment ideas about religion. It might also be pointed out that while Browne was a keen advocate for the Babi movement, his interest did not extend to him acknowledging their role in the Constitutional Movement, a role which may might have considered impolitic to highlight. See Amanat's introduction to *The Persian Revolution*, p. XIV & XIX.

contextualise their views within this frame of reference. This has of course subsequently led to problems of its own as critiques of the Enlightenment gathered pace after 1945, which tended to argue that all the ills of radical *nationalism* – most obviously in its promotion of race theory – and imperialism, could be traced to and laid at the door of the Enlightenment.[6]

In this re-reading of the narrative, the Enlightenment gave birth to notions of race, nationalism, and imperialism in Europe, which was soon transported and transplanted, often through the agency of a willing local elite to the non-European world, where these alien ideas obviously failed to take root, and led ultimately to further dislocation and the emergence of nativist movements, which were instinctively 'anti-nationalist' and increasingly beholden to 'authentic' cultural and ideological values often identified around religion. Edward Said was to epitomise this narrative in his eponymous critique of 'Orientalism', but it is also not difficult to see how Browne with his apparent sympathy for pan-Islamism, could be recruited to this narrative. It does not necessarily sit well with Browne's support for the constitutional movement – no narrative, especially those driven by an explicitly ideological template is clean and tidy in its analytical categories – but Browne's apparent support for the 'subaltern' in the Iranian political awakening helps exonerate him from any responsibility in not seeing the flaws of a movement drawn from an inauthentic nationalist ideology, and which, despite its idealism, ultimately resulted in the restoration of autocracy, under the Pahlavis.

At the same time, it is worth acknowledging that the Enlightenment was not a homogenous movement and that Browne engaged with particular *narratives* of the Enlightenment and, like other intellectuals, absorbed, adapted and reproduced these ideas according to his own needs, rationalisation and prejudices. Intellectual history, in short, is neither clean nor tidy, nor does it follow a disciplined template in which one idea clearly leads to another.[7] It is our retrospective analytical conceit – as well of course our need to provide didactic explanation – that seeks to simplify complex processes into neat categories. Browne, for example, is clear in his *Persian Revolution* that ties of faith are a good deal more rational than ties of race.[8] Yet in an earlier exposition, his unfavourable comparison of the Turks

6 A key text in this regard being Horkheimer, M. and Adorno, T., *Dialectic of the Enlightenment*, Stanford, 2002 (first published 1947).

7 For a useful introduction see: Whatmore, R., *What is Intellectual History?*, Cambridge, 2016, pp. 137.

8 Browne, *The Persian Revolution*, p. 1.

against the Iranians could certainly be read as racist[9] while his continued passion and enthusiasm for the Iranians could be viewed as holding them up as a people of innate superior intellect. To quote Browne: 'However grievous their fate and however cruel their destiny, [Iranians were] a chosen people, unique and apart from all other nations'.[10]

Far more interesting in this respect is our interpretation of Afghani, long considered the champion of pan-Islamism and the scourge of imperialism. Yet depending on where you look quite different impressions can be drawn about Afghani's intellectual inheritance and worldview. His debate with the French philosopher Ernest Renan was impressive for its progressive perspective on questions of race and more intriguingly religion, such that many of his more religious followers found this particular text awkward to explain.[11] It is less difficult when one considers that, in reality, Afghani drew many of his ideas from various narratives of the Enlightenment, his awareness of which, drew him the accolades of the salons of both Paris and London. It also undoubtedly helped that he was a Freemason, and a politically active one at that. If this comes as a surprise to those who might view such an association as incompatible with his 'pan-Islamism', it may prove even more problematic that he was, according to some reports, encouraged in his membership by the British vice-consul in Cairo.[12] Indeed this scourge of imperialism appears to have had had a somewhat ambivalent relationship with the British Empire, as a particularly angry article entitled, 'The Reign of terror in Persian' reveals. In this piece Afghani excoriates the British for not living up their ideals and *intervening* in support of Iranian rights:

> What made the Persian believe that England meant to help them? I pray you, did not your Ministers a year or two ago urge upon the Shah a firman granting security of life and property to his subjects. Did not the Shah issue such a firman, and, after considerable pressure and long debate and hesitation, frankly communicate to the Powers? Did not her Majesty [Queen Victoria] upon hearing this express to Malcom [*sic*] Khan her

9 Browne, E., *A Year among the Persians*, London, 1893, p. 109.

10 Quoted in Bonakdarian, 'Edward G Browne', p. 22.

11 Afghani, Sayyid Jamal al-Din, 'Answer of Jamal al Din to Renan', in *Journal des Debats* May 18, 1883, reprinted in: Keddie, N. (ed.), *An Islamic Response to Imperialism*, Los Angeles, pp. 181–87.

12 Albert Kudsi-Zadeh, A., 'Afghani and Freemasonry in Egypt', in *Journal of the American Oriental Society*, vol. 92, no. 1, pp. 27–28.

> profound satisfaction, and was not your Minister at Teheran regarded as a party to the transaction? All Persians believed that a firman thus issued and *communicated* to the European Powers gave the Powers, England first and foremost, the diplomatic right to insist upon its due observance, or at least to demand the explanation for any gross violation of it. Well, what followed? I, Sheikh Djemal ed Din, soon after became the natural and respectful mouthpiece of the people's joyful aspirations. I am received with favour by His Majesty, my words are approved, the regeneration of Persia is at hand; law is to be given, life and property are to be safe, our wives and daughters protected from outrage, our bread winners from cruel and ruinous exactions – all is going well. Suddenly I am seized, banished, imprisoned: my friends were imprisoned and tortured, without explanation, without trial… the peoples eyes were opened; they felt they could place no reliance on the Shah…But their eyes were then to the Powers, to England first and foremost. Now would the British minister, at least, certainly speak on little word at Teheran, if only to ask for some explanation of so gross a violation of the blessed firman. But no not a word![13]

Few passages express so clearly the complex relationship between Iranian intellectuals and their Western – in this case specifically British – interlocutors. Moreover, the piece was reproduced in a British journal *The Contemporary Review*, with an enthusiastic endorsement. It reinforces what a number of historians have more recently sought to articulate and introduce into the debate: that the intellectual dialogue between Iran and the West was more subtle and reciprocal than earlier studies may have suggested, and that the engagement – as even Browne's study shows – approximated more towards a dialectical exchange where each side drew on and interpreted, for their own intellectual audience, the ideas of the other.[14] This question of interpretation is crucial, not only in the way in which

13 Afghani, Sayyid Jamal al-Din, 'The Reign of Terror in Persia', in *The Contemporary Review*, LXI, 1892, pp. 238–48, reprinted in Ridgeon, L. (ed.), *Religion and Politics in Modern Iran*, London, 2005, p. 12.

14 These important works include: Bonakdarian, M., *Britain and the Constitutional Revolution of 1906–1911: Foreign Policy, Imperialism and Dissent*, New York, 2006; Chehabi, H. and Martin, V. (eds.), *Iran's Constitutional Revolution: Popular Politics, Cultural Transformations and Transnational Connections,* London, 2010, p. 504; Gheissari, A., *Iranian Intellectuals in the twentieth century*, Austin, 1997, p. 268; Amanat A. and Vejdani F. (eds.), *Iran Facing Others*, New York, 2012, p. 292; Bonakdarian, M., 'The Persia Committee and the Constitutional Revolution in Iran', in *The British Journal of Middle Eastern Studies*, vol. 18, no. 2, 1991, pp. 186–207; Ekhtiar,

we, from our modern perspective, reach back to understand the particular vocabulary of the past but also how they interpreted these terms and ideas, not only cross culturally but historically. It is worth bearing in mind for example that nineteenth-century intellectuals were themselves inheriting a lexicon from the past that was not fixed but fluid. All this ensures that not only do we look at the inheritance from the Enlightenment, but question the parameters of that Enlightenment, or more accurately, look at the various *narratives* that were on offer.

Matters are complicated further by the realities of Iranian historiography and historical writing through this formative period. If historical writing was changing in Europe from the preserve of gentleman amateurs to professional historians, newly equipped with the tools of their trade, and an acute awareness of the importance of sources and the need for diligent and precise referencing, this skill set took time to transfer into the Iranian world, where the concept of referencing was frequently viewed as offensive.[15] Indeed well into the contemporary period it is often difficult to convince writers to reference their works with the consequence that any work of intellectual history that seeks to provide some sort of credible genealogy of thought faces serious obstacles. All the more so because in the earlier period, and certainly in the nineteenth century, there are few, if any, bibliographical lists and we are faced with reconstructing what we think would have been available and would have been read, whether the material would have been read in translation, and if so how that translation mediated the language being used. As Seidel in his chapter [Early Translations of Modern European philosophy] shows, in the nineteenth century there was a relative paucity in resources not helped by the limitations of the legacy itself which left little clue as to the inheritance. We know for example that many intellectuals acquired a knowledge of French and Russian (in addition to a knowledge of Ottoman Turkish and Arabic), few would have initially at least, been fluent in English.[16] How this affected their acquisition

M., 'An Encounter with the Russian Czar: The Image of Peter the Great in Early Qajar Historical Writings', in *Iranian Studies*, 29(1/2), 1996, pp. 57–70; Masroori, C., 'European Thought in Nineteenth-Century Iran: David Hume and Others', in *The Journal of the History of Ideas*, vol. 61, no. 4, 2000, pp. 657–674; Sanjabi, M. B., 'Rereading the Enlightenment: Akhundzada and his Voltaire', in *Iranian Studies*, 2010, vol. 28, no. 1/2, pp. 39–60.

15 '…excessive display of learning could only impair, not enhance, the moral and pragmatic impact of a history. Gentlemen must write as they rode – with great skill but no apparent effort. In the seventeenth and eighteenth century Republic of Letters. Bayle's and Gibbon's footnotes could win them a reputation for both impudence and erudition.' Grafton, A., *The Footnote: A Curious History*, Cambridge, Massachusetts, 1997, pp. 225–226

16 A good example in this regard is Taqizadeh's autobiography which remains tantalisingly brief

of knowledge, and narratives of the Enlightenment remains, as yet, difficult to ascertain and if, for example as we know, a rich flow of intellectual traffic came via Russia, to what extent did Russian intellectualism affect the interpretation and transmission of those texts?

Moreover, European texts aside, it is still unclear to what extent these Iranian intellectuals communicated with each other, had access to original material (as opposed to hearsay), and how selective this may have been. Until publishing became more systematic and widespread in Iran the level of internal communication is not clear and to take but one example from the 1920s, Taqizadeh's controversial call to arms about the adoption of European civilisation which was first articulated in the newspaper *Kaveh*, it is clear that a number of later critics did not have access to the original text.[17]

Consequently any re-creation of the intellectual environment is a very real exercise in the 'archaeology' of knowledge. Given the paucity of material, and even the occasional tendency of some Iranian writers to invent sources to further their cause the student of Iranian intellectual history is required to reconstruct the intellectual frame of reference, brick-by-brick, drawing on common references and extrapolating, within reason, from the clues left to us.[18] Paradoxically, a window into this particular milieu might be provided by one of the very facts that serves to disguise this dynamic, and this is the persistence of secret societies and organisations, most obviously the Freemasons (Seigel provides an interesting insight into one of these in the city of Tabriz in this volume [In Search of the Secret Center in Constitutional Tabriz]). Membership of the Masons, by its very nature remained clouded in secrecy, not helped by the subsequent association of the Masons with foreign conspiracies of all varieties resulting in further obfuscation by members (to say nothing of the abrupt discrediting of important intellectuals known to be Masons such as Mohammad Ali Foroughi).[19] We now know for example that

on his education, providing the reader with only the broadest of brushstrokes, Taqizadeh, H., *Zendegi-ye Tufani*, Tehran, 1990, p. 421.

17 See for example: Aryanpur Y., *Az Saba ta Nima* (From Saba till Nima), Tehran 1350, p. 232. Another critic was Ahmad Kasravi, whose dislike of referencing makes it unclear whether he had access to the original text.

18 It is worth bearing in mind that published collections of papers and reissues of books have come relatively late and it largely down to the Herculean efforts of Iraj Afshar that Iranian students of intellectual history have a comprehensive corpus of material to work with by the end of the twentieth-century.

19 Foroughi is interestingly enjoying something of a renaissance in Iran, see the special issue of *Andisheye Puya*, 31, Azar/Dey 1394, (2015) dedicated to his life and thought and entitled, 'the patient liberal'.

almost every leader of the Constitutional Revolution belonged to a single lodge in Tehran, and even if this lodge enjoyed a tenuous relationship with European lodges, it is clear that some sort of intellectual relationship existed.[20] Taqizadeh, while he demurred in later life about his association, is generally accepted to have been one such member, but more than that, two important influences on his own intellectual development, Malkom Khan and Jamal al Din al Afghani, were both known in the very least, to have sympathies in that direction (Afghani perhaps more formally than Malkom Khan whose famed 'faramush-khaneh'[21] appears to have been an attempt to imitate the Masonic movement).[22] In a similar vein we are now more aware of the role of adherents of the Babi movement whose iconoclasm created further space for new 'provocative' ideas to flourish.[23]

This of course begs the question of what the Masons at this time represented and, given their secrecy, how we could know? We do know, for example from Afghani's own experience, that lodges tended to operate according to their own political parameters – some were more radical and/or active than others, and Afghani's apparent decision to move and indeed found his own lodge was dictated in part by his unhappiness with the political passivity of the Egyptian lodge he had originally joined. Assessing the operation of lodges within Europe, especially in the eighteenth and early-nineteenth century, when the first Iranians would have become acquainted with Freemasonry, there is evidence of their political radicalness, liberal attitude towards politics and society, and determination to challenge the orthodoxies of the day. Its belief in progress through the application of reason and the dissemination of education could perhaps best be described as a form of radical Whiggism,[24] in the British conception of the term, and this central idea that mankind could and should improve itself and was not

---

20 Bayat, M., 'The Rowshanfekr in the Constitutional period', in Chehabi and Martin, *Iran's Constitutional Revolution,* p. 179.

21 This term, literally, 'House of Forgetfulness' has been interpreted by some to suggest the conspiratorial nature of Malkom Khan's enterprise. It could of course simply imply the confidentiality of the gatherings and to remind participants not to divulge information about the meetings.

22 Malkom Khan and Talabof are specified in his autobiography: Taqizadeh, *Zendegi-ye Tufani*, p. 26. He wrote widely and admired Afghani, Taqizadeh, H., 'Seyyed Jamal al Din ma'roof be afghani', in Afshar, I. (ed.), *Maqallat-e Taqizadeh*, vol. 2, (Tehran, *Bist-o panjum-e sharivar*, 1350/1972), pp. 75–83.

23 see note 5 above.

24 See: Jacob, M., *The Radical Enlightenment: Pantheists, Freemasons and Republicans*, Louisiana, 2006 (first published 1981), especially pp. 80–111.

fated to suffer a miserable existence, was one that was to gain considerable traction in the minds of Iranian intellectuals. It offered a clear route out of the malaise and committed no one to an existence from which they could not liberate themselves.

This radical Whiggism offered, in short, a highly attractive – and in its divorce from any specific religion – a remarkably transferable, myth of *emancipation* and *salvation*. In its British manifestation at least, it did not denigrate religion, but eschewed and condemned superstition; it demanded a belief in a creator, but did not insist on an acknowledgement of the Christian Trinity (an important distinction for those members from the Islamic world), and in its promotion of the idea of an international brotherhood of man, it projected a humanism that was both cosmopolitan and inclusive. Beyond the individual, the building blocks of the nation if you will, these ideas encouraged the belief in the rule of law, constitutionalism and a specifically civic nationalism defined by rights and responsibilities, and *not* beholden to race. It is difficult not to see the influence of some of these ideas in the writings of individuals such as Afghani, Taqizadeh and indeed Foroughi.

But it is likewise worth bearing in mind that this was a particular narrative of the Enlightenment which contested and competed with other readings and while those proponents of such ideas sought a cosmopolitan, one might even say, unitary vision, the reality of course more complex and subject to interpretation. While it is counter-intuitive to argue for 'national' enlightenments (although nationalists do not tire of making the attempt), differing experiences did lead to different readings and definitions of terms. It is clear for example that by the end of the nineteenth century, in part perhaps as a reflection of the dominance of European power, that cosmopolitanism gave way to a more racially delimited view of civilisation and progress and that these views were more entrenched (though by no means limited to) the European continent, and for example the southern States of the United States. As racial theories crystallised, it becomes clear that the concept of race itself, along with ideas such as 'ethnicity' were redefined and tied to biological parameters. Nonetheless, it is worth remembering for example that the term 'ethnick' in its early usage tended to relate to a mentality rather than a biological distinction,[25] and if such terms did become effectively identified with race in its biological sense (as opposed to kinship or wider consanguinity), not

25 Kidd, C., 'Ethnicity in the British Atlantic World, 1688–1830', in Wilson K. (ed.), 'A New Imperial History: Culture, Identity and Modernity in Britain and the Empire, 1660–1840', Cambridge, 2004, p. 261.

all users would have been aware of the new distinction, agreed with it or indeed applied it.[26]

A similar problem confronts us with the use of the term 'civilisation', that acquisition of which in the Iranian world appears to be largely drawn from English, and perhaps early French usage, but not German, where the term, especially after 1919 (following the Great War 'for civilisation'), German intellectuals sought to effectively replace with the term 'culture'. In English usage the term civilisation, while contrasted with barbarism, and later savagery, was much more neutral in its application than later readings suggest. It simply defined descent from Greco-Roman civilisation and, while this had distinct qualities to it, the 'barbarism' of the Germanic tribes that overthrew the empire also had its uses. Above all civilisation was regarded as a process to be acquired and developed through manners and education, and as Gibbon argued in his *Decline and Fall*, civilisation could indeed rise and fall. Moreover, as even Gibbon accepted, civilisation was not a preserve of the West or the Europeans. For the Germans, 'culture' and the cultivation of culture took on this more didactic meaning, while civilisation, while undoubtedly of value, was both superficial and by extension of secondary importance.[27]

The narratives of the Enlightenment are therefore many and varied. If we choose to argue about an intellectual inheritance we need to have some understanding of the intellectual environment in all its diversity. As well as the means and ways in which these ideas were absorbed, interpreted and reproduced for particular audiences. The collection of essays in this volume attempt to contribute to this wider debate in the developing field of Iranian intellectual history, drawing on different perspectives, specific writers and particular themes. Seidel, as noted above, looks at the broader canvas of intellectual appropriation by analysing the nineteenth-century environment for the translation of European philosophical texts, before Mohammad Ali Foroughi's comprehensive introduction and review of European philosophy in the twentieth century, drawing attention to the relative paucity of translations and it implications for engagement. Gheissari, one of the pioneers of Iranian intellectual history assesses the broader engagement with ideas of modernity and modernisation, while Matin takes an unabashedly Marxian approach to the encounter between Iran's constitutionalists and the narratives of the Enlightenment, in particular those

26 See in this respect: Barkan E., 'Race and the Social Sciences', in Porter T. M. and Ross D. (eds.), *The Cambridge History of Science: The Modern Social Sciences*, vol. 7, Cambridge, 2003, pp. 693–707.

27 See: Elias, N., *The Civilising Process*, London, 2000 (first published in 1939), pp. 5–30. On the distinctive use in French see pp. 30–43

readings that seek to define it as a 'bourgeois revolution'. Goesken looks at the way later twentieth-century thinkers challenged the Enlightenment inheritance with a 'counter-enlightenment' – itself of course influenced by similar movements within Europe – a long view continued by Randjbar-Daemi in his analysis of late Pahlavi narratives on the Constitutional Revolution.

Seigel looks at the mechanics of intellectual acquisition with a closer look at the secret societies that operated in Tabriz with all the problems for historiography that this implies, effectively seeking to piece together the influence of the society from the limited evidence that is available. The lens narrows further with Odabaei and Seidel. Odabaei takes a critical and vitally important look at the way in which ideas and vocabulary were translated into Persian, while Helbig provides a fascinating insight into how memory was constructed through the relatively widespread application of the modern medium of photography.

Abdolmohammadi and Malayeri look at specific aspects of the political thought of Kermani and Akhundzadeh, key thinkers in the appropriation of European thought, initially brought to public attention through the intellectual biographies written by Fereydoun Adamiyat, but whose influence on their immediate intellectual successors is probably more difficult to ascertain. Adamiyat may be considered the father of Iranian intellectual history, applying a discipline and method towards his studies that were unprecedented within an Iranian context, even if, as critics have rightly pointed out, he was not able to free himself of the many biases of which he liberally accused others.[28]

Adamiyat is a useful reminder of the complexity of the Enlightenment inheritance, at once rigorous and empowered with the tools of a new discipline for the acquisition of knowledge. Yet at the same time flawed and dangerously vulnerable to the very tendencies the radical Enlightenment sought to consign to pre-modern superstition. Adamiyat was not alone, and kept company with some of the luminaries of Western thought, in harbouring ideas which contradicted the philosophy he sought to impart.[29] But the key point in seeking to understand trends in

28 For a critical assessment of Adamiyat's contribution to Iranian historiography, see Chehabi, H., 'The Paranoid Style in Iranian historiography', in Atabaki, T., *Iran in the 20th Century: Historiography and political culture*, London, 2009, pp. 162–164. See also: Bast, O., *Occidentalism and Historiography in Modern Iran: Fereydoun Adamiyat, one of 20th century Iran's foremost historians and his assessment of the rise of National Socialism and the Fall of the Weimar Republic*, LIV.I, Iran, 2016, pp. 73–98.

29 See for example: Adamiyat, F., (transl. by Ricks, T. M.), 'Problems in Iranian Historiography' *Iranian Studies*, vol. 4, no. 4, 1971, pp. 132–156.

intellectual history is not to reduce, simplify or identify individuals outside the complex inheritance and dialectical process which they inhabit but to appreciate and understand this *process* of development and to recognise that contradictions are often part of this process and arguably progress of intellectual growth.[30] For the historian, to paraphrase Max Weber, the purpose should not be to confirm or condemn the narratives of the Enlightenment but to recognise that if our investigation, 'does not serve as the preparation, but as the conclusion of an investigation, accomplishes equally little in the interest of historical truth'.[31]

30 See for example: Matin-Asgari, A. on Taqizadeh and the question of 'Orientalism' in his 'The Berlin Circle: Iranian Nationalism meets German Countermodernity', in Aghaie, K. S. and Marashi, A. (eds), *Rethinking Iranian Nationalism and Modernity*, Austin, 2014, p. 57.

31 Weber, M., *The Protestant Ethic and the Spirit of capitalism*, London, 1992 (first published 1930), p. 183.

Bibliography

Adamiyat, F., (transl. by Ricks, T. M.), 'Problems in Iranian Historiography' *Iranian Studies*, vol. 4, no. 4, 1971, pp. 132–156.

Afghani, Sayyid Jamal al-Din, 'Answer of Jamal al Din to Renan', in *Journal des Debats* May 18, 1883, reprinted in: Keddie, N. (ed.), *An Islamic Response to Imperialism*, Los Angeles, pp. 181–87.

Afghani, Sayyid Jamal al-Din, 'The Reign of Terror in Persia', in *The Contemporary Review*, LXI, 1892, pp. 238–48, reprinted in Ridgeon, L. (ed.), *Religion and Politics in Modern Iran*, London, 2005.

Albert Kudsi-Zadeh, A., 'Afghani and Freemasonry in Egypt', in *Journal of the American Oriental Society,* vol. 92, no. 1, pp. 25–35.

Amanat A. and Vejdani F. (eds.), *Iran Facing Others*, New York, 2012.

Amanat, A., 'Memory and Amnesia in the Historiography of the Constitutional Revolution', in Atabaki, T. (ed.), *Iran in the Twentieth Century*, London, 2009.

Aryanpur Y., *Az Saba ta Nima* (From Saba till Nima), Tehran 1350.

Barkan E., 'Race and the Social Sciences', in Porter T. M. and Ross D. (eds.), *The Cambridge History of Science: The Modern Social Sciences*, vol. 7, Cambridge, 2003.

Bast, O., *Occidentalism and Historiography in Modern Iran: Fereydoun Adamiyat, one of 20th century Iran's foremost historians and his assessment of the rise of National Socialism and the Fall of the Weimar Republic*, LIV.I, Iran, 2016.

Bayat, M., 'The Rowshanfekr in the Constitutional period', in Chehabi, H. and Martin, V. (eds.), *Iran's Constitutional Revolution: Popular Politics, Cultural Transformations and Transnational Connections,* London, 2010.

Bonakdarian, M. 'Edward G Browne and the Iranian Constitutional Struggle: From Academic Orientalism to Political Activism' in *Iranian Studies*, vol. 26, no. 1/2, 1993, pp. 7–31.

Bonakdarian, M., 'The Persia Committee and the Constitutional Revolution in Iran', in *The British Journal of Middle Eastern Studies*, vol. 18, no. 2, 1991, pp. 186–287.

Bonakdarian, M., *Britain and the Constitutional Revolution of 1906–1911: Foreign Policy, Imperialism and Dissent*, New York, 2006.

Browne, E. G., *The Persian Revolution 1905–1909*, Washington DC, 1995, (first published by Cambridge University Press in 1910).

Browne, E., *A Year among the Persians*, London, 1893.

Chehabi, H. and Martin, V. (eds.), *Iran's Constitutional Revolution: Popular Politics, Cultural Transformations and Transnational Connections,* London, 2010.

Chehabi, H., 'The Paranoid Style in Iranian historiography', in Atabaki, T., *Iran in the 20th Century: Historiography and political culture*, London, 2009.

Ekhtiar, M., 'An Encounter with the Russian Czar: The Image of Peter the Great in Early Qajar Historical Writings', in *Iranian Studies*, 29(1/2), 1996, pp. 57–70.

Elias, N., *The Civilising Process*, London, Blackwell, 2000 (first published in 1939).

Gheissari, A., *Iranian Intellectuals in the twentieth century*, Austin, 1997.

Horkheimer, M. and Adorno, T., *Dialectic of the Enlightenment*, Stanford, 2002 (first published 1947).

Jacob, M., *The Radical Enlightenment: Pantheists, Freemasons and Republicans*, Louisiana, 2006 (first published 1981).

Kidd, C., 'Ethnicity in the British Atlantic World, 1688–1830', in Wilson K. (ed.), 'A New Imperial History: Culture, Identity and Modernity in Britain and the Empire, 1660–1840', Cambridge, 2004.

Masroori, C., 'European Thought in Nineteenth-Century Iran: David Hume and Others', in *The Journal of the History of Ideas*, vol. 61, no. 4, 2000, pp. 657–674.

Matin-Asgari, A., 'The Berlin Circle: Iranian Nationalism meets German Countermodernity', in Aghaie, K. S. and Marashi, A. (eds), *Rethinking Iranian Nationalism and Modernity*, Austin, 2014.

Ridgeon, L., 'Ahmad Kasravi's Criticisms of Edward Granville Browne', in *Iran* vol, 42, 2004, pp. 219–233.

Sanjabi, M. B., 'Rereading the Enlightenment: Akhundzada and his Voltaire', in *Iranian Studies*, 2010, vol. 28, no. 1/2, pp. 39–60.

Taqizadeh, H., 'Seyyed Jamal al Din ma'roof be afghani', in Afshar, I. (ed.), *Maqallat-e Taqizadeh*, vol. 2, (Tehran, *Bist-o panjum-e sharivar*, 1350/1972), pp. 75–83.

Taqizadeh, H., *Zendegi-ye Tufani*, Tehran, 1990.

Weber, M., *The Protestant Ethic and the Spirit of capitalism*, London, 1992 (first published 1930).

Whatmore, R., *What is Intellectual History?*, Cambridge, 2016.

1

Iran's Dialectic of the Enlightenment: Constitutional Experience, Transregional Connections, and Conflicting Narratives of Modernity[1]

Ali Gheissari

Iran's Constitutional Revolution of 1906 aimed at changing the structure of the monarchy from despotic to constitutional and to adopt representative governance by introducing the country to a parliamentary system. It further resulted in a written constitution in which a separation between different branches of government was recognised. Intellectually, however, it drew on a diverse range of ideas and orientations that in good measure were associated with the Enlightenment – either directly from European sources or, more regularly, through elaborate routes of transregional contacts, notably from India, the Ottoman Empire, and the Caucasus.

By drawing on a select range of primary and secondary source material, this paper examines the intellectual encounter of Iran's constitutional movement with various types of Enlightenment ideas and the general intellectual debates and textual production of that period in areas such as representative governance and the rule of law. Such diverse trends, for instance, can be seen in terms of combining liberal as well as étatiste approaches in the composition of the constitutional laws and subsequent interpretations of constitutional principles and methods of implementation.

Further complexities of Iran's constitutional experience can also be noted in terms of the impact of Shi'ism on the one hand and prerogatives of autocratic state on the other – as in, for example, the articulation of Iran's civil code and the subsequent range of procedural laws that were adopted in the 1920s and 1930s. In both of these domains Iran's constitutional experience included an underlying religious element in its conceptualization of popular sovereignty, and thus the ideal of a constitutional governance emerged with a strong religious component and emphasis on the rule of law rather than demand for liberty. By juxtaposing such divergent trends the paper also elucidates the broad range of intellectual imports of the Enlightenment and their impact on Iran's political and intellectual landscape during the constitutional period and beyond.

---

1 An earlier version of this essay was presented at the conference on 'Iran's Constitutional Revolution of 1906 and the Narratives of the Enlightenment', organised by Gingko Library and the British Institute of Persian Studies, at the British Academy, London, 15 September 2015. My thanks are due to the conference organisers for their hospitality and to participants for their fruitful discussions. I am also grateful to Ali Ansari, Mohsen Ashtiany, Mansour Bonakdarian, Rasool Jafarian, Ranin Kazemi, and Vanessa Martin for providing me with valuable comments, and to Matthew Eastwood for editorial assistance. However, the responsibility for all shortcomings is entirely mine.

The main argument in *Dialectic of Enlightenment*, an influential book that was first published in 1944, co-authored by German critical social theorists, Max Horkheimer and Theodor Adorno, was to show how in the course of its historical development under capitalism, a fundamental premise of the European Enlightenment turned into its opposite – that is, to show how the Enlightenment idea of man's ability and right to dominate nature gave way to the idea and the practice of domination of man over man.[2] Accordingly, various forms of totalitarian and autocratic regimes that appeared in the twentieth century were, in fact, the manifestations of how the Enlightenment ideas of individualism, universalism, and liberty gave way to their opposites.[3]

---

2 Horkheimer, M. and Adorno, T. W., *Dialektik der Aufklärung*, first published in 1944, revised version, Amesterdam, 1947; also in English by John Cumming, J. (transl.) as *Dialectic of Enlightenment*, New York, 1972; new edition by Noerr, G., S. (ed.) and Edmund Jephcott, E. (transl.), as *Dialectic of Enlightenment: Philosophical Fragments*, Stanford, CA, 2002 (transl. from Vol. 5 of Horkheimer, M., *Gesammelte Schriften: Dialektik der Aufklärung und Schriften 1940–1950*, (ed. by Noerr, G., S.), Frankfurt, 1987). By focusing on its totalising, totalitarian, and universalist modalities, these theorists were also generalising the historical progression of the Enlightenment principles. However, regardless of their analytical shortcomings, they represented the self-reflective and anti-authoritarian principles of the Enlightenment – as such, this juxtaposition reflects the interplay between the universalist versus particularist tendencies of the Enlightenment, which could just as easily give rise to hierarchical, racist, capitalist, and imperialist platforms in the name of collective and/or individual rights and disinterested scientific objectivity, as well as to opposing platforms that ranged from Karl Marx's (1818–1883) own totalizing vision of history and universal human liberation to anarchist and other comparable platforms.

3 Here the notion of 'individual' is taken in the broad sense, including individual with respect to rights as well as duties, as the notion is understood in constitutional political theory formulated by, for example, John Locke (1632–1704); and also individual as 'subject' in the sense of it being simultaneously susceptible to two divergent possibilities – i.e. of being empowered by autonomy as well as of being prone to heteronomy. These two defining perspectives have been examined in considerable theoretical extent by, for example, Immanuel Kant (1724–1804) and Michel Foucault (1926–1984), respectively. See, Kant, I., '*Beantwortung der Frage: Was ist Aufklärung?*' (originally published 1784) available online: http://www.allmendeberlin.de/What-is-Enlightenment.pdf , English edition: 'Answering the Question: What is Enlightenment?', (transl. by Smith, M. C.), available online: http://www.columbia.edu/acis/ets/CCREAD/etscc/kant.html ; Kant, I., 'An Answer to the Question: What is Enlightenment?', in Gregor, M. J. (ed.), *The Cambridge Edition of the Works of Immanuel Kant: Practical Philosophy*, Cambridge, 1996, pp. 11–22; Foucault, M., '*Qu'est-ce que les Lumières?*' (originally published 1984) available in English: 'What is Enlightenment?', in Rabinow, P. (ed.), *The Foucault Reader*, New York, 1984, pp. 32–50, also available online: http://foucault.info/documents/whatIsEnlightenment/foucault.whatIsEnlightenment.en.html.

Within the broader context of modern European intellectual history there has been a diverse

In Iran such divergent approaches were further marked by random and unsystematic familiarity of Iranian writers with European sources as well as by Iran's own heterogeneous social makeup, intellectual background, and historical experience. Iranians' reading of the European material was also impacted by two distinct yet interrelated factors, namely, the tradition of reacting to domestic autocracy, a tendency with certain similarities to the teachings of the eighteenth-century French Enlightenment as well as the example of the nineteenth century British parliamentary system, and the ideological consequences of Iran's semi-colonial situation, which was specific to Iran – although Iran was never directly colonised, it was affected by imperial politics and economic incursions during the Qajar period (1785–1925). Opposition to autocracy and resistance to imperialist advances gradually assumed a nationalist form in some elite and non-elite circles – for instance, it was experienced firsthand by segments of the merchant classes, intellectuals, some members of the clergy, and also by some covertly dissenting members of the political elite. In particular such opposition and resistance were aroused by concessions granted to foreign interests and capitulations to foreign states. Domestically, however, opposition to local or central authorities was often expressed in measures such as seeking individual justice out of grievance (*tazallom*), and resorting to the normative paradigm of '*circle of justice*.'[4]

---

reception of Enlightenment ideas at times leading to different political and ideological trajectories – such as different interpretations regarding the writings of, for example, Jean-Jacques Rousseau (1712–1778) or G. W. F. Hegel (1770–1831), or of earlier thinkers such as Thomas Hobbes (1588–1679), that often led to individualist or collectivist, conservative or critical, perspectives. For assessments on ideologically diverse readings of Hobbes, Rousseau, and Hegel see, respectively, Macpherson, C. B., *The Political Theory of Possessive Individualism: Hobbes to Locke*, Oxford, 1962, (reprinted 2011); Lauritsen H. R., and Thorup, M. (eds.), 'Rousseau and Revolution', *Continuum Studies in Political Philosophy Series,* London & New York, 2011; Marcuse, H., *Reason and Revolution: Hegel and the Rise of Social Theory*, New York, 1999. See further, Althusser, L., *Politics and History: Montesquieu, Rousseau, Marx* (transl. by Ben Brewster), London, 2007.

4 For *tazallom* and *circle of justice* traditions in nineteenth-century Iran, see Sohrabi, N., 'Revolution and State Culture: The Circle of Justice and Constitutionalism in 19th-Century Iran', in Steinmetz, G.(ed.), *State/Culture: State-Formation after the Colonial Turn*, London, 1999, pp. 253–288; Sohrabi, N., *Revolution and Constitutionalism in the Ottoman Empire and Iran*, Cambridge, 2011, pp. 293–299; Perry, J. R., 'Justice for the Underprivileged: The Ombudsman Tradition of Iran', in *Journal of Near Eastern Studies*, no. 37, 1978, pp. 203–215; Schneider, I., *The Petitioning System in Iran: State, Society and Power Relations in the Late 19th Century*, Wiesbaden, 2006. For a general study in the wider Middle Eastern context, see Darling, L. T., *History of Social Justice and Political Power in the Middle East: The Circle of Justice from Mesopotamia to Globalization*, London, 2012.

Seeking a solution to both domestic autocracy and the semi-colonial situation, was a central concern of Iran's constitutional movement that was later articulated in the text of the Constitution (1906) and its Supplement (1907).[5] During the late-nineteenth and early-twentieth centuries these concerns also provided a window for the reception of counter-Enlightenment ideas, such as romanticism, socialism, and anarchism, that were, by and large, Western in origin – although it ought to be noted that it was not always an either/or situation, as Iranians often selectively combined Enlightenment and 'counter'-Enlightenment thoughts in ways that conformed to their perceived and desired sense of personal, social, religious-cultural, and national identities and overall objectives. They also gave way to the development of anti-Enlightenment ideas by Iranians, such as Islamic attempts to provide either a synthesis, and accommodation with, or a dismissal of Western ideas or, as was more often the case, reaching at a limited incorporation of Englighten-ment ideas and other facets of modernities in general – as can be seen in, for example, some of the writings of Mo'ayyed al-Islam Kāshāni and Sayyed Jamāl al-Din (al-Afghāni), among others.[6] Indeed both of these figures were modernising

5 Browne, E. G., *A Brief Narrative of Recent Events in Persia followed by a translation of 'The Four Pillars of the Persian Constitution'*, London, 1909; Browne, E. G., 'Appendix A: The Bases of the Persian Constitution', in *The Persian Revolution of 1905–1909*, Washington, DC, 1995, pp. 351–400 (Available online through the Foundation for Iranian Studies: 'Iran's 1906 Constitution and its Supplement', http://fis-iran.org/en/resources/legaldoc/iranconstitution). See further: Arjomand, S., A., 'Constitutional Revolution III. The Constitution', in *Encyclopaedia Iranica*, vol. VI, fasc. 2, 1992, pp. 187–192, (available online: http://www.iranicaonline.org/articles/constitutional-revolution-iii).

6 Sayyed Jalāl al-Din Mo'ayyed al-Islam Kāshāni (1863–1930) was the editor of the influential periodical *Habl al-Matin* that he published in Calcutta, India (1893–1930). In turn, he could have been influenced by the pragmatist ideas of Sir Syed Ahmad Khan (1817–1898) who, in late nineteenth-century British India, was an influential advocate of accommodation between Islamic and Western traditions, mostly on political and juristic coexistence. Sayyed Jamāl al-Din (al-Afghāni) (c.1838–1897), on the other hand, was an influential Muslim activist, ideologue, and agitator, and although he was a Freemason and his polemics certainly showed some adherence to the ideas of the Enlightenment, his public profile moved increasingly towards rejecting accommodation with the West and advocating 'Muslim Unity' instead. It should further be noted that in al-Afghāni's case, given the existing conditions of Iran in that time period and the general conservative attitudes that existed in the country, in occasions he also advocated modern educational reforms, some measure of religious tolerance, and greater rights for women. These latter tendencies, however, were certainly indicative of his receptivity toward Enlightenment influences. Also, in al-Afghāni's case, it was not just living in British-administered India that shaped his views, but similar to many other Iranian reformists at the time, he too was enamored

reformers, defending certain key Enlightenment ideas (such as popular sovereignty) and many features of 'modernity,' but at the same time rejecting the notion that one had to uncritically imitate the West as the sole proprietor of modernity. In Iran of the early twentieth century there were a number of debates over the ideas and teachings that were associated with the Enlightenment, but such arguments, although carrying over some basic tenets of the Enlightenment, treaded on a different path that was just as dialectical but differed with its European counterpart in philosophical substance and political scope.

Iran and the Enlightenment

There is a shared, yet seldom clearly substantiated, opinion among various authors and commentators, that 'sources of the self' in modern Iran often consist of a mixture of loosely perceived concepts and values that involve nationalism (or more generally, themes and values associated with the so-called 'idea of Iran' and the power of Persian language), Shiʿism (in its outward as well as inward dimensions), and a combination of modern European or Western ideas and divergent trends that stemmed from the Enlightenment (in both its individualist and collectivist traditions).[7] Yet these are not internally exclusionary qualities applied

---

by developments in Japan. For Kāshāni and *Habl al-Matin* see, for example, Golbon, M., '*Habl al-Matin* va Zamineh-hā-ye Mashrutiyat', in Sanjari, Ā. (ed.), *Barresi-ye Mabāni-ye Fekri va Ejtemāʿi-ye Mashrutiyat-e Iran: Bozorgdāsht-e Āyatollāh Mohammad-Kāzem Khorāsāni*, Tehran, Mo'asseseh-ye Tahqiqāt va Towseʿeh-ye ʿOlum-e Ensāni, 1383 (2004), pp. 260–265; Parvin, N., 'Habl al-Matin' , in *Encyclopaedia Iranica,* vol. XI, fasc. 4, 2002, pp. 431–434 (available online: http://www.iranicaonline.org/articles/habl-al-matin). Al-Afghāni's fluctuating position has been briefly discussed elsewhere; see Gheissari, A., *Iranian Intellectuals in the Twentieth Century*, Austin, TX, 1998, pp. 28–31. For al-Afghāni and his interactions with certain European intellectual trends, see also Keddie, N. R., *Sayyid Jamal ad-Din al-Afghani: A Political Biography*, Berkeley, CA, 1972; Kia, M., 'Pan Islamism in late nineteenth-Century Iran', in *Middle Eastern Studies*, vol. 32, no. 1, 1996, pp. 30–52; and Ansari, A. M., *The Politics of Nationalism in Modern Iran*, Cambridge, 2012, pp. 26–29. It should further be noted that in fact Kāshāni himself was initially motivated by al-Afghāni to embark on journalism and propagating reformist ideas, differences in their later ideological convictions and activities notwithstanding.

7 Here the reference to 'sources of the self' is borrowed from Charles Taylor's seminal philosophical/ethical inquiry into the question of identity in modern west, see Taylor, C., *Sources of the Self: The Making of the Modern Identity*, Cambridge, MA, 1999. An earlier reference to the 'idea of Iran' was given by Gherardo Gnoli in his *The Idea of Iran: An Essay on Its Origin*, Leiden, 1989. Bibliography on the question of Iranian identity is vast and with varying scope and substance. For general observations and summary of various arguments

to the bare majority of the population, given the variant constructs of the self when it comes to non-Persian or non-Shi'i Iranians. Also, in regards to the self and its corresponding question of agency, such definitions can be traced in both the ideological discourse of the state or in the ideological counter-discourse of its critics in different periods of Iran's modern history. In this view each of these sources has maintained a complex and at the same time flexible composition, yet the level and manner of their interaction has been subject to historical and sociological variables – for instance, along typological, sociological (including variables relating to gender, class, ethnicity, and religion), educational, and city/country demarcations. Also in the course of the past two centuries each of these trends and tendencies, in varying degree, has had certain intellectual, ideological, and political implications, ranging from random reception of post-Enlightenment thought, to the impact of nationalism and later socialism, to various approaches to constitutional government. Further implications can also be noted in the ideological and institutional framework of Iran's autocratic state-nationalism in the interwar period (1920s and 1930s).

In this context a clear impact of Enlightenment ideas can further be noted in terms of the positive light in which the very term 'revolution' came to be viewed and appraised.[8] In contrast to its former negative connotation as reversal of fortune, 'revolution' (*enqelāb*) was now viewed as a necessary measure for change and a turning point which could deliver the society to the threshold of progress. This semantic shift was also associated with varying degrees of subscription to Jacobin ethics, according to which revolutionary transformation may well involve, if not require, violence. Seen in this light *violence* would be taken as a secondary concern, and the choice of whether to employ or avoid it would be determined by the exigencies of the revolutionary moment.[9] (This is not to ignore or neglect prior historical patterns of violence in Iranian society, nor to suggest a complete break between older and newer patterns of violence.) Another semantic impact of

---

see, for example, Ashraf, A., 'Iranian Identity, i. Perspectives', in *Encyclopaedia Iranica*, vol. XIII, fasc. 5, 2006, pp. 501–504 (available online: http://www.iranicaonline.org/articles/iranian-identity-i-perspectives).

8 For a historical survey of the concept of revolution in Persian political thought, see Arjomand, S. A., 'The Conception of Revolution in Persianate Political Thought,' in Journal of Persianate Studies, vol. 5, no. 1, 2012, pp. 1–16.

9 For an analysis of violence in the Iranian Constitutional Revolution, see Bonakdarian, M. 'A World Born through the Chamber of a Revolver: Revolutionary Violence, Culture, and Modernity in Iran, 1906–1911,' in Comparative Studies of South Asia, Africa and the Middle East, vol. 25, no. 2, 2005, pp. 318–40.

the Enlightenment on the ideological composition of Iran's constitutional movement was the almost universal adoption of the metaphor of 'light' when referring to the agency that was most associated with the task of propagating the conceptual principles and values of modern reforms (and by extension, modernity in general), namely the intellectuals.[10] As briefly argued elsewhere, in the late-nineteenth and early-twentieth centuries the term *monavvar al-fekr* (common for 'intellectual'), which had already gained currency in the Ottoman Empire, was also used in reference to a wide range of Iranian educated elite, both inside Iran and abroad, who were in favor of reform, modernisation, and constitutional government. Furthermore, the term *intellectual* in its initial form of *monavvar al-fekr* (lit. one who has been enlightened), resembled the French usage, *illuminé*, and also almost simultaneously implied 'someone who enlightens others' (*monavver al-fekr*) which had a clear Promethean connotation. However, later in the twentieth century these semantic variations seem to have been conclusively merged into a widely used Persian neologism *rowshanfekr* (lit. 'enlightened'), which delineates both of these attributes. Early Iranian intellectuals, somewhat similar to their counterparts elsewhere, were preoccupied with diagnosing the broad range of economic, social, cultural, and political ills of their country; writing as physicians of the body politic, they prescribed remedies in accordance with their ideological orientations.[11]

In this context the Enlightenment emphasis on free trade also appealed to merchants and traders and posed further challenges to the authority of the state to regulate the economy or to interfere with it at will. This would later also generate a tension between the *bazaar*-based class and the state, as was manifested during the constitutional period and beyond.

10 In this regard, there was also the Masonic reference to light and 'illumination' and its emphasis on universal humanism that had certain appeal with intellectuals and some among the reform-minded members of the elite; in addition, both of these groups could also relate more readily to private networks and connections. In this context, although there were certain formal similarities in the use of symbols (light), themes (universalism), and interactive patterns (such as selective belonging to circles and networks), with the Illuminationist (*Ishrāqi*) tradition in philosophy, their substantive distinctions were such that one cannot be considered as continuation of the other. Furthermore, it can be noted that the Enlightenment reference to 'light' also resonated among many Iranians, given that it also in some ways paralleled the Zoroastrian concept of the world as a battle between the opposite forces of darkness and light, as well as the Islamic notion of rationality and progress (in theory at least) as denoted in the concept of *ijtihād* (i.e. offering independent judgement on *shari'a* related questions, in accordance with the exigencies of time and place).

11 Gheissari, A., 'Iranian Intellectuals, Past and Present', interview by Ali Ahmadi Motlagh, *Muftah*, posted on March 10, 2011, (available online: http://muftah.org/?p=923).

Transregional Connections

Iran's Constitutional Revolution of 1906 aimed at changing the structure of the monarchy from despotic to constitutional, and to adopt representative governance by introducing the country to a parliamentary system. It further resulted in a written constitution in which a separation between different branches of government was recognised.[12] Intellectually, however, Iran's constitutional movement drew on a diverse range of ideas and orientations that in good measure were associated with the Enlightenment – either directly from European sources or, more regularly, through certain elaborate routes of transregional contacts, notably from India, the Ottoman Empire, and the Caucasus, all of which could be traced back to the Safavid period. These routes were primarily commercial and economic, through which not only goods and capital travelled but also ideas and a broad range of cultural styles and comportment.[13] In addition to these there was also the route which connected Iran to Ottoman Iraq, with its Shiʿi pilgrimage destinations in the south, such as Najaf, Karbalā, and Kāzemayn among others, referred to collectively as the *ʿAtabāt* (lit. Sanctuaries) – some of these locations, notably Najaf, also housed a cluster of Shiʿi seminaries which, as will be noted later, had important doctrinal and leadership impact on the events in Iran during the constitutional period.

By the time of Iran's constitutional movement, a considerable volume of printed material ranging from periodicals and reformist tracts to literary and historical works that were produced in each of these zones regularly reached Iran, while also circulating among the expatriate Iranian communities in each of these regional centers. These materials were generally well received by an emerging community of interested readers and followers. Although it would be inaccurate to generalise, certain patterns or trends (notably liberal, étatiste, and radical tendencies) can be

---

12 For a brief and general entry, see Gheissari, A., 'Constitutional Revolution in Iran', in Martin, R. C. (ed.), *Encyclopedia of Islam and the Muslim World*, 2nd edition, New York, NY, 2016, pp. 253–256.

13 Such as European-style outfits, translations of European novels, European-style theatre, the phonograph, and so forth. This topic has further been briefly discussed elsewhere, see Gheissari, A., *Iranian Intellectuals in the Twentieth Century*, Austin, TX, 1998, p. 18; Gheissari, A., 'Merchants without Borders: Trade, Travel, and a Revolution in late Qajar Iran', in Farmanfarmaian, R. (ed.), *War and Peace in Qajar Persia: Implications Past and Present*, London, 2008, pp. 183–212. For a broad range of information on Iran's economy and transregional connections in this period, see Jamālzādeh, M. A., *Ganj-e Shāygān yā Owzāʿ-e Eqtesādi-ye Iran*, (first edition, Berlin, 1917), reissued, Tehran, 1362 (1983); and Issawi, C., *The Economic History of Iran, 1800–1914*, Chicago and London, 1971.

discerned in the overall tone and orientation of the ideas that originated in each of these transregional zones. These ideas echoed certain discourses or range of debates that were also current among their respective intelligentsia, each of which, in turn, echoed a certain tonality and intellectual, as well as ideological, orientation of their place or zone of origin in modern Europe.[14] In this context, in addition to the European connection itself, three zones or circuits of contact and transmission of ideas that were referred to above, reflected distinct types of European ideas and exposed Iran to a range of European intellectual traditions and ideologies – namely, India, the Ottoman Empire (including post-Ottoman Egypt after 1805), and the Caucasus.[15] In the nineteenth century there was also a random and limited familiarity of Iranians with topics in modern European philosophy.[16] Nevertheless it should be stressed that liberal, étatiste, and radical tendencies more or less existed in all three regions: British India, the Ottoman world, and the Russian Caucasus. For example, there were clear liberal, étatiste, and radical currents in key parts of the Ottoman world in places such as Beirut and Istanbul, and also in Cairo and Alexandria.

---

14 The topic of center-periphery is a major analytical concern in comparative and transregional historiography. However, in spite of its importance, this topic is beyond the scope of the present paper. For an in-depth study of transregional interactions, see Bonakdarian, M., *Britain and the Iranian Constitutional Revolution of 1906–1911: Foreign Policy, Imperialism, and Dissent*, Syracuse, N.Y., 2006. There were also additional locations (such as London and Paris and several other European cities), termed as 'third contact zones,' where reformists and nationalists from Iran as well as from the neighboring regions met outside their own homelands and shared a variety of ideas and political experiences. See in particular Bonakdarian, M., 'Iranian Nationalism and Global Solidarity Networks, 1906–1918: Internationalism, Transnationalism, Globalization, and Nationalist Cosmopolitanism' in Chehabi, H. E., Jafari, P., and Jafroudi, M. (eds.), *Iran in the Middle East: Transnational Encounters and Social History*, London, 2015, pp. 77–119.

15 It can further be pointed out that during the opening years of the twentieth century other than Western societies or the Ottoman Empire, Egypt, and British-India, a major model of Asian modernisation in Iranian circles was Japan, noted for its scientific, parliamentary, educational, and military modernisation, without necessarily having imitated all Western social mores. See, for example, the letter on the urgency of reforms written by Abu al-Qāsem Nāser al-Molk (Qaragozlu) (1866–1927) to Āyatollāh Sayyed Mohammad Tabātabā'i (1842–1920), a noted constitutionalist leader based in Tehran, in which the author praised Japan and its Emperor, Meiji Mutsuhito (r. 1867–1912), for having initiated constitutional reforms; letter partially quoted in Kasravi, A., *Tārikh-e Mashruteh-ye Iran*, 13th edition, Tehran, 1356 (1977), p. 94. Another example is Mirzā Hosayn-ʿAli Tājer-e Shirāzi, *Mikādo-Nāmeh*, in verse, Calcutta: Habl al-Matin, 1906, p. 112, praising Japan in its 1905 victory in war with Russia.

16 See, for example, Mojtahedi, K., *Āshnā'i-ye Iranian bā Falsafeh-hā-ye Jadid-e Gharb* ([Early] Encounters of Iranians with Modern Western Philosophies), Tehran, 1388 (2009).

Invariably some of these currents influenced individuals such as Mirzā Aqā Khān Kermāni (1854–1896), Shaykh Ahmad Ruhi (1865–1896), Sayyed Jamāl al-Din (al-Afghāni), and Mirzā Malkam Khān (1833–1908), among many others, who spent time in various parts of the Ottoman world as Qajar officials, merchants, or intellectuals and radicals. With respect to Shiʿi debates regarding constitutional movement and the clerical participation and leadership role in it, as will be noted later, the *ʿAtabāt* connection was particularly significant.

There was also a heterodoxical current in the writings of some of Azali and early Bahāʾi authors who resided in the Ottoman Empire or in the Russian Caucasus during the late-nineteenth and early-twentieth centuries. A notable example is Mirzā ʿAbbās Nuri (ʿAbd al-Bahāʾ) (1844–1921) and his *Resāleh-ye Modoniyyeh* (Essay on Polity) written in Persian in 1875 and circulated in Iran anonymously.[17] In this text the author proposed the creation of representative institutions not unlike those envisioned by the Young Ottomans, some of whom were also in exile at the time, with several Bahāʾi leaders residing in ʿAkkā in Ottoman Palestine. Echoing certain key notions of the Enlightenment for representative governance, ʿAbd al-Bahāʾ suggested the creation of 'councils' (*majāles*) and 'consultative assemblies' (*mahāfel-e mashverat*) of 'elected representatives' of people (*aʿzā-ye montakhabeh*) in Iran to address the political, cultural, and economic problems of the country.

European Connection

The present essay specifically deals with regional connections and cross-influences. However, the impact of ideas and ideologies that in one way or another were associated with the Enlightenment and influenced Iranian authors and commentators more directly as a consequence of their first-hand exposure while traveling to, or residing in, European locations during this period cannot be overlooked. Similarly significant was the perceptions of Iran and themes related to Persian culture among various European writers who were identified with the Enlightenment.[18] Yet, given their broad and varied scope, these indispensable historical components, each in its own right, require separate studies. Thus relevant topics for further investigation would include cases of direct exposure of some Iranians to

17 N.n. [Mirzā ʿAbbās Nuri (ʿAbd al-Bahāʾ)], *Resāleh-ye Modoniyyeh*, Bombay, 1882.

18 Literature on this topic is vast. For a succinct survey of various Enlightenment perceptions of early modern Iran, see Matthee, R. 'The Imaginary Realm: Europe's Enlightenment Image of Early Modern Iran,' in *Comparative Studies of South Asia, Africa and the Middle East*, vol. 30, no. 2, 2010, pp. 449–62.

European Enlightenment thought inside Iran itself, as in the case of contacts with European (or American) diplomats, travelers, staff of various commercial agencies, such as telegraph or other departments, or, occasionally, even some Christian missionaries such as the American Presbyterians who, despite their religious orientation, valued greater political and social rights. Direct influence of Europe can also be noted through the works of people who visited or spent a considerable amount of time in Europe. Individual authors such Malkam Khān, Hājj Sayyāh (1836–1925), Eʿtemād al-Saltaneh (1843–1896), Kāshef al-Saltaneh (1865–1929), to name only a few, wrote diaries, newspapers, pamphlets, histories, or else tracts that contributed to raise awareness about popular as well as individual rights and a social contract between the government and the people.[19] For example, one of the most conservative of these figures, Eʿtemād al-Saltaneh, was in many ways a forerunner for a broad range of ideas that later became commonplace during the Constitutional Revolution. By the late nineteenth century there is also a considerable body of material produced in Persian about law and legal reform in the works of authors such as Mostashār al-Dawleh (1813–1895) and Mirzā Malkam Khān.[20]

Indian Connection

A dominant tone that often transpired from the Persian texts that were produced in India and sent to Iran or read elsewhere by the Iranian expatriate community, had a distinct flavour of being preoccupied by issues relating to political economy.

---

19 For samples of Malkam Khān's writings, see Nāzem al-Dowleh, M. M. K., *Majmuʿeh-ye Āsār-e Mirzā Malkam Khān, Vol. 1*, Tehran, 1327/1948; Nāzem al-Dowleh, M. M. K., *Ruznāmeh-ye Qānun* (2nd Ed.), Tehran, 1355 (1976). For a brief study of Iranian students who were sent to Europe during the Qajar period, see Minovi, M., 'Avvalin Kārevān-e Maʿrefat', in *Yaghmā*, no. 62, 1332 (1953), pp. 181–85; and Mahbubi-Ardakāni, H., 'Dovvomin Kārevān Maʿrefat', *Yaghmā*, no. 211, 1344 (1966), p. 592–98. For further study of Iranians visiting Europe in the nineteenth century, see Green, N., *The Love of Strangers: What Six Muslim Students Learned in Jane Austen's London*, Princeton, NJ, 2015.

20 See Mostashār al-Dowleh's treatise *Yek Kalameh* (One Word) which was initially completed in 1871 and was later published in various editions in 1891 onwards. For an English translation, see Seyed-Gohrab, A. A. and McGlinn, S. (eds.), *One Word – Yek kalameh: 19th century Persian Treatise Introducing Western Codified Law*, Leiden, 2010; for Mostashār-al-Dowle, see further Kia, M., 'Constitutionalism, Economic Modernization and Islam in the Writings of Mirza Yusef Khan Mostashar od-Dowleh', *Middle Eastern Studies* vol. 30, no. 4, 1994, pp. 751–77. An early reference to the French concept of 'liberté' (*horiyyat*) in Persian can be traced to Mustashār al-Dowleh's writings.

In line with prevailing British economic views at the time, particular attention was devoted by some Iranian reformers to improving customs and ports, introducing a modern banking system, and developing the country's infrastructure, with construction of railways as an often repeated mantra.[21] The major outlets for expression of such views included the influential periodical *Habl al-Matin* published in Calcutta. In these sources economic development was generally seen as a precondition for progress in other fields. In articulating their economic remedies these texts were also influenced by critique-of-colonialism perspectives. Hence, in their overall composition we can often detect a clear sense of mercantile nationalism. This goal fell on receptive ears inside Iran – in particular among the *bazaar* merchants who already were critical of the state's inability or unwillingness to protect their interests and offset foreign semi-colonial reach into Iranian markets and were calling for the development and protection of native manufactures and industries. The fresh memory of the 1891–1892 Tobacco Protest was carried over to the general discourse of the constitutional movement. However, the discourse of merchant nationalism had to grapple with a profound dilemma which it never succeeded to resolve during the constitutional period. On the one hand, in line with its ideological and social memory, merchant nationalism was largely articulated on the premise of expressing itself via grievances and basing its demands on a seemingly liberal claim that rights of the nation must be protected by a new governing order from the intrusions and abuses of the state (and of foreign competitors). Yet on the other hand its belief in the necessity of economic development and the urgency of investment in the country's infrastructure would have required the existence of a strong state which could exercise and implement central planning; a postulate that in principle and in practice would have contradicted any hypothetically liberal premise of Iranian merchant nationalism in the early twentieth century.[22]

21 Construction of a railway network had universal appeal among Iranian reformists and was resonated in a wide range of reformist writings produced in India or elsewhere. For a brief discussion and additional references, see Gheissari, *Iranian Intellectuals in the Twentieth Century*, p. 33, p. 140 (n. 89).

22 Theoretically, however, it can be noted that these two premises were not entirely contradictory to the point of being mutually exclusive options – there could be protectionist economy and internal infrastructural development carried out by the state, without state intrusion in the realm of commerce and free market. This ambivalence and dilemma with regard to the prospects for economic development can be clearly seen in the material that was published in the periodical *Habl al-Matin* itself. In view of its regular and long-time publication, *Habl al-Matin* had secured loyal readership among constitutionalists, but the periodical's own opinion pieces and analyses,

The reform literature that travelled through the Indian route and reached Iran were adamant in their anti-colonial, anti-despotic, and anti-patrimonial tendencies but less vocal on practicalities of institution-building and the type of state that was needed in order to deliver such reforms. Although the general tone of many reformist material on political economy that were produced within the Indian zone was particularly impacted by English and Scottish economic theories and to a significant extent by British administration in India, they were also informed of and influenced by comparable experience elsewhere, notably in central Asia or the Caucasus.[23] The Indian route was also significant in such fields as educational and legal reforms, British colonial inequities notwithstanding. In any transregional analysis, therefore, particular attention should be given to the fact that none of these routes were passive channels of transmitting ideas from their European origins to Iran or elsewhere. For instance, the Indian circuit itself had an elaborate network of connections with various other places and contexts.[24] We know that a major supporter of *Habl al-Matin*, for instance, was Hājj Zain al-ʿĀbedin Marāghaʾi (1839–1910), a reform minded merchant and author in his own right, who had initially resided in Baku and was later established in Istanbul. In other words, the transregional context of communication was exposed to European centers but also very dynamically to surrounding regions within the Middle East, southwest, southern, and central Asia, the Caucasus, and beyond.[25]

---

which were often written by Moʾayyed al-Islam Kāshāni himself as chief editor, were not always supportive of constitutionalism for Iran. In fact Moʾayyed al-Islam's own position shifted from time to time, in part because of his concerns with *Habl al-Matin*'s survival, and also because he had not resolved his own conflicting views on this topic. See, for example, Kasravi's criticism of Mo'ayyed al-Islam in Kasravi, *Tārikh-e Mashruteh-ye Iran*, pp. 42–44.

23 Note, for example, the supporting role that some Iranians of Baku had towards the periodical *Habl al-Matin*, or the close links that existed between Indian circles and those in Afghan centers in the early twentieth century and contemporary to the Iranian constitutional movement.

24 For a transregional survey of contacts in southwest and central Asia, see Green, N., *Bombay Islam: The Religious Economy of the West Indian Ocean, 1840–1915*, Cambridge, 2011; Khazeni, A. 'The City of Balkh and the Central Eurasian Caravan Trade in the Early Nineteenth Century,' in Comparative Studies of South Asia, Africa and the Middle East, vol. 30, no. 2, 2010, pp. 463–72.

25 See also Matthee R. and Baron, B. (eds.), *Iran and Beyond: Essays in Middle Eastern History in Honor of Nikki R. Keddie*, Costa Mesa (CA), 2000; Keddie, N. R. and Matthee, R. (eds.), *Iran and the Surrounding World: Interactions in Culture and Cultural Politics*, Seattle (WA), 2002; Chehabi, H. E., Jafari, P., and Jafroudi, M. (eds.), *Iran in the Middle East: Transnational Encounters and Social History* (London, 2015); Amanat, A. and Vejdani, F. (eds.), *Iran Facing Others: Identity Boundaries in a Historical Perspective*, New York, NY, 2012.

Ottoman Connection

Another significant route that connected Iran to its surrounding world and beyond that to Europe, was via the Ottoman Empire, notably Istanbul, Izmir, and Beirut, and also Alexandria and Cairo in Egypt.[26] These centres were, each in its own way, hubs of diverse social, cultural, and ideological trends and transregional connections extending from the Middle East and North Africa to the Caucasus, Russia, and Central and Western Europe. The connection to Istanbul took place through a number of routes which included the Caucasus (Baku, Tbilisi), Iraq (Baghdad, and the *'Atabāt*), or through the Mediterranean maritime routes (Alexandria, Beirut, Izmir). During the second half of the nineteenth century both Beirut and Istanbul were active scenes of Ottoman attempts at reform – they both had a highly dynamic social, cultural, and ideological climate which influenced Ottoman subjects as well as Iranian expatriate communities that were mostly comprised of merchants – and, as noted earlier, merchant nationalism was a recurrent theme in many influential Persian periodicals that were published outside Iran in the late nineteenth century. In these periodicals one can simultaneously trace echoes of not just one but all different currents of influence emanating from India, the Ottoman Empire, and the Caucasus.[27] Here another major part of the Ottoman state that could be added as a source of influence is Egypt. For instance, al-Afghāni had a network of supporters in Egypt and there was a sizable community of Iranians in Cairo and Alexandria.[28]

26 In this context we are dealing with British-occupied Egypt after 1882, which had a large European diasporic population and direct ties to Europe as well as to the intellectual circles in the Ottoman Greater Syria. On the Beirut-Iran links, see also Chehabi, H. E., 'The Paris of the Middle East: Iranians in Cosmopolitan Beirut', in Chehabi H. E., Jafari, P., and Jefroudi M. (eds.), *Iran in the Middle East: Transnational Encounters and Social History*, London, 2015, pp. 120–136.

27 A good case in point was the influential Persian periodical *Akhtar* that was published in Istanbul during the last quarter of the nineteenth century. For *Akhtar*, see Koloğlu, O., *'Akhtar*, journal person d'Istanbul,' and Pistor Hatam, A., 'The Persian Newspaper *Akhtar* as a Transmitter of Ottoman Political Ideas,' both in Zarcone, T., and Zarinebaf-Shahr, F. (eds.), *Les Iraniens d'Istanbul*, Istanbul and Tehran, 1993, pp. 133–140 and 141–147 respectively; and Lawrence, T. E., *Akhtar: A Persian Language Newspaper Published in Istanbul and the Iranian Community of the Ottoman Empire in the Late Nineteenth Century,* Istanbul, 2015. See further Algar, H., *Mirzā Malkum Khān: A Biographical Study in Iranian Modernism*, Berkeley, CA, 1973, pp. 186–187; and Zarinebaf, F., 'From Istanbul to Tabriz: Modernity and Constitutionalism in the Ottoman Empire and Iran', in *Comparative Studies of South Asia, Africa and the Middle East*, vol. 28, no. 1, 2008, pp. 154–169. For the Iranian community in Cairo in the early twentieth century, see Luesink, A. W. M., 'The Iranian Community in Cairo at the Turn of the Century,' in Zarcone, T., and Zarinebaf-Shahr, F. (eds.), *Les Iraniens d'Istanbul*, pp. 193–200

28 Persian periodicals supported by the expatriate mercantile community of Egypt, included

The above-mentioned centers and routes, each in its own way, were particularly exposed to, and receptive of, European debates regarding modernization and reform. These debates were carried out simultaneously on several fronts, ranging from economy and industry to education, law, culture, gender rights, and government administration. In this context French influence in Alexandria and Beirut, and the Central European, notably German, influence in Istanbul were particularly visible.[29] Although in the case of the Ottoman connection debates regarding reforms also touched on improvements, the general tone in the Persian publications produced in the Ottoman Empire, particularly in Istanbul, was that of romantic nationalism and with a clear étatiste orientation. Also themes such as 'purification' of Persian language from 'alien' influence (generally implying Arabic), were also discernible in these debates. Some of the advocates of this debate were receptive to texts produced by members of the Parsi Zoroastrian community in India, who were being regarded as living custodians of authentic Persian.[30]

In this context, there were also idealised references to Iran's ancient pre-Islamic civilisations which, thanks in part to some recent Western archeological findings, juxtaposed the ancient glories of 'Iran' with its contemporary weaknesses and, by way of offering a remedy, concluded that for the success of any project of national recovery the state had to be revived first. Here the state was both the embodiment of the nation's soul and the only viable medium that could deliver the nation to its destiny.

Another significant aspect of the Ottoman connection was that it generated a considerable volume of debates concerning nationality as a political and also a

---

Sorayyā and *Parvaresh* which began publication in 1899 and 1900 respectively. See Browne, E. G., *The Press and Poetry of Modern Persia*, Cambridge, 1914, pp. 66–67 and pp. 58–59; for *Sorayyā*, see further Motallebi, M.,'Sorayyā', in *Dāneshnāmeh-ye Jahān-e Islam*, Tehran, vol. 1, p. 4231 (available online: http://lib.eshia.ir/23019/1/4231). Similar to *Akhtar* these periodicals were important during the period leading to the Constitutional Revolution in Iran.

29 The Italian influence, in including the large presence of Italian workers and anarchist activities, were also important. See, for example, Khuri-Makdisi, I., *The Eastern Mediterranean and the Making of Global Radicalism, 1860–1914*, Berkeley, CA, 2010.

30 One such example was Mirzā Rezā Afshār, whose epistolary tract, *Parvaz-e Negāresh-e Pārsi* (Method of Writing [clear] Persian) published in Istanbul in 1883, was influenced by the *Dasātir* model developed by Āzar Keyvān (d. between 1609 and 1618), an influential Parsi Zoroastrian leader in India well over two centuries earlier. For a brief discussion, see, Gheissari, *Iranian Intellectuals in the Twentieth Century*, pp. 23–24 (and p. 133, n. 32); and Gheissari, A., '*Maqāle, Resāle, Ketāb*: An Overview of Persian Expository and Analytical Prose', in Yarshater, E. (ed.), *A History of Persian Literature*, vol. V: *Persian Prose*, (ed. by Bo Utas), London, (forthcoming).

cultural paradigm. This in part stemmed from the intensive debate already underway among the nineteenth-century Ottoman elite regarding the boundaries and attributes of 'nationality.' Early expressions of this concept were voiced by the Young Ottomans in 1870s and later by the Young Turks movement in 1900s.[31] It was clearly anticipated that the trajectory of these debates would sooner or later also lead to the introduction of new regulations concerning citizenship requirements for those residing in the Ottoman Empire. Iranian subjects in the Ottoman Empire were alarmed by the potential repercussions of such regulations on their long term prospects in the Ottoman Empire. These various Ottoman debates on nationality predictably resonated in Iranian circles as well.[32]

During the second half of the nineteenth century many aspects of social life in the Ottoman Empire were impacted by attempts at legal reform and the implementation of the *Mecelle* code in private transactions and in state-society relations. The idea of codification of the law and procedural uniformity that was associated with the Ottoman *Mecelle* captured the attention of many Iranian reformists prior to the Constitutional Revolution. However, at a substantive level (regarding the exact nature of such laws and procedures), there is relatively lesser reflection of this issue in the debates among Iranian intellectuals at home or abroad and there is little trace of this subject in Persian publications outside Iran, be it in the Ottoman Empire or elsewhere. One plausible explanation for this absence can be noted in the Shiʿi-Sunni differences on juristic questions and methodologies. But another, and perhaps more consequential, reason was the very difference between state institutions in Iran and in the Ottoman Empire. By all standards the Ottoman state was a *complex state*. It was far more centralised than its counterpart in Iran, and it also had a different institutional memory and experience in dealing with diverse confessional communities (*millets*) within its own domain and in interacting with Europe. Iranian exile or diasporic communities, in Istanbul, Izmir, or elsewhere, had a markedly different experience dealing with the Ottoman state than what they had experienced in Iran. By extension, their concrete and direct experience with

---

31 For the question of nationality in late Ottoman Empire, see Zürcher, E. J., *The Young Turk Legacy and Nation Building: From the Ottoman Empire to Atatürk's Turkey*, London, 2010; Kayali, H., *Arabs and Young Turks: Ottomanism, Arabism, and Islamism in the Ottoman Empire, 1908–1918*, California, 1997; Hanioglu, M. S., *The Young Turks in Opposition, Oxford, 1995.*

32 Regarding nationality and citizenship, further attention should be given to such circumstances as the large-scale presence of Iranian nationals working in Russian-controlled Caucasus, or the Iranians residing in the Indian subcontinent, as well as the existing Iranian passport law. These topics, however, fall beyond the scope of the present paper.

the Ottoman state was not something from which they could draw much immediate practical use for dealing with the Qajar state or in contemplating its future contours. Instead, their insights into and expectations of the state grew increasingly abstract, meta-historical, and romantic.[33]

During the constitutional period the Iranian community in Istanbul was also in regular contact with various Shiʿi centers in Ottoman Iraq, as well as with Iranian expatriate communities in the Caucasus – and these contacts further augmented the Istanbul community's complex ideological profile.[34] This community was as much exposed to ideas of the Enlightenment (notably nationalism and étatisme), as it was to more recent involvement in Iran's domestic politics by some of the high-ranking clerics residing in Shiʿi centers in Iraq and their leadership role in articulating popular grievances to the Qajar state.[35]

The Caucasus and the Russian Connection

This zone, which connected Tabriz and Rasht to Yerevan, Baku, Tbilisi, and other centers in the Caucasus, was also a major route connecting Iran to Europe during the constitutional period.[36] Via this route we can identify some of the earliest instances of the exposures of Iranian intellectuals to more radical strands of European Enlightenment, namely socialism, Marxism, and anarchism. These ideas reached Iran through Russia and had distinctly Russian inflections that continued to resonate well after the constitutional movement. Ideas that transmitted through this route had two distinct characteristics. On the one hand they entailed conceptually radical approaches to politics, society, and culture that respectively challenged absolutism, social class structure, and religious conservatism. On the other hand, these ideas were conceptually launched from outside the institutional

33 Concern with the question of nationality continued among Iranians living in the Ottoman Empire during the constitutional period and beyond. New citizenship laws introduced in the 1920s under the new Turkish Republic, prompted many, though not all, Iranian subjects either to return to Iran or move to Europe, with many among the latter group choosing to go to Germany.

34 For various aspects of the Iranian community in Istanbul see: Zarcone, T., and Zarinebaf-Shahr, F. (eds.), *Les Iraniens d'Istanbul, Istanbul and Tehran, 1993.*

35 However, it should further be noted that the only prior example of a constitutional and parliamentary system in the predominantly Muslim territories prior to the Iranian revolution of 1906 had been the short-lived Ottoman constitution of 1876–1877.

36 Gocheleishvili, I., 'Georgian Sources on the Iranian Constitutional Revolution (1905–1911): Sergo Gamdlishvili's Memoirs of the Gilan Resistance', in *Iranian Studies*, vol. 40, no.1, 2007, pp. 59–85.

boundaries of the state and, hence, some of their advocates considered that any prospect for reform would have to be contingent upon the breakdown of the existing state, rather than its piecemeal incremental reform. Among the influential writers and critics of this milieu during the period prior to the Constitutional Revolution was Mirzā Fath-ʿAli Ākhundzādeh (1812–1878), whose attacks on conservatism and religious obscurantism left a lasting influence on the later generation of Iranian political and cultural critics such as the influential authors Mirzā Yusof Khān Mostashār al-Dowleh (1813–1895), Mirzā Āqā Khān Kermāni (1854–1896), Mirzā Malkam Khān Nāzem al-Dowleh, and Mirzā ʿAbd al-Rahim Tālebof Tabrizi (1834–1911), within Iran or abroad.[37]

As an important center in the Caucasus, Baku was linked to Georgia and Russia and to the Ottoman ports on the Black Sea and to Istanbul. Also, in the absence of a direct and reliable overland road connecting Azerbaijan to Khorasan, Baku was frequently used by those who wanted to travel between Tabriz and Mashhad, using the trans-Caspian steamboat service.[38] From an ideological point of view the Caucasus zone more directly impacted Iran's Constitutional Revolution, especially in Azerbaijan and Gilan. The constitutionalist societies (*anjomans*) in Tabriz and Rasht clearly reflected the considerable level of interaction that existed between Iran and the Caucasus, both in terms of their member composition and the range of topics that they put to debate.[39] The Caucasus connection was particularly significant in the introduction of socialist ideas to ideological debates of the constitutional period and after, as can be noted in groups such as *Ejtemāʿiyun Eʿtedāiyun* (Social Moderates) and the radical minority *Ejtemāʿiyun ʿĀmiyun* (Social Democrats).[40]

---

37 On Ākhundzādeh, see Ādamiyat, F., *Andisheh-hā-ye Mirzā Fath-ʿAli Akhundzādeh*, Tehran, 1970; Algar, H., 'Ākundzāda', in *Encyclopaedia Iranica*, vol. I, fasc. 7, 1984, pp. 735–740 (available online: http://www.iranicaonline.org/articles/akundzada-playwright).

38 See Gheissari, 'Merchants without Borders', p. 184.

39 Rafiʿi, M. (ed.), *Anjoman: Orgān-e Anjoman-e Ayālati-ye Āzarbāijān* (*Anjoman*: Journal of the Provincial Council of Azerbaijan), Tehran, 1983; Ettehadieh, M.,'Anjoman-e Eyālāti-e Tabriz', in *Encyclopaedia Iranica*, online edition, originally published: July 20, 2002: http://www.iranicaonline.org/articles/anjoman-e-eyalati-e-tabriz (last updated: August 5, 2011).

40 For a pioneering study of this impact and various personalities involved in these debates, see Ādamiyat, F., *Fekr-e Demokrāsi-ye Ejtemāʿi dar Nahzat-e Mashrutiyat-e Iran* (The Idea of Social Democracy in the Iranian Constitutional Movement), Tehran, 1976. See also Afary, J., *The Iranian Constitutional Revolution, 1906–1911: Grassroots Democracy, Social Democracy, and the Origins of Feminism*, New York, NY, 1996, note in particular chapter 3: 'The First National Assembly, the Urban Councils, and the Iranian Organization of Social Democrats: 1906–1907', and chapter 10: 'The Second National Assembly and the Formation of Political Parties: The Democrat Party and Its

Among the influential activists and ideologues with connections with to both Tabriz and Baku, was Āvetis Sultānzādeh (1889–1938) who was also one of the early advocates and organizers of communism in Iran.[41] Baku and other centers in the Caucasus continued to impact Iran's post-constitutional politics, particularly in Azerbaijan and Gilan.[42] Moreover, the Caucasus were significant in so far as the overwhelming majority of mercenary and volunteer fighters joining the constitutionalist camp during the 1908–1909 Civil War came from the Caucasus. There was also a sizeable Iranian émigré community residing in the Caucasus as well as the existence of a major Iranian trade route that connected Iran to Russia and beyond, and a wide range of pro-reform newspapers in Azeri (and occasionally in Persian) were published there.[43]

The ʿAtabāt

By the late nineteenth century a significant Iranian community (or people of Iranian descent) was residing in the *ʿAtabāt* as well as elsewhere in Ottoman Iraq, and Iran's connection to the region was not limited to pilgrimage destinations and seminary centers. In fact the *ʿAtabāt* together with different largely Shiʿi-populated parts of Iraq were long under the influence of Persian culture and as such provided a conduit for Ottoman and Arab influence on Iran. Iraq was thus open to a considerable volume of economic, social, cultural and intellectual exchange and transactions with Iran.[44] Also by the late nineteenth century some

---

Organ, *Iran-i Naw*', pp. 63–88 and pp. 257–283 respectively.

41 Chaqueri, C., 'Sultanzade: The Forgotten Revolutionary Theoretician of Iran: A Biographical Sketch', in *Iranian Studies*, vol. XVII, no 2–3, 1984, pp. 215–235; Chaqueri, C., *The Soviet Socialist Republic of Iran, 1920–1921: Birth of the Trauma*, Pittsburgh and London, 1995.

42 For a valuable range of studies on the impact of the Caucasus zone on Iran's constitutional movement and the period that followed, see Cronin, S., (ed.), *Iranian-Russian Encounters: Empires and Revolutions since 1800*, London, 2013; and Cronin, S., *Reformers and Revolutionaries in Modern Iran: New Perspectives on the Iranian Left*, London, 2009.

43 For reference to many of these periodicals, see Browne, *The Press and Poetry of Modern Persia*; for further listing, see Atabaki, T. and Rustamova-Towhidi, S., *Baku Documents: Union Catalog of Persian, Azerbaijani, Ottoman Turkish and Arabic Serials and Newspapers in the Libraries of the Republic of Azerbaijan*. London: I.B. Tauris, 1995.

44 For works on the influence and impact of Persian culture in Iraq, see for example, Chalabi al-Mawsili, D., *Kalimāt Fārsiyya mustaʿmila fi ʿāmiyya al-Mawsil wa fi inhāʾ al-ʿIrāq*, Baghdad, 1380AH (1960), which is a dictionary of Persian words used in the colloquial language of Mosul; see also Mujāni, S., Khātami, S., and Moqarrab N. (eds.), *Akhbār-e Najaf*, 2 Volumes, Tehran, 1391

of the Iranian *ulema* of Iraq came to leave a significant impact on political events inside Iran, most notably the Tobacco Protest of early 1890s and ultimately the Constitutional Revolution of 1906.

The *ulema*'s relation with the monarchy was strained during the long reign of Nāser al-Din Shah (r. 1848–1896). The alienation of the *ulema* and the *bazaar* merchants with the monarchy erupted into the open in 1890 following the government's decision to grant a British-owned company exclusive monopoly for the purchase and sale of all tobacco that was grown in Iran. The tobacco concession caused protests among the *bazaar* merchants who in turn mobilised the *ulema* to openly oppose it. The tobacco merchants' fear that the concession would make them redundant also alarmed other merchants of the possible extension of foreign monopolies to their own spheres of trade as well as the clergy who were the recipient of religious alms and donations from merchants. Ultimately Mirzā Hasan Shirazi (c.1814-c.1896), a senior member of the Shiʿa *ulema* residing in Iraq, issued a *fatwā* that forbade his followers to consume tobacco so long as it was handled by a foreign monopoly. The protest forced the government to eventually rescind the concession in 1892. The tobacco protest was one of the early episodes of joint participation by different opposition groups, both clergy-led and those with secular orientations, and on the whole it has been noted by later historians as a 'dress rehearsal' for Iran's Constitutional Revolution in 1906.[45]

Initially the central idea that ultimately led to the Constitutional Revolution was the demand for setting up a 'House of Justice' (*ʿAdālat Khāneh*) – following a number of economic and political events of 1905, such as public opposition to increase taxation and the negative impact of public punishment of some prominent merchants over price increase. The ideal of justice also echoed a wider demand

(2012). A personal account and testimony on the Persian seminary students studying in Najaf in the late Qajar period is given by Āqā Sayyed Mohammad-Hasan Hosayni Quchāni (1877–1943), known as Āqā Najafi Quchāni, who was also among Khorāsāni's students; see Quchāni, A. N., *Siyāhat-e Sharq*, Tehran, first edition: 1347 (1929), new edition: 1378 (1999). For a general study of the Shiʿa community in Iraq in historical perspective, see for example, Nakash, Y., *The Shiʿis of Iraq*, Princeton, NJ, 2003.

45 Abrahamian, E., *Iran between Two Revolutions*, Princeton, NJ, 1982, p. 73. For contemporary observations, see for example, Browne, *The Persian Revolution of 1905–1909*, pp. 31–58; and Nāzem al-Islam Kermāni, M. M., *Tārikh-e Bidāri-ye Irāniān*, ed. by ʿA. A. Saʿidi-Sirjāni, vol. 1, 3rd edition, Tehran, 1363 (1984), pp. 11–45. For an analysis of the role of social groups in these events and the dynamics of Iran's public sphere and its broader transnational connections, see Kazemi, R., 'The Tobacco Protest in Nineteenth-Century Iran: The View from a Provincial Town,' in *Journal of Persianate Studies*, vol. 7, no. 2, 2014, pp. 251–95.

for stability and order, and for protection of national interests from foreign interference. Justice was then seen as synonymous with curbing the powers of the monarchy since the monarchy, somehow against its own self-interests, had been repeatedly ignoring or violating the unwritten 'Qajar Pact' – the normative system of elaborate negotiations between the center and different segments of the society.[46] The monarchy had thus become associated with arbitrary rule and injustice – which the people, especially those associated with the *bazaar*, viewed as evident in the concessions that foreign interests received in economic matters. Thus the term 'Constitutionalism' was rendered as *Mashrutiyat* (setting conditions), which implied placing conditions on the monarchy. The Constitutional Revolution was therefore not an anti-monarchist movement, but an anti-absolutist one. It was also a movement that advocated protection of civil and constitutional rights or, as stated in the text of the Constitution itself, 'rights of the nation' (*Supplement*, Arts. 8–25). It was concerned with national sovereignty, good government, economic progress, and demanding a unified and uniformly applied legal system. It therefore enmeshed the idea of political rights and administration of justice with goals that were expressed in the language of nationalism – both political and economic.

The Constitutional Revolution therefore sought to provide not a restoration or repair of the Qajar Pact nor a revival of an even earlier '*circle of justice*' paradigm – in fact the assassination of Nāser al-Din Shah in 1896 by a petitioner-turned-assassin was a clear indication of the breakdown of that paradigm for good. The Constitutional Revolution proposed a systematic change in the structure and exercise of political authority, one that would ideally be an alternative to *fatwa*s and assassinations as the means of contending with absolutism.

As it has been argued elsewhere, the *ulema* had consistently supported the absolute monarchy when the Safavid dynasty (1501–1722) established a Shiʿa monarchy in Iran. They had viewed the monarchy as the protector of the Shiʿa domain and propagator of the faith. During the Constitutional Revolution, some of the *ulema*, such as Shaykh Fazlollāh Nuri (c. 1842–1909) of Tehran or Mirzā Hasan Mojtahed (1851–1918) of Tabriz, continued to defend absolute monarchy on those lines. Nuri viewed constitutionalism as a Western idea that would ultimately subvert Shiʿism and the insular sanctity of the Shiʿa domain. On the other hand, other senior *ulema*, such as Mohammad-Kāzem Khorāsāni (1839–1911) and Mohammad-Hosayn Nāʾini (1860–1936), who were residing in Najaf, saw no tension between the requirements of Shiʿa piety and the imperatives of Shiʿa

46 For a valuable elaboration of this analysis, see Martin, V., *The Qajar Pact: Bargaining, Protest and the State in Nineteenth-Century Persia*, London, 2005.

authority on the one hand and constitutionalism on the other.[47] In fact the *ulema* had supported the monarchy insofar as it was capable of protecting the interests of the people and the nation – which they had equated with the Shi'a domain. If the powers vested in the monarchy were manipulated by foreign interests to the detriment of the nation, and if arbitrary rule alienated the masses and caused instability, then limiting those powers under a constitution was necessary.[48] Such arguments embodied certain similarities with the general strand of Enlightenment political theory where, irrespective of methods, the state draws its legitimacy both from its willingness and its ability to fulfill common good.

Addressing these questions Nā'ini, in his noted 1909 treatise, *Tanbih al-Umma va Tanzih al-Milla* (Awakening the Community and Purifying the Nation), argued for the compatibility of constitutionalism and Islam.[49] The short text is divided into one introduction, five chapters, and a conclusion. The first chapter gives a general account of a government based on religious precepts and equates it with government based on reason. Chapters two, three, and four provide a defense of constitutional government based on consultation, consensus and setting limits on the powers of the government. Chapter five defines the qualifications of those who would be eligible to be representatives at the consultative assembly or the parliament (the *majles*). In this text Nā'ini argues that the religious questions (*omur-e shar'i*) have already been clarified in the *Qur'an*. For clarification of public, social, and non-religious questions (*omur-e 'urfi*) the community must rely on experts in these areas. Accordingly, the relationship between the people and the ruler belongs to *omur-e 'urfi*. Although as a Shi'i thinker, Nā'ini considered the only just rule to be that of the Hidden Imam, in practice, during the period of Occultation before the

---

47 For studies on Khorāsāni and Nā'ini, see Farzaneh, M. M., *The Iranian Constitutional Revolution and the Clerical Leadership of Khurasani*, Syracuse, NY, 2015; Hairi, A. H., *Shi'ism and Constitutionalism in Iran: A Study of the Role Played by the Persian Residents of Iraq in Iranian Politics*, Leiden, 1977. See also Afary, J., 'The Place of Shi'i Clerics in the First Iranian Constitution,' in Critical Research on Religion, vol. 1, no. 3, 2013, pp. 327–46.

48 Gheissari, A. and Nasr, V., *Democracy in Iran: History and the Quest for Liberty*, Oxford, 2006, pp. 27–28.

49 For later editions, see Nā'ini, M., *Tanbih al-Umma va Tanzih al-Milla* (edited by Tāleqāni, S.M., Tehran, 1955) and (edited by Vara'i, S. J., Tehran, 2003). For a general study of Nā'ini, see Hairi, *Shi'ism and Constitutionalism in Iran*; see further Nouraie, F. M., 'The Constitutional Ideas of a Shi'ite Mujtahid: Muhammad Husayn Nâ'înî', in *Iranian Studies*, vol. 8, no. 4, 1975, pp. 234–47. For a detailed examination and commentary on *Tanbih al-Umma*, see Feyrahi, D., *Āstāneh-ye Tajaddod: dar sharh-e Tanbih al-Umma va Tanzih al-Milla (*Threshold of Modernity: On Tanbih al-Umma va Tanzih al-Milla), Tehran, 1394 (2015).

reappearance of the Imam, it is not only possible but also legitimate to regulate the relationships between the people and the government in accordance with certain laws and instructions that are offered by experts. Although in a real sense the constitution was designed to replace the *shariʿa*, Nāʾini nevertheless dismissed the conservative (or quasi *Akhbāri*) criticism that constitutional legislation in Islamic countries would be a heretical innovation (*bidʿa*).

Furthermore, the pro-constitutionalist *ulema*, such as Nāʾini, focused their attention to replace arbitrary rule with a 'conditional' (*mashrut*, hence *mashruteh* or 'constitutional') form of government that would be compatible with Islamic recommendations in favour of justice, consultation, and consensus. Therefore constitutionalism was not seen as a threat to the integrity of the Shiʿa domain, but as a necessary measure to protecting it. In this context political reform was sanctioned by the imperative of both preserving the faith and the nation that embodied it. Looking closely at the language of Nāʾini's text, it can be noted that he was also arguing that such 'innovations' complied with Islamic practice of *ijtihād*. In fact, similar to al-Afghāni and others in different frameworks, many clerical and non-clerical reformers argued that emulating certain western practices and institutions were not contradictory to Islam, but were rather compatible with basic tenets of Islamic 'rational' approach as in the practice of *ijtihād*.

On the other hand the constitutionalists did not see themselves exclusively concerned with religious law (the *shariʿa*), nor with secularism and liberty, but with popular sovereignty and justice. They also viewed the *ulema* as an important ally in the quest for a constitution. In this context constitutionalism was clearly not a secular ideal, and it was not expected to cut off the individual from the hold of religious law. It was neither anti-clerical nor an expression of a Muslim 'Enlightenment.' To the extent that constitutionalism was a demand for the rule of law, it reinforced the writ of the *shariʿa*, the position of which vis-à-vis the monarchy reinforced the demands of the constitutionalists.[50] Eventually, influential members of the elite, grasping the urgency of political reforms, persuaded Mozaffar al-Din Shah (r. 1896–1907) to compromise and agree to convene a representative assembly that would then draw a constitution.

The Constitutional Revolution produced Iran's first parliamentary system. The new constitution, which was modeled after the Belgian Constitution of 1831, was promulgated in 1906, and a Parliament (*Majles*) was convened for the first time in October of that year.[51] It effectively transferred some of the powers of the monarchy

---

50 For further discussion, see Gheissari and Nasr, *Democracy in Iran*, p. 28.

51 See Gheissari and Nasr, *Democracy in Iran*, p. 30. See also Afary, J. 'Civil Liberties and the

to the legislature and it provided the representatives with a forum through which to influence legislation and, ultimately, governance.

The constitution further specified that the monarchy would be subservient to a representative government that would be produced by the parliament, yet it was less clear in delineating the relations between religion and politics and it did not draw boundary lines between the two. Regardless of the long-term implications of this omission, its immediate significance was that it included religion in the emerging Iranian conception of popular sovereignty. The ideal of a constitutional governance therefore emerged with a strong religious component and emphasis on the rule of law rather than demand for liberty.

Conflicting Narratives of Modernity

As shown in the preceding sections, Iran's constitutional experience drew on a wide range of ideas that in one way or the other were associated with the Enlightenment as well as with Iran's own intellectual and political context. Ideas that were associated with the Enlightenment came from different quarters, some directly from Europe while others through the neighboring regions and countries. In this vein, Iran's written constitution introduced modern concepts of citizenship and political rights to Iranian politics. It also provided the necessary framework for institutionalising these notions through new and uniform legislations in civil and procedural laws which, after several attempts in the 1910s, took place from the late 1920s onwards – a process that unfolded under the overriding prerogative of the state. Iran's legal reforms in the twentieth century were largely facilitated, indeed were made possible, by such constitutional experience and framework.[52]

Moreover, Iran's constitutional experience to the extent that it echoed merchant nationalism, did not produce a substantive transformation in the ideological formation of the Iranian bourgeoisie (in its broad and conventional sense, 'the middle class'), its aspirations, political culture, and its overall world outlook. Whereas

---

Making of Iran's First Constitution,' in *Comparative Studies of South Asia, Africa, and the Middle East*, vol. 25, no. 2, 2005, pp. 341–59; Arjomand, S. A., 'The 1906–07 Iranian Constitution and the Constitutional Debate on Islam,' in *Journal of Persianate Studies*, vol. 5, no. 2, 2012, pp. 152–74.

52 For a brief discussion on legal reforms in the context of post-constitutional history, see Gheissari, A., 'Constitutional Rights and the Development of Civil Law in Iran, 1907–1941', in Chehabi, H. E. and Martin, V. (eds.), *Iran's Constitutional Revolution: Politics, Cultural Transformations, and Transnational Connections*, London, 2010, pp. 60–79 (notes, pp. 419–427).

the constitutional movements in Europe and North America, having experienced turbulent and often violent tensions between proponents and opponents of constitutionalism and Enlightenment, in one way or the other paved the way for a more assertive individualism which in turn helped capitalism (or more accurately, manufacturing capitalism) to consolidate, expand, and develop its representative institutions with regard to policy making and governance, in Iran the constitutional aspirations of the Enlightenment often remained a private abstraction among many of those who considered themselves constitutionalist, while in practice constitutional institutions remained at the mercy of either too much or too little state.[53] However, Iran's constitutional experience, similar to its counterparts elsewhere, involved diverse, often conflicting, narratives of modernity which, in all 'honesty of purpose,' sought to synthesise fundamentally opposite concepts, values, and methodologies.[54] Indications of coexistence and simultaneous association among opposites during the constitutional movement and the periods that followed, are abundant – these include, among others, textual representations, personal deeds and biographies, and political behavior. While studying Iran's constitutional history we routinely encounter diverse tendencies and binary orientations such as patrimonialism vs. embryonic syndicalism, Shiʿism vs. liberalism, traditionalism vs. modernism, centralism vs. regionalism, tribalism vs. urbanism, internationalism and pan-Islamism vs. nationalism, parliamentarism vs. clericalism (as implied by the combined expression '*mashruteh-ye mashruʿeh*', constitutionalism based on the *shariʿa*), state nationalism vs. popular nationalism, etc. – all of which were indicative of the complexity of Iran's constitutional experience.

A discussion of Iran's dialectic of the Enlightenment in the post-constitutional era would also entail addressing the question of the autocratic path to state formation during the interwar period as a historical means and catalyst to achieve modernisation.[55] Unlike the 'enlightened despotism' that had appeared in European history during the eighteenth and early nineteenth centuries, Iran's autocratic states in the twentieth century during the interwar period and beyond, adopted centralisation and state-nationalism. Although chronologically this topic falls beyond the

53 For a classic study of the typology of individualism in modern European political theory, see Macpherson, *The Political Theory of Possessive Individualism*.

54 The term 'honesty of purpose' is taken here in the sense used in Kant, I., *Groundwork of the Metaphysics of Morals*, (transl. and ed. by Gregor, M.), Cambridge, 1998, p. 59.

55 See, for example, Atabaki, T. and Zürcher, E. J. (eds.), *Men of Order: Authoritarian Modernization under Ataturk and Reza Shah*, London, 2003; Enayat, H., *Law, State, and Society in Modern Iran: Constitutionalism, Autocracy, and Legal Reform, 1906–1941*, New York, 2013.

constitutional period and is therefore beyond the scope of the present essay, it impacted the popular perception of the Enlightenment and of its associated modes of modernity in Iran.

Bibliography

Abrahamian, E., *Iran between Two Revolutions*, Princeton, NJ, 1982.

Ādamiyat, F., *Andisheh-hā-ye Mirzā Fath-ʿAli Akhundzādeh* [The Ideas of Mirzā Fath-ʿAli Akhundzādeh)], Tehran, 1970.

Ādamiyat, F., *Fekr-e Demokrāsi-ye Ejtemāʿi dar Nahzat-e Mashrutiyat-e Iran* (The Idea of Social Democracy in the Iranian Constitutional Movement), Tehran, 1976.

Afary, J., *The Iranian Constitutional Revolution, 1906–1911: Grassroots Democracy, Social Democracy, and the Origins of Feminism*, New York, NY, 1996.

Afary, J. 'Civil Liberties and the Making of Iran's First Constitution,' in *Comparative Studies of South Asia, Africa, and the Middle East*, vol. 25, no. 2, 2005.

Afary, J. 'The Place of Shiʿi Clerics in the First Iranian Constitution,' in *Critical Research on Religion*, vol. 1, no. 3, 2013.

Afshār, Mirzā Rezā. *Parvaz-e Negāresh-e Pārsi* (Method of Writing [clear] Persian), Istanbul, 1883.

Algar, H., 'Ākundzāda', in *Encyclopaedia Iranica*, vol. I, fasc. 7, 1984, pp. 735–740, (available online: http://www.iranicaonline.org/articles/akundzada-playwright).

Algar, H., *Mirzā Malkum Khān: A Biographical Study in Iranian Modernism*, Berkeley, CA, 1973.

Althusser, L., *Politics and History: Montesquieu, Rousseau, Marx* (transl. by Ben Brewster), London, 2007.

Amanat, A. and Vejdani, F. (eds.), *Iran Facing Others: Identity Boundaries in a Historical Perspective*, New York, NY, 2012.

Ansari, A. M., *The Politics of Nationalism in Modern Iran*, Cambridge, 2012.

Arjomand, S. A., 'Constitutional Revolution III. The Constitution', in *Encyclopaedia Iranica*, vol. VI, fasc. 2, 1992, pp. 187–192, (available online: http://www.iranicaonline.org/articles/constitutional-revolution-iii).

Arjomand, S. A., 'The Conception of Revolution in Persianate Political Thought,' in *Journal of Persianate Studies*, vol. 5, no. 1, 2012.

Arjomand, S. A., 'The 1906–07 Iranian Constitution and the Constitutional Debate on Islam,' in *Journal of Persianate Studies*, vol. 5, no. 2, 2012.

Ashraf, A., 'Iranian Identity, i. Perspectives', in *Encyclopaedia Iranica*, vol. XIII, fasc. 5, 2006, (available online: http://www.iranicaonline.org/articles/iranian-identity-i-perspectives).

Atabaki, T. and Rustamova-Towhidi, S., *Baku Documents: Union Catalog of Persian, Azerbaijani, Ottoman Turkish and Arabic Serials and Newspapers in the Libraries of the Republic of Azerbaijan*. London: I.B. Tauris, 1995.

Atabaki, T. and Zürcher, E. J. (eds.), *Men of Order: Authoritarian Modernization under Ataturk and Reza Shah*, London, 2003.

Bonakdarian, M. 'A World Born through the Chamber of a Revolver: Revolutionary Violence, Culture, and Modernity in Iran, 1906–1911,' in *Comparative Studies of South Asia, Africa and the Middle East*, vol. 25, no. 2, 2005.

Bonakdarian, M., *Britain and the Iranian Constitutional Revolution of 1906–1911: Foreign Policy, Imperialism, and Dissent*, Syracuse, N.Y., 2006.

Bonakdarian, M., 'Iranian Nationalism and Global Solidarity Networks, 1906–1918: Internationalism, Transnationalism, Globalization, and Nationalist Cosmopolitanism' in Chehabi, H. E., Jafari, P., and Jafroudi, M. (eds.), *Iran in the Middle East: Transnational Encounters and Social History*, London, 2015, pp. 77–119.

Browne, E. G., *The Press and Poetry of Modern Persia*, Cambridge, 1914.

Browne, E. G., *A Brief Narrative of Recent Events in Persia followed by a translation of 'The Four Pillars of the Persian Constitution'*, London, 1909

Browne, E. G., 'Appendix A: The Bases of the Persian Constitution', in *The Persian Revolution of 1905–1909*, Washington, DC, 1995, (Available online through the Foundation for Iranian Studies: 'Iran's 1906 Constitution and its Supplement', http://fis-iran.org/en/resources/legaldoc/iranconstitution).

Chalabi al-Mawsili, D., *Kalimāt Fārsiyya musta'mila fi 'āmiyya al-Mawsil wa fi inhā' al-'Irāq* [Persian Words used in Mosul and across Iraq], Baghdad, 1380AH (1960).

Chaqueri, C., 'Sultanzade: The Forgotten Revolutionary Theoretician of Iran: A Biographical Sketch', in *Iranian Studies*, vol. XVII, no 2–3, 1984.

Chaqueri, C., *The Soviet Socialist Republic of Iran, 1920–1921: Birth of the Trauma*, Pittsburgh and London, 1995.

Chehabi, H. E., 'The Paris of the Middle East: Iranians in Cosmopolitan Beirut', in Chehabi H. E., Jafari, P., and Jefroudi M. (eds.), *Iran in the Middle East: Transnational Encounters and Social History*, London, 2015.

Chehabi H. E., Jafari, P., and Jefroudi M. (eds.), *Iran in the Middle East: Transnational Encounters and Social History*, London, 2015.

Cronin, S., (ed.), *Iranian-Russian Encounters: Empires and Revolutions since 1800*, London, 2013.

Cronin, S., *Reformers and Revolutionaries in Modern Iran: New Perspectives on the Iranian Left*, London, 2009.

Darling, L. T., *History of Social Justice and Political Power in the Middle East: The Circle of Justice from Mesopotamia to Globalization*, London, 2012.

Enayat, H., *Law, State, and Society in Modern Iran: Constitutionalism, Autocracy, and Legal Reform, 1906–1941*, New York, 2013.

Ettehadieh, M.,'Anjoman-e Eyālāti-e Tabriz', in *Encyclopaedia Iranica*, online edition, originally published: July 20, 2002: http://www.iranicaonline.org/articles/anjoman-e-eyalati-e-tabriz (last updated: August 5, 2011)

Farzaneh, M. M., *The Iranian Constitutional Revolution and the Clerical Leadership of Khurasani*, Syracuse, NY, 2015.

Feyrahi, D., *Āstāneh-ye Tajaddod: dar sharh-e Tanbih al-Umma va Tanzih al-Milla* (Threshold of Modernity: On Tanbih al-Umma va Tanzih al-Milla), Tehran, 1394 (2015).

Foucault, M., '*Qu'est-ce que les Lumières?*' (originally published 1984) available in English: '*What is Enlightenment?*', in Rabinow, P. (ed.), *The Foucault Reader*, New York, 1984, also available online: http://foucault.info/documents/whatIsEnlightenment/foucault.whatIsEnlightenment.en.html.

Gheissari, A., *Iranian Intellectuals in the Twentieth Century*, Austin, TX, 1998.

Gheissari, A. and Nasr, V., *Democracy in Iran: History and the Quest for Liberty*, Oxford, 2006.

Gheissari, A., 'Merchants without Borders: Trade, Travel, and a Revolution in late Qajar Iran', in Farmanfarmaian, R.(ed.), *War and Peace in Qajar Persia: Implications Past and Present*, London, 2008, pp. 183–212.

Gheissari, A., 'Constitutional Rights and the Development of Civil Law in Iran, 1907–1941', in Chehabi, H. E. and Martin, V. (eds.), *Iran's Constitutional Revolution: Politics, Cultural Transformations, and Transnational Connections*, London, 2010, pp. 60–79 (notes, pp. 419–427).

Gheissari, A., 'Iranian Intellectuals, Past and Present', interview by Ali Ahmadi Motlagh, Muftah, posted on March 10, 2011, available: http://muftah.org/?p=923.

Gheissari, A., 'Constitutional Revolution in Iran', in Martin, R. C. (ed.), *Encyclopedia of Islam and the Muslim World*, 2nd edition, New York, NY, 2016.

Gheissari, A., '*Maqāle*, *Resāle*, *Ketāb*: An Overview of Persian Expository and Analytical Prose', in Yarshater, E. (ed.), *A History of Persian Literature*, vol. V: *Persian Prose*, (ed. by Bo Utas), London, (forthcoming).

Gnoli, G., *The Idea of Iran: An Essay on Its Origin*, Leiden, 1989

Gocheleishvili, I., 'Georgian Sources on the Iranian Constitutional Revolution (1905–1911): Sergo Gamdlishvili's Memoirs of the Gilan Resistance', in *Iranian Studies*, vol. 40, no.1, 2007.

Golbon, M., '*Habl al-Matin* va Zamineh-hā-ye Mashrutiyat', in Sanjari, Ā. (ed.), *Barresi-ye Mabāni-ye Fekri va Ejtemā'i-ye Mashrutiyat-e Iran: Bozorgdāsht-e Āyatollāh Mohammad-Kāzem Khorāsāni*, Tehran, Mo'asseseh-ye Tahqiqāt va Towse'eh-ye 'Olum-e Ensāni, 1383 (2004).

Green, N., *Bombay Islam: The Religious Economy of the West Indian Ocean, 1840–1915*, Cambridge, 2011.

Green, N., *The Love of Strangers: What Six Muslim Students Learned in Jane Austen's London*, Princeton, NJ, 2015.

Hairi, A. H., *Shi'ism and Constitutionalism in Iran: A Study of the Role Played by the Persian Residents of Iraq in Iranian Politics*, Leiden, 1977.

Hanioglu, M. S., *The Young Turks in Opposition*, Oxford, 1995.

Horkheimer, M. and Adorno, T. W., *Dialektik der Aufklärung*, first published in 1944, revised version, Amesterdam, 1947; also in English by John Cumming, J. (transl.) as *Dialectic of Enlightenment*, New York, 1972; new edition by Noerr, G., S. (ed.) and Edmund Jephcott, E. (transl.), as *Dialectic of Enlightenment: Philosophical Fragments*, Stanford, CA, 2002 (translated from Volume 5 of Horkheimer, M., *Gesammelte Schriften: Dialektik der Aufklärung und Schriften 1940–1950*, (edited by Noerr, G., S.), Frankfurt, 1987).

Issawi, C., *The Economic History of Iran, 1800–1914*, Chicago and London, 1971.

Jamālzādeh, M. A., *Ganj-e Shāygān yā Owzā'-e Eqtesādi-ye Iran*, (first edition, Berlin, 1917), reissued, Tehran, 1362 (1983).

Kant, I., '*Beantwortung der Frage: Was ist Aufklärung?*' (originally published 1784) available online: http://www.allmendeberlin.de/What-is-Enlightenment.pdf, English edition: 'Answering the Question: What is Enlightenment?', (transl. by Smith, M. C.), available online: http://www.columbia.edu/acis/ets/CCREAD/etscc/kant.html

Kant, I., 'An Answer to the Question: What is Enlightenment?', in Gregor, M. J. (ed.), *The Cambridge Edition of the Works of Immanuel Kant: Practical Philosophy*, Cambridge, 1996.

Kant, I., *Groundwork of the Metaphysics of Morals*, (transl. and ed. by Gregor, M.), Cambridge, 1998, p. 59.

Kasravi, A., *Tārikh-e Mashruteh-ye Iran*, 13th edition, Tehran, 1356 (1977).

Kayali, H., *Arabs and Young Turks: Ottomanism, Arabism, and Islamism in the Ottoman Empire, 1908–1918*, California, 1997.

Kazemi, R., 'The Tobacco Protest in Nineteenth-Century Iran: The View from a Provincial Town,' in *Journal of Persianate Studies*, vol. 7, no. 2, 2014.

Keddie, N. R., *Sayyid Jamal ad-Din al-Afghani: A Political Biography*, Berkeley, CA, 1972.

Keddie, N. R. and Matthee, R. (eds.), Iran and the Surrounding World: Interactions in Culture and Cultural Politics. Seattle (WA), 2002.

Khazeni, A. 'The City of Balkh and the Central Eurasian Caravan Trade in the Early Nineteenth Century,' in *Comparative Studies of South Asia, Africa and the Middle East*, vol. 30, no. 2, 2010.

Khuri-Makdisi, I., *The Eastern Mediterranean and the Making of Global Radicalism, 1860–1914*, Berkeley, CA, 2010.

Kia, M., 'Constitutionalism, Economic Modernization and Islam in the Writings of Mirza Yusef Khan Mostashar od-Dowleh', *Middle Eastern Studies* vol. 30, no. 4, 1994.

Kia, M., 'Pan Islamism in late nineteenth-Century Iran', in *Middle Eastern Studies*, vol. 32, no. 1, 1996.

Lauritsen H. R., and Thorup, M. (eds.), 'Rousseau and Revolution', *Continuum Studies in Political Philosophy Series,* London & New York, 2011

Lawrence, T. E., *Akhtar: A Persian Language Newspaper Published in Istanbul and the Iranian Community of the Ottoman Empire in the Late Nineteenth Century,* Istanbul, 2015.

Macpherson, C. B., *The Political Theory of Possessive Individualism: Hobbes to Locke*, Oxford, 1962 (reprinted 2011)

Mahbubi-Ardakāni, H., 'Dovvomin Kārevān Ma'refat', *Yaghmā*, no. 211, 1344 (1966).

Malkam Khān, see Nāzem al-Dowleh, Mirzā Malkam Khān.

Marcuse, H., *Reason and Revolution: Hegel and the Rise of Social Theory*, New York, 1999.

Martin, V., *The Qajar Pact: Bargaining, Protest and the State in Nineteenth-Century Persia*, London, 2005.

Matthee R. and Baron, B. (eds.), *Iran and Beyond: Essays in Middle Eastern History in Honor of Nikki R. Keddie*, Costa Mesa (CA), 2000.

Matthee, R. 'The Imaginary Realm: Europe's Enlightenment Image of Early Modern Iran,' in *Comparative Studies of South Asia, Africa and the Middle East*, vol. 30, no. 2, 2010.

Minovi, M., 'Avvalin Kārevān-e Ma'refat', in *Yaghmā*, no. 62, 1332 (1953).

Mojtahedi, K., *Āshnā'i-ye Iranian bā Falsafeh-hā-ye Jadid-e Gharb* ([Early] Encounters of Iranians with Modern Western Philosophies), Tehran, 1388 (2009).

Motallebi, M.,'Sorayyā', in *Dāneshnāmeh-ye Jahān-e Islam*, Tehran, vol. 1, p. 4231 (available online: http://lib.eshia.ir/23019/1/4231).

Mujāni, S., Khātami, S., and Moqarrab N. (eds.), *Akhbār-e Najaf*, 2 Volumes, Tehran, 1391 (2012).

N.n. [Mirzā ʿAbbās Nuri (ʿAbd al-Bahāʾ)], *Resāleh-ye Modoniyyeh* Bombay, 1882.

Nā'ini, M., *Tanbih al-Umma va Tanzih al-Milla* (ed. by Tāleqāni, S. M.), Tehran, 1955) and (ed. by Varaʿi, S. J., Tehran, 2003).

Nakash, Y., *The Shiʿis of Iraq*, Princeton, NJ, 2003.

Nāzem al-Dowleh, M. M. K., *Majmuʿeh-ye Āsār-e Mirzā Malkam Khān, Vol. 1*, Tehran, 1327/1948.

Nāzem al-Dowleh, M. M. K., *Ruznāmeh-ye Qānun* (2nd Edition), Tehran, 1355 (1976).

Nāzem al-Islam Kermāni, M. M., *Tārikh-e Bidāri-ye Irāniān* [A History of the Iranian Awakening], edited by ʿA. A. Saʿidi-Sirjāni, vol. 1, 3rd edition, Tehran, 1363 (1984).

Nouraie, F. M., 'The Constitutional Ideas of a Shiʿite Mujtahid: Muhammad Husayn Nâ'înî', in *Iranian Studies*, vol. 8, no. 4, 1975.

Parvin, N., 'Habl al-Matin', in *Encyclopaedia Iranica,* vol. XI, fasc. 4, 2002 (available online: http://www.iranicaonline.org/articles/habl-al-matin).

Perry, J. R., 'Justice for the Underprivileged: The Ombudsman Tradition of Iran', in *Journal of Near Eastern Studies*, no. 37, 1978.

Pistor Hatam, A., 'The Persian Newspaper Akhtar as a Transmitter of Ottoman Political Ideas', in Zarcone, T. and Zarinebaf-Shahr, F. (eds.), *Les Iraniens d'Istanbul*, Istanbul and Tehran, 1993, pp. 141–147.

Quchāni, A. N., *Siyāhat-e Sharq* [Touring the East], Tehran, first edition: 1347 (1929), new edition: 1378 (1999).

Rafiʿi, M. (ed.), *Anjoman: Orgān-e Anjoman-e Ayālati-ye Āzarbāijān* (*Anjoman*: Journal of the Provincial Council of Azerbaijan), Tehran, 1983.

Schneider, I., *The Petitioning System in Iran: State, Society and Power Relations in the Late 19th Century*, Wiesbaden, 2006.

Seyed-Gohrab, A. A. and McGlinn, S. (eds.), *One Word – Yek kalameh: 19th century Persian Treatise Introducing Western Codified Law*, Leiden, 2010.

Sohrabi, N., 'Revolution and State Culture: The Circle of Justice and Constitutionalism in 19th-Century Iran', in Steinmetz, G.(ed.), *State/Culture: State-Formation after the Colonial Turn*, London, 1999.

Sohrabi, N., *Revolution and Constitutionalism in the Ottoman Empire and Iran*, Cambridge, 2011.

Taylor, C., *Sources of the Self: The Making of the Modern Identity*, Cambridge, MA, 1999.

Zarcone, T., and Zarinebaf-Shahr, F. (eds.), *Les Iraniens d'Istanbul*, Istanbul and Tehran, 1993.

Zarinebaf, F., 'From Istanbul to Tabriz: Modernity and Constitutionalism in the Ottoman Empire and Iran', in *Comparative Studies of South Asia, Africa and the Middle East*, vol. 28, no. 1, 2008.

Zürcher, E. J., *The Young Turk Legacy and Nation Building: From the Ottoman Empire to Atatürk's Turkey*, London, 2010.

2

From Narrating History to Constructing Memory: The Role of Photography in the Iranian Constitutional Revolution

Elahe Helbig

The Iranian Constitutional Revolution (1905–1911) has left an enormous visual legacy, largely consisting of photographs and postcards. The significance of this visual legacy extends from forming a collective self-conception in the process of nation-building all the way to the retrospective construction of individual and collective memories of a nation. Photography, or generally images, has been recognised to be a powerful medium in materialising and authenticating national iconographies, icons and symbols. Thereby, the visual legacy of the Constitutional Revolution constructed a collective narrative and/or a 'counter narrative' of history, through which people could conceive themselves as a coherent nation. Hence, for the first time in its Iranian history, photography corresponded with the entire realm of civil society. It injected the ideas of enlightenment into the public sphere and crucially shaped the notions of 'nation', 'nationhood', and 'national identity'. This only fortified with the passage of time as the visual legacy of the Constitutional Revolution intricately bound up with its historiography and evolved into a 'location of remembrance' for the salvaging of histories. Various cultural practices arose, such as supplementing photographs or postcards with historical statements, national and personal comments, colouring and adorning them with popular symbols and national metaphors. These are performative acts of remembrance that elevated many photographs and postcards to the status of commemorative icons. In applying image theories that have become increasingly prominent over the last decades to a set of selected postcards, reproduced from photographs, this paper examines the multifold spheres of significance of photography during and in the aftermath of the Constitutional Revolution.

> 'By remembering, we form an idea of our self and shape a sense of our identity: thus, we end up embodying the memory that inhabits us. But memory is a dynamic phenomenon for any individual, but also for a culture as a whole.'
>
> *Liedeke Plate and Anneke Smelik*[1]

> 'Memory projects itself toward the future, and it constitutes the presence of present.'
>
> *Jacques Derrida*[2]

The Iranian Constitutional Revolution (1905–1911) has left an enormous visual legacy, largely consisting of photographs and postcards. Widely scattered across national archives, private and public collections, and family estates, partly gathered just after the event, partly collected across decades thereafter, this visual legacy has come to constitute a collective memory of an emerging nation. Equally significant, it is intricately bound up with the historiography of the Constitutional Revolution in being repeatedly invoked in the narrative that surrounds nation-building. Such narrative, as Elisabeth Edwards puts it, is constructed through, on the one hand, 'honorific portraits of leaders and great men [...] and, on the other hand the application of photographs of atrocity, violence and oppression as a forceful and reinforcing counter-narrative to a sense of nation – one united in suffering.'[3]

It is no coincidence that a large number of photographs and postcards were elevated to the status of commemorative icons; they embody and manifest the ideas fundamental to the Constitutional Revolution. In a similar way as Pierre Nora argues for other cultural sites, this visual legacy has become a 'location of remembrance' upon which the collective memory of an emerging nation elucidates and releases itself. Such collective memory is central to the self-awareness of a nation in giving a sense of continuity to the endless flow from past to present.[4]

The visual legacy of the Iranian Constitutional Revolution has increasingly

1 Plate, L. and Smelik, A. (eds.), *Technologies of Memory in the Arts*, London, 2009, p. 1.

2 Derrida, J., *Memories for Paul de Man*, (Rev. Ed., transl. by Lindsay, C., Culler, J., and Cadava, E.), New York, 1986, p. 57.

3 Edwards, E., 'Photographs as Strong History?', in Caraffa, C. and Serena T. (eds.), *Photo Archives and the Idea of Nation*, 2015, p. 323.

4 Nora, P., 'Between Memory and History: Les Lieux de Mémoire' [1984], in *Representations* no. 26, 1989, pp. 7–27.

come to the fore over the course of the last four decades for various reasons. Two of these are especially important to recognise: First, the Constitutional Revolution is taking an increasingly important place in today's national consciousness. It has been traced and revisited as a historical event, during which the foundations of a modern Iranian state were laid. In spite of its eminent and pragmatic failings, the causes and consequences of the Constitutional Revolution for the political discourse of the country retain contemporary relevance in the political landscape. Second, and of central importance to this paper, recent discourses in cultural studies have paid growing attention to the role of image, including photography, as a constitutive part of national narratives and salvaging histories. It has thus been commonly argued for the contribution of photography within a wide range of media of commemorative practices 'to master narratives of nation-building and collective understandings of the past.'[5] Photographs became a dominant force in the visual politics of the second half of the nineteenth and early-twentieth centuries, for they contribute to a strong sense of historical continuity, which is required for a nation to find and negotiate its place in the modern world. This is a historical timeframe in which the idea of nation and national identity required a consolidated narrative of history, both in establishing narratives of existing nations and in reinforcing counter-narratives of resistance and revolutions that imparted a sense of nation-building. Such narratives provide sources of coherence in the imagined discourse of a nation; legitimating, validating and authenticating a sense of national identity in a modern, evolving and interconnected world.[6]

Facing up to the manifold visual legacy of the Constitutional Revolution forces a set of pressing questions, regarding both the impacts of photography on the movement and the retrospective constructing of the memory of an emerging nation. What was the significance of photography within the societal and political shifts in Iran, as part of which the idea of a modern nation emerged? How did photographs visually record the notions of 'nation', 'nationhood', and 'national identity', widely inject them into the public sphere, and articulate such ideological notions to a broader audience? How did photography visually narrate the Iranian Constitutional Revolution in line with the ideas and thoughts of the enlightenment and, related to this, how did photography retrospectively determine the perception of such within the public sphere? Finally, and of central concern to this paper,

---

5 Schwartz, J., 'Photographic Archives and the Idea of Nation: Images, Imaginings, and Imagined Community', in Caraffa, C. and Serena, T. (eds.), *Photo Archives and the Idea of Nation*, Berlin, 2015, p. 24.

6 Edwards, E., 'Photographs as Strong History?', p. 321.

how were memories, both individual and collective, constructed through photographs, and more significantly, how do such memories irrevocably interconnect with national identity and national consciousness?

This paper elaborates on these questions, which range from the narration of the Constitutional Revolution all the way to the construction of the collective memory of a nation. From the midst of the tremendous visual legacy of the Constitutional Revolution it examines a set of carefully selected postcards that have often, and in various ways, been reprinted from photographs. The cultural practices surrounding such images – supplemented with historical statements, national poems and personal comments, coloured and adorned with popular symbols and national metaphors – are performative acts of remembrance of the Constitutional Revolution. In being interwoven with these cultural practices, the images transform into commemorative icons that, having been circulated in private and remaining preserved in family albums, perpetuated individual memories of the Constitutional movement. Individual memories, however, take place within a social context and, being socially mediated,[7] serve to actively construct the identity of social groups and are of special importance the nation.

Memory is a social and cultural act. As such it is grounded in the here and the now, embedded in a variety of cultural practices and institutionalised discourses.[8] While memory may initially be involuntary, it evolves into an act of active remembrance. Conceiving of memory as performative in determining *what* and *how* a culture remembers presupposes its agency. Hence, memory makes the past become the present in ways that can be experienced and (re)negotiated. The past is put to serve the interests of the present, either at the level of the individual yearning to recall their personal past, or, more significantly, at the level of the nation recollecting its collective history. Consolidating this collective memory of the Constitutional Revolution has become central to forming a collective self-conception as a nation and supporting the process of nation-building.

Photography and Nation-Building

Ever since Anderson postulated his hypothesis of 'imagined communities', a nation has more and more been conceived through imaginative and symbolic

7 Halbwachs, M., *Das Gedächtnis und seine sozialen Bedingungen*, (transl. by Geldsetzer, L.), Frankfurt am Main, 1985.

8 Plate, L. and Smelik, A. (eds.), *Performing Memory in Art and Popular Culture,* New York and London, 2013, p. 2.

acts. For, as much as a nation is territorially bound, it is constituted by a collective self-conception and identification with a cohesive national body that shares traditions, rituals, beliefs, attitudes, sentiments, images and various other symbols. Anderson asserts that nationalism has to be understood by aligning it not with 'self-consciously held political ideologies', but rather with 'the large cultural systems that preceded it, out of which – as well as against which – it came into being.'[9] National identity is embodied in a unit that endorses itself by gathering around a historical and homogeneous common core that sets it apart from other people. A nation, or as Ernest Renan calls it, 'a soul, a spiritual principle', thus combines past and present into one: 'One is the possession in common of a rich legacy of memories; the other is present-day consent, the desire to live together, the will to perpetuate the value of the heritage that one has received in an undivided form.'[10]

Most modern nations in Europe were built in the nineteenth century. Anderson suggests that the crucial engine to the initial forming of national communities was the intersection of capitalism and print. The same function as print can be attributed to images, including photography. Discussing landscape photography in Britain and Germany, Jens Jäger argues for the significance of nationalistic reinterpretations and (re)definitions of all kinds of images during the process of nation-building in the nineteenth and early twentieth centuries. As part of this, photography proved an invaluable tool in the wide diffusion and acceptance of national iconographies and symbols, which 'whether already existing, invented or emerging, carry the weight of symbolizing, strengthening or sustaining the cohesion of a nation.'[11]

Photography played an analogous role in the process of nation-building in Iran, although this transpired in a different social and cultural context. For the creation and (re)definition of national iconographies and popularisation of photographs of the Constitutional Revolution enforced the vision of a cohesive nation. Juxtaposing the following two postcards (see Fig. 1 in the plate section) and (Fig. 2), dated roughly the same time, manifests the reinterpretation of political iconographies immediately after the Constitutional Revolution – while one justifies the Qajar

9 Anderson, B., *Imagined Communities,* (Rev. Ed.), London and New York, 1991, p. 12.

10 Renan, E., 'What is a Nation', (transl. by Thom, M.), in Bhabha, H. (ed.), *Nation and Narration*, London, 1990, p. 19.

11 Jäger, J., 'Picturing Nations: Landscape Photography and National Identity in Britain and Germany in the Mid-Nineteenth Century', in Schwartz, J. M. and Ryan, J. R., *Picturing Place: Photography and the Geographical Imagination*, London, 2006, p. 117.

dynasty's claim to power, the other stages the reconfiguration of power balances. The former displays the portraits of all eight Qajar kings, two kings of the preceding dynasty and two reformers loyal to the dynasty. This consolidates and transmits the dynastic claim to power – even if depicting the two reformers, and stressing Aḥmad Shah over the abdicated Moḥammad Ali Mīrzā, points to a political change. The latter postcard, by contrast, artistically assembles members of the first parliament (October 7, 1906 – June 23, 1908) with two religious leaders of the Constitution, underscoring an analogous claim of the parliament to legitimate authority on behalf of the emerging nation.

Political iconography undergoes a transformation during the Constitutional Revolution. Images of propagators of the Constitution, religious advocates and national heroes forced themselves into the public sphere. Together with images of protests, resistance, and celebrations, these redefined the nation's political iconography. In drawing upon newly established symbols and attributes emblematic of a nation, such images construct a 'counter-representation' to the dynastic iconography of the Qajar, which traditionally consolidates and manifests their ultimate authority.[12]

The political and social role of photography during the Constitutional Revolution is well-established. Within this, it is important to recognise that it consisted not merely in recording and reporting, but rather in ideologically representing images in the public sphere. Pictures are not just a description of events and practices, but rather a specific *representation* of them, enabling a way of gaining access to them. They contain signs and symbols through which they communicate and exert influence over, or rather bring about, human emotions and behaviours. It follows that pictures, as William Mitchell calls attention to, are 'ways of world-*making* not just world-mirroring'.[13] He expands on this thought by reference to the paradoxical double consciousness of pictures. They vacillate between their power and abjection, being meaningful and meaningless, between 'magical beliefs and

12 For an elaborate discussion on images of 'dynastic power' in early Persian painting and photography see Diba, L. S., 'Images of Power and the Power of Images: Intention and response in early Qajar painting (1785–1834)', in Diba, L. S. and Ekhtiar, M. (eds.), *Royal Persian Paintings: The Qajar Epoch, 1785–1925*, London, 1998, pp. 30–49; Behdad, A., 'The Powerful Art of Qajar Photography: Orientalism and (Self)-Orientalizing in Nineteenth-Century Iran', in *Journal of Iranian Studies*, vol. 34, no. 1–4, 2001, pp. 141–152.

13 Mitchell, W. J. T., *What Do Pictures Want?: The Lives and Loves of Images*, Chicago, 2005, pp. xiv–xv. Mitchell here alludes to the title of the publication by Goodman, N., *Ways of Worldmaking*, Indianapolis, 1978.

sceptical doubts, naive animism and hard-headed materialism, mystical and critical attitude.'[14]

The ambiguous duality of images reveals itself in the ideological function of photographs of the Constitutional Revolution: intrinsic to them are not only authenticity, evidence and materiality, but also affectivity and emotionality. On the one hand, photographs record the visible world with accuracy and certainty, a claim photography has held since its very inception. On the other hand, they stir up intangible, affective experiences. While photographs enlarge human capacities for observation, concurrently they invoke an act of imagination, a subjective reality. It is this ambiguous duality that makes photography a powerful medium to affirm ideas of nations as 'imagined communities'. Photographs have the power to materialise and authenticate national iconographies, symbols and icons and thus construct a collective narrative through which people can conceive themselves as a cohesive nation. Simultaneously, photographs command an emotional legitimacy that induces a present sense of identification with, and identity as, this cohesive community. Or, to use the words of Edward, 'photographs have been used to reinforce a sense of being, of possession, of identity and of belonging through the establishment of key tropes which have addressed both the physical reality and the imagined discourse of nation.'[15]

Photography and Salvaging History

In the aftermath of the Constitutional Revolution its visual legacy immediately started being recalled and revisited in the public sphere. The presentation of Iran as a nation to a global public constituted one vital source for collecting and compiling photographs of the Constitutional Revolution right after its occurrence. Yahyā Dowlatābādi compiled four photo albums, containing about 400 photographs altogether, which he presented in the summer of 1911, following an invitation to the First Universal Congress of Race in London. The last album he presented is filled with photographs of the Constitutional Revolution, including photographs of *mojāhedīn* that are compiled under the heading of 'Iranian People'. To the end of compiling his presentation, Dowlatābādi did partly rely on the photo archive of the College of Dār al-Fonūn, but the majority of the photographs and information he gathered from sources spread over the entire country.[16]

14 Mitchell, *What Do Pictures Want?*, p. 7.

15 Edwards, 'Photographs as Strong History?', p. 322.

16 Reza Sheikh offers an insight into this collection, sourcing his depictions in Dowlatābādi's

Yet personal interest also led to the collection and circulation of photographs and postcards of the Constitutional Revolution. A telling example is the collection of a Turkish merchant residing in Iran at the time. It consists of postcards, which he sent home around 1911, with such descriptive titles as 'Souvenirs from Iran', and 'Souvenirs from the Constitutional Revolution'.[17] He intended to publish these postcards in a book upon his return to Turkey, being aware that they were probably unknown outside of Iran. It contains, for example, the portrait of Moḥammad-Walī Khan (1847–1926), later honoured as *Sepah-sālār* (Supreme Commander). Initially sent to crush the resistance in Tabriz, he eventually became a leader of the Constitutionalists and anti-royalist forces, leading them to Qazvin and, in the end, to Tehran. In this picture, he was still titled *Sepah-dār A'ẓam* (Commander), and 'leader of the revolutionaries in Gīlān and Qazvīn' (Fig. 3). However, the interest that culminated in collecting photographs and postcards of the Constitutional Revolution was by no means restricted to publicly presenting Iran as a nation. Worth mentioning in this context is a collection of postcards that was part of the vast family estate of Mo'ir-al-Mamālek, himself a passionate photographer and collector.[18]

It was the historiography of the Constitutional Revolution, however, that effected the sustained imprinting of its visual legacy into the collective memory of the nation. A witness of the Constitutional Revolution, Aḥmad Kasravi (1891–1946) wrote *History* in order to avoid that 'the stories were being lost and that no one would be able to gather them in the future.'[19] In his endeavour he did not restrict himself to accessible Persian or English documents. On the contrary he sought insight into the accounts of surviving contemporary witnesses, or rather of those who participated in the movement. Initially, between September 1923 and July 1924, he published these accounts in the Shi'ite journal *al-'Irfān*, a literary journal published in Saïda (Sidon), Lebanon. After that, between 1934 and 1942,

own memoirs, *Tarikh-e mo' aser yā ḥayaāt-e Yaḥyā*. See: Sheikh, R., 'National identity and photographs of the Constitutional Revolution', in Chehabi, H. and Martin, V. (eds.), *Iran's Constitutional Revolution: Popular Politics, Cultural Transformations and Transnational Connections*, London, 2010, p. 255 and pp. 273–274.

17 For further information see: Sheikh, 'National identity and photographs of the Constitutional Revolution', p. 274, and p. 258.

18 Qāsem Sāfī tells of this collection and generally of the postcards of the Constitutional Revolution in an interview with Mehrdād Oskoueī. The collection has meanwhile been donated to the archive of the Tehran University Library.

19 Kasravi, A., *History of the Iranian Constitutional Revolution*, (transl. by Siegel, E.), Tehran, 2006. p. 2.

he published stories of the events in Azerbaijan – from the Constitutional Revolution and across the following eighteen years – in the magazine *Peymān*, which he had founded himself.[20] Kasravi himself emphasised the great recognition and endorsement that this magazine series enjoyed amongst its readers, moving them to send their stories, memoirs, documents, newspapers, books and images, 'as if a group of people had been jolted into action.'[21] These contemporary textual and visual documents recalled to consciousness long-forgotten memories of the great deeds of the 'class of the forgotten and simple', in whose name 'history should be written'.[22] In employing the art of storytelling, Kasravi forcefully conveys the entire spectrum of sentiments, strivings, aspirations and limitations of the generation that unleashed a popular and unprecedented movement in the cause of liberty and the establishment of a constitutional state.[23]

In the context of such a political, nationalistically inclined historiography, Kasravi makes full use of photographs, for which he went to great lengths to formulate appropriate captions. The photographs are diverse, telling tales of historical events, street protests and siege and resistance, victory and celebrations. Further, they include portrait photographs of numerous protagonists. By purposefully juxtaposing the faces of broadly unknown revolutionaries, activists and ordinary people with images of statesmen, clerics, political leaders and intellectuals, Kasravi gave birth to new icons, the national heroes of an entire nation. Kasravi thereby ensures that those 'who made the movement'[24], the ordinary people and the many anonymous *mojāhedīn* (revolutionary militia), who stood up for their rights and the rights of the nation would obtain their rightful place in history. The associated images evolved into symbols emblematic of an entire national movement.

When Kasravi furnished *Tārikh-e hejdah sāla-ye Āẕarbāijān* (Eighteen-year history of Azerbaijan) and *Tārikh-e mashruṭa-ye Irān* (History of the Iranian Constitutional Revolution) with images, the visual legacy of the Constitutional Revolution became an integral part of its narrative. In their retrospective function of narrating and constructing national history, such images have been unanimously equated with their representational meaning as either iconic messages or historical

20 Kasravi, *History of the Iranian Constitutional Revolution*, p. xix.

21 Kasravi, *History of the Iranian Constitutional Revolution*, p.1.

22 Kasravi, *History of the Iranian Constitutional Revolution*, p. 3.

23 For more information about Kasravi and his historical works see Manafzadeh, A., 'Aḥmad Kasravi as Historian', in *Encyclopaedia Iranica,* vol. XVI, fasc. 1, 2012, pp. 94–97.

24 Kasravi, *History of the Iranian Constitutional Revolution*, p. 4.

documents. Narration and image thereby came to intertwine into a single unit, irrevocably advancing themselves to an integral element of the narrative discourse of the Constitutional Revolution. Over the course of decades this visual legacy came to decisively shape the collective memory of a nation in multifarious ways.

However, it is important to recognise that the historiography of the Constitutional Revolution inevitably assigned a narrative layer to its visual legacy. For, reciprocally, the enormous body of images of key personalities and occurrences has become inseparable from the national storytelling of the events. The additional layer of meaning thereby bestowed upon images clearly comes to bear in the image of Māshāllāh Khan (Fig. 4). Taking advantage of the weakening of the central government, Naīeb Hossein-e Kāshī and his son Māshāllāh Khan established themselves as a local force in Kāshān, gathering a group of looters around them. They primarily raided caravan routes but also harassed local inhabitants. After numerous fruitless attempts, finally the central government's constant efforts to control the group paid off, and they surrendered in the hope of amnesty.[25] In being interwoven into the national storytelling – from a sense of helplessness and uncertainty all the way to civil aspirations, social advancement, and victory – images like this become evidence embodiment and manifestation of history. Equipped with this narrative layer, the photographs and postcards of the Constitutional Revolution circulated in public for decades, being passed from hand to hand, from generation to generation. In being unfailingly bound into oral storytelling and national narratives, images are associated with the ideas of 'nation', 'nationhood' and 'national identity'. Enabling encounters and interactions with past, they not only sustain individual memories but they also construct the collective memory of the Constitutional Revolution. Indeed, in mediating this relationship, images become integral determinants of national consciousness.

25 It is not obvious when this photograph was taken. For while the caption presents Māshāllāh Khan and Ḥājī Mīr-Panj as prisoners, the image indicates a certain status on their part. It is therefore questionable whether the photograph was really taken during their imprisonment, or, indeed, when they reached Tehran in hope of amnesty. The atrocities of Naīeb Hossein-e Kāshī and the government's efforts to secure these areas and routes are accounted for in: Kasravi, A., *Tārikh-e hejdah sāla-ye Āẕarbāijān: bāzmānda-ye Tārikh-e mashruṭa-ye Irān* [Eighteen-year History of Āẕarbāijān: The Rest of the History of the Iranian Constitutional Revolution], (2nd Ed.), Tehran, 1333(1954), p. 570, pp. 807–809, pp. 820–822, pp. 828–831.

Visualising 'awakened' Iranians

The retrospective analysis of photographs as instrumental embodiments of conceptual ideas, icons and symbols is to be complemented with an examination of the immediate ramifications effected by photography at the time of the Constitutional Movement, a time when photography in Iran was undergoing a significant transformation. By then, photography – initially introduced in 1842 – had already been employed for almost five decades in manifold applications in Qajar Iran. In line with the political agenda of the Nasiri Era, it was being used in many ways to transfer knowledge of Persian domains and its population, to record present history, to codify the past, and to manifest dynastic representation.[26]

Yet during the constitutional movement a decisive change took place: for the first time in its history in Iran, photography called the political legitimacy of the ruling power into question and instead started to correspond directly with civil society. Photographs were being produced and disseminated across wide social strata, primarily addressing ordinary people. This eminent shift in the intended recipient from the ruling class and elite circles to the subjects of the *mamālek-e mashrūṭeh-ye Īran* (Guarded Domains)[27] is fundamental to the shift in the function and meaning of photography. Similar transitions in intended audience can be noted in other cultural domains, encompassing education and the press,[28] a transition that

26 The history of photography during the Qajar period is extensively discussed in many publications. For just a small exemplary selection, see: Adle, Ch. and Zokā', Y., 'Notes et documents sur la photographie Iranniene et son histoire: I. Les premiers daguerréotypistes c. 1844–1854/1260–1270', in *Studia Iranica*, no. 12, 1983, pp. 249–280; Afshār, I., *Ganjīneh-ye 'akshaā-ye Īrān: Hamraāh-e tārikh-e voruūd-e 'akkāsi beh Īrān* [A Treasury of Early Iranian Photographs, Together with a Concise Account of How Photography Was First Introduced in Iran], Tehran, 1370(1992); Pérez González, C., *Local Portraiture. Through the Lens of the 19th century Iranian Photographer*, Leiden, 2012; Zokā', Y., *Tarikh-e 'akkāsi va 'aākkāsaān-e pishgām dar Īran* [History of Photography and Pioneer Photographers in Iran], Tehran, 1376(1997). For the transferring of knowledge on Persian domains and its population see Helbig, E., 'Geographies Traced and Histories Told: Photographic Documentation of Land and People by 'Abdullah Mirza Qajar, 1880s-1890s', in Ritter, M. and Scheiwiller, S. G. (eds.), *The Indigenous Lens: Early Photography in the Near and Middle East*, Zurich, 2016 (forthcoming); An excellent overview of the expeditions of European photographers and their documentations of archaeological sites is provided in Bonetti, M. F. and Prandi, A., *La Persia Qajar. Fotografi italiani in Iran 1848–1864*, Roma, 2010.

27 Abbas Amanat defines this notion. See Amanat, A., *Pivot of the Universe: Nasir-al-Din Shah Qajar and the Iranian Monarchy, 1831–1896*. Berkeley and Los Angeles, 1997, p. 15.

28 For more information about readership and the press see: Nabavi, N., 'Readership, the Press and the Public Sphere in the First Constitutional Era', in Chehabi, H. and Martin, V. (eds.),

supported the ideas and thoughts of enlightenment that had been inflamed in Iran.[29] This constitutes a major turning point in the history of Iranian photography, since it advanced photography to the status of a mass medium during the last decades of Qajar rule – a role which photography had occupied in Europe ever since its invention. From this very moment, photography continuously corresponded with the entire realm of civil society, acting as an agent in evolving and shaping a coherent vision of nation.

How was the Constitutional Revolution visually narrated? How was the notion of a nation articulated, in line with the ideas and thoughts of the enlightenment? How did photographers visually express their commitment to the movement? What aesthetic strategies did they employ to this end? And what effects of group identifications and national identities did these images evoke?

Although the Constitutional Revolution left behind an enormous body of photographs, their authorship mostly remains unknown. Nevertheless, it can be deduced from contemporary sources that a number of photographers took part in the movement themselves, or at the very least were sympathetic to it. These photographers participated in the political effervescence, fighting for and enduring various reprisals for the Constitution. Even though this cost some of them their lives, the stories of their own lives and photographic works remain incomplete, for sketchy and scattered notes and remarks reveal all that is known.

For example, Mīrzā Javād Khan, who operated a photography studio with his brother in Lālehzār, was executed during the Lesser Autocracy. As Nāẓem-al-Eslām Kermāni describes, this was not just due to his reproducing and disseminating photos of revolutionaries but also of those photographs of his that brought the opponents of the constitution to public recognition.[30] Yet such sketchy accounts, commonly not more than marginal notes in memoirs, are insufficient to provide grounded insights into the production, distribution and reception of this vast body of photographs. They do not even permit well-justified views of the reprisals and fears that were associated with taking photographs of that kind, with circulating

Iran's Constitutional Revolution: Popular Politics, Cultural Transformations and Transnational Connections, London, 2010, pp. 213–223.

29 For a discussion on Iranian enlightenment see: Ansari, A., *The Politics of Nationalism in Modern Iran*, New York, 2012, pp. 36–65.

30 Nāẓem-al-Eslām Kermāni, *Tārikh-e bidāri-e Irāniān* [*History of the Awakening of Iranians*], vol. 2, (7th Ed., ed. by Sa'idi Sirjāni, A.), Tehran, 2005, p. 566. Zokā'provided brief information about a few photographers who sympathised with the Constitutional Revolution. See Zokā', *Tarikh-e 'akkāsi va 'aākkāsaān-e pishgām dar Īran*, p.216, p. 263, p. 273, p. 284.

these in the public sphere, with merely selling them, or with being depicted on them.

The change in recipient from the ruling to the subordinate class inevitably effected a change in the displayed motifs and contents as well as the representational modes, and aesthetic strategies, ultimately culminating in the emergence of photo assemblage as a commemorative cultural practice. The broadened variety of depicted motifs ranges all the way from clerics and political proponents of the movement to activists and freedom fighters. Motifs in especially high demand included the *bast* (sanctuary) in the British legation, images from the uprising of Tabriz, and the victory of the freedom fighters in Tehran and other cities. Images of the parliament and its members, anniversaries and celebrations also circulated in great numbers. Of particular importance are also various images of political prisoners and public executions.

From this diverse spectrum of themes, this paper primarily examines two sets of images, those displaying the *bast* in the British legation in 1906 and those portraying the resistance in Tabriz in 1909. They display two key occurrences: the start and the end point of the Constitutional Revolution respectively – both shedding light on the patriotic rhetoric incurred by aesthetic strategies within the processes of nation-building.

The *bast* at the British legation, initially intended to force the regime into political concessions, started on the nineteenth of July and ended on the fourteenth of August 1906 when finally the founding of a national assembly was agreed on by Moẓaffar ad-Din Shah. It is widely known that the demand for a constitution and a national assembly had only evolved during this event.[31] While a small group of merchants, accompanied by *ṭollāb* (theology students), initiated this protest, soon thereafter representatives from almost all societal groups, including merchants, craftsmen, clerics, the simple staff of the administration, and even students, had joined in. Consequently, the number of protesters, starting at just 50, came to reach 14,000 by the end. While the odd photograph of the *bast* shows groups of dispersed and scattered people, many photographs portray a well-organised protest either of individual groups and guilds or of the entire protest (Fig. 5). For example, this postcard of clerics gathered in the British legation, reprinted from a photograph, has obtained great popularity as a memento of the constitution years thereafter. The camera perspective is such that it conveys the impression of a never-ending mass of protesters, sanctioned by their status as clerics. This induces a feeling of

31 Martin, V., 'Constitutional Revolution', in *Encyclopaedia Iranica*, vol. VI, fasc. 2, 1992, pp. 176–187.

identification and identity where the group takes precedence over the individual lost amidst the mass.

Contemporary accounts, such as that of Nāẓem-al-Eslām Kermāni, reveal that professional photographers were frequently asked to take photographs of this occurrence.[32] However, who these photographers were and on whose behalf they acted is not mentioned. In spite of the different authorships of this large number of photographs and their distinct aesthetic strategies, they are united in one thing: they uniformly focus on ordinary people, telling their story of awakening. It is not only political authorities, royal elites, intellectual leaders or even clergy but also common men who take centre stage of such photographs. This is aptly illustrated by the image of the provisional kitchen in the British legation (Fig. 6). The inscription on this postcard, written in elegant handwriting, states 'photographs of the cauldrons for cooking in the English legation'. There are a variety of such images of the kitchen, most of the expenses for which were defrayed by the merchants who initiated the protests.[33] Furthermore a personal comment on the postcard reads 'the kitchen for the Constitution'. This exemplifies how ordinary stories were purposefully put in the context of the Constitution, elevating their images to memories, through the lens of which the constitution was recalled in the decades that ensued.

These images show the guild mercers (Fig. 7), gathered together in the court of the British Legation, and the guild of traders of tea, sugar, pepper and similar goods (Fig. 8) in its respective tents. Nearly all the trade and craft guilds took part in the protest, locating themselves in their respective tents as representatives of their communities. Wandering from tent to tent, activists gave speeches during the *bast,* discussed political thoughts with such representative groups and addressed issues that ultimately culminated in the demand for a constitution.[34] Giving the impression of a well-organised gathering, the members of the group deliberately interact with the camera to communicate their claims. In purposefully representing themselves as a group, the members of the guild become aware of their social status, not as passive subordinates but as active members of an emerging 'civil society'.

The photographs of the *bast* at the British legation visually narrate how a 'civil society' was being formed. Such images show how ordinary men from various social classes come together, jointly share ideas and step up for their demands. Just as they 'entered the public visual space and as Iranians revisited them through the

32 Nāẓem-al-Eslām Kermāni, *Tārikh-e bidāri-e Irāniān*, p. 561, p. 566.

33 Martin, 'Constitutional Revolution', pp. 176–187.

34 Nāẓem-al-Eslām Kermāni, *Tārikh-e bidāri-e Irāniān*, pp. 542–545.

years, they assisted them as a "nation" to acquire a face and a body.'[35] The novel ideas of a civil society, and value systems – such as *ḥorriyat, mosāvāt, okhovvat, ʿedālat* (freedom, equality, brotherhood, and justice) – that were essential to promote a political change were inherent in all cultural areas. Negin Nabavi argues that the constitutional press, such as *Ḥabl al-matin* (Firm Cord), *Ṣur-e Esrāfil* (The Trumpet of Esrafil) and *Mosaāvāt* (Equality), were not satisfied with simply reporting news but rather saw their role as 'transforming former passive subjects into the active members of a nation.'[36] Yet the medium of photography visually narrated these values and communicated them to a broader audience. By representing diverse social groups as actively participating in political processes, and affirming their willingness to enforce their claims, photography encouraged ordinary people to get involved in the movement.

Staging of Power

The photographs of the resistance in Tabriz distinguish themselves from those of the *bast* at the British legation in Tehran with regard to both content and mode of representation. They display a civil society, not one that is emerging, but rather one that is organising itself for the unanimous defence of the Constitution. While the photographs of the *bast* constituted snapshots recording the unfolding scenes, a large number of photographs of the Tabriz resistance display scenes purposefully arranged in an act of self-presentation. Accordingly, the aesthetic strategies transformed from communicating ideological and political thoughts to the 'Staging of Power' and calls for armed resistance. This induced the development of a new photographic mode of representation, a genre in which armed revolutionaries are staged and arranged as the main motif.

The Constitutional Revolution entered into a new phase when, simultaneously with the bombardment of the *Majles* in Tehran on 23 June 1908, a civil war broke out in Tabriz. Along with the coup d'état in Tehran, Moḥammad ʿAli Shah (1872–1925; reg. 1907–1909), now in a position to bring Tehran back under his control, ordered an assault on the Constitutionalists in Tabriz. This relocated the focal point of resistance to Tabriz, which for a long time effectively constituted the only opposition to Moḥammad ʿAli Shah. The city, which had started preparing itself for possible attacks and initiated the military training for the freedom fighters, put up resistance to the forces that the Shah had sent to pacify Tabriz. For

35 Sheikh, 'National identity and photographs of the Constitutional Revolution', p. 251.

36 Nabavi, 'Readership, the Press and the Public Sphere in the First Constitutional Era', p. 217.

a whole eleven months Tabriz was torn by a civil war, while also being besieged by government troops. This success story of military resistance was crucial to the Constitutional Revolution as it functioned as a source of encouragement for other centres of resistance, and ultimately led to the abdication of Moḥammad ʿAli Shah on the sixteenth of July 1909.[37]

In the months leading up to August 1908, when the reinforced government troops started a new offensive, and besieged the city, the coalition of the two militant leaders – Sattār Khan and Bāqer Khan – effectively forced anti-constitutionalist tribesmen out of the city, reorganised the *mojāhedīn* (revolutionary militia), and unified most quarters in their defensive strategy, which ultimately lifted the siege. Once *lūṭīs* they were initially recruited into the constitutionalist police force in Tabriz and eventually emerged as its military leaders.[38] Through their continued fierce resistance Sattār Khan *sardār-e melli* (the people's commander) and Bāqer Khan *sālār-e melli* (national chieftain) emerged as popular heroes who stood up in defence of the city and its inhabitants. Their integral role in the resistance and its successful reverberations irrevocably interwove them as national icons with the Constitutional Revolution, as enforced through historical narratives of eyewitnesses and chroniclers. This interweaving is so strong that Pistor-Hatam argues that popular heroes, paradigmatically referring to Sattār Khan, are 'transformed in a *lieu de memoire* because he possesses a symbolic function that turns him into a long-lasting focal point of memory and identity.'[39] This draws on Nora's idea of *lieux de memoires* as sites with a sense of historical continuity where a past memory can live in the present.[40] Accordingly, the images of such 'mythical personages', Sattār Khan but also Bāqer Khan, firmly anchored themselves in the collective memory of the nation.

This portrait (Fig. 9) displays Bāqer Khan who was born in Tabriz in the 1870s. Bāqer Khan was a bricklayer by profession, before he emerged as the chief *lūṭī*

37 See, among other sources: Martin, 'Constitutional Revolution', pp. 176–187. For an extensive account of the events see: Kasravi, A., *Tarikh-e Mashrute-ye Iran* [History of the Iranian Constitutional Revolution], vol. 2, (16th Ed.), Tehran, 1363(1984).

38 Regarding the lives of Sattār Khan and Bāqer Khan and their role during the resistance see: Pistor-Hatam, A., 'The Iranian Constitutional Revolution as *lieu(x) de mémoire*: Sattar Khan', in Chehabi, H. and Martin, V. (eds.), *Iran's Constitutional Revolution: Popular Politics, Cultural Transformations and Transnational Connections*, London, 2010, pp. 33–44; Amanat, A., 'Bāqer Kkan Sālār-e Melli', in *Encyclopaedia Iranica,* vol. III, fasc. 7, 1988, pp. 726–728.

39 Pistor-Hatam, 'The Iranian Constitutional Revolution as *lieu(x) de mémoire*: Sattar Khan', p. 39.

40 See: Nora, 'Between Memory and History: Les Lieux de Mémoire', pp. 7–25.

of a quarter, which later became one of the strongholds of resistance in Tabriz. After joining the *mojāhedīn*, the political climate was suitable for his immediate advance in military succession. Following the Constitutionalists' victory, Bāqer Khan, together with Sāttar Khan, was invited to Tehran, received with an effusive welcome indicative of their popularity, though in reality it was condemnation to exile. He died in 1916 in Kermānshāh. Showing him in his uniform, and rifle in hand, this portrait, like many others of its kind, enjoyed vast popularity, and appeared in numerous publications, including Kasravi's *Tārikh-e mashruṭa-ye Irān.*[41] It was reprinted as a postcard, and the careful colouring and adorning with floral ornaments undermines his status as *sālār-e melli* and defender of the constitutional cause. Pistor-Hatam states that historical events selectively imprint themselves into the individual or collective memory from 'a collectively felt desire for meaningfulness'.[42] Along this line, the collective attempt at remembrance rendered not just Bāqer Khan's person, remembered through his devotion to the Constitutional Revolution and his bravery in its defence, but also his images circulating in the public sphere into 'locations of memory' that are used to construct a national identity.

Most photographs of the Tabriz resistance display groups of freedom fighters and their leaders. Yet a considerable number of photographs tell the tales of resistance by depicting the national army in Tabriz (Fig. 10), street fights, and barricades (Fig. 11).

Both postcards have been numerously reproduced, also in coloured versions. These coloured reproductions are very detailed so much so that both, the soldiers in the foreground, each individually emphasised, and the surrounding landscape, are coloured. Kasravi details precise information about the latter photograph, which was taken in the citadel in Tabriz. The person in front and to the left of the cannon is Khalīl Khan, leader of the *mojāhedīn.*[43] The contrastive colouring employed in the numerous reproductions highlights the rifles, cannon and cannon balls, making them stand out for the viewer. In colouring the face and garments of some of the fighters, their appearance as proud and assertive is underwritten. This snapshot was most likely taken by Estepān Estepāniān (1868–1914), who went to the barricades every day to take photographs, though at times he was also helping or even fighting. Sympathising with the Constitutional Movement himself, he photographed the events in Tabriz from the very first day and distributed the images of resistance

41 Kasravi, *Tārikh-e mashruṭa-ye Irān*, p. 602, Fig. 187.

42 Pistor-Hatam, 'The Iranian Constitutional Revolutio as *lieu(x) de mémoire*: Sattar Khan', p. 34.

43 Kasravi, *Tārikh-e mashruṭa-ye Irān*, p. 684, Fig. 213.

widely amongst its inhabitants. Aḥmad Kasravi published numerous of his images in *Tārikh-e hejdah sāla-ye Āẕarbāijān* and acknowledges Estepān Estepāniān's efforts to shine a light on the resistance as a substantial reason why many photographs of the resistance in Tabriz still survive.[44] According to Zokā', Estepāniān commissioned many postcards of the resistance and its leaders in Europe, disseminating them in Tehran and in other cities. Many such images were once again reproduced in Tehran.[45]

Just as images of the leaders of the resistance, particularly Sattār Khan sardār-e melli (the people's commander) and Bāqer Khan sālār-e melli (national chieftain), enjoyed great popularity and were widely circulated, so did group photographs of *mojāhedīn*. Uniting both elements, this postcard shows the two leading figures of the Tabriz resistance amidst his group (Fig. 12). The group comes together for the photograph, arranging itself around their leaders and a cannon. This forces the gaze upon them and thus (en)forces the status of their leaders and the fierceness of the resistance movement. Most of the displayed actively interact with the gaze of the camera, in an act of comradeship, cohesion and power. This mode of representation is brought to bear even more strongly in this photograph of the group of Bāqer Khan gathered in the Blue Mosque in Tabriz (Fig. 13). The members of the group consciously staged themselves, their meaningful expressions entrap the observer, and immediately transmit their political claims. The chosen mode of representation symbolises their determination and readiness to fight, and glorifies armed struggle as an expression of patriotism. This mode of representation supports the political message inherent in the images of the resistance in Tabriz.

Analogously, John Mraz recognises that the efforts of Emiliano Zapata, a leading figure in the Mexican revolution, to have himself photographed in emblems of resistance present a conscious attempt to legitimate his movement.[46] In a similar vein, freedom fighters present themselves fully armed to reinforce their claim as righteous fighters in defence of the Constitution. In positioning themselves as a closed group that readily embraces a fighting position, they are aware of their self-presentation as objectified through the camera. Group photographs of Sāttar Khan, Bāqer Khan and other leaders of revolutionary groups, in the midst of their military group, made use of photography's power to authenticate their political messages.

---

44 Kasravi, *Tārikh-e hejdah sāla-ye Āẕarbāijān*, p. 115, p. 552.

45 Zokā', *Tarikh-e 'akkāsi va 'aākkāsaān-e pishgām dar Iran*, p. 284.

46 Mraz, J., 'Archives and Icons: Constructing Post-Revolutionary Identities in Mexico', in Caraffa, C. and Serena, T. (eds.), *Photo Archives and the Idea of Nation*, Berlin, 2015, pp. 241–242.

Photographs of armed revolutionaries reaped such vast popularity that public photography studios started equipping themselves with the relevant backdrops and accessories allowing not only activists and sympathisers but also ordinary clients to portray themselves as freedom fighters (Fig. 14). Although these staged scenes appear theatrical, they nevertheless framed the national identity and consciousness.

At the time of the Constitutional Revolution, photographic self-representation had ceased to be a novelty restricted to the royal authorities and ruling class. By contrast, following the increase in the number of public photographic studios being set up in the 1880s, portrait photography had become widely accessible.[47] Then, these studios had provided diverse settings, most frequently with European accessories and backdrops to let everyone to present themselves as a 'modern citizen'. On a similar pattern, the staged photographs of the resistance in Tabriz embodied and framed nationalism and expressed national identity. Drawing on this, common people, independent of their background, could have themselves portrayed as freedom fighters as an individual memento of the Constitutional Revolution, its struggles and victories even years afterwards. Contemporaneous memoirs, like those of Moʿir-al-Mamālek, indicate the popularity of this trend, so that even servants of the elite took such photographs.[48] Photographs of this kind have imprinted themselves in the memories that form the aftermath of the Constitutional Revolution.

The images of the *bast* and the resistance paradigmatically exhibit the significance of photography in its manifold facets. In interweaving the events, their stories and faces, into the national narrative, photography gave birth to national symbols, metaphors and icons. Their popularisation evoked a collective self-conception as a cohesive community, sustainably interconnecting them with national identity and national consciousness.

From Photographs to 'Commemorative Image-Objects'

The visual politics of the Constitutional Revolution centrally invokes photography – one of the most popular media of the time – in order to reach a broad audience, responding to the needs of a semi-illiterate mass. Many photographs of the Constitutional Revolution, in turn, were reprinted as postcards, either immediately, or

47 The first public photographic studio was founded in 1868 by ʿAbbāsʿAli beyk in Tehran. For a chronology regarding the spread of public photographic studios see Tahmasbpour, M., 'Photography in Iran: A Chronology', in *History of Photography* no. 37, 2013, pp. 9–11.

48 Tahmasbpour, M., *Of Silver & Light*, Tehran, 2012, pp. 61–62.

even many years later. These postcards are of immense significance, for they constitute a vivid manifestation of the *zeitgeist*. As historical documents, postcards display popular personalities, national sites, symbolic landscapes, and significant societal events, which were of immediate concern to the public. Commonly, postcards contain personal notes and additional information that illuminatingly reveal the circulation of information, making them invaluable as testimonies of history. This studio portrait of Ḥājī Mīrzā Naṣr-Allāh Eṣfahāni, known as Malek-al-Motakallemīn (1860–1908), was reproduced into a postcard after his execution (Fig. 15). Malek-al-Motakallemīn (King of Rhetoric) was a radical advocate of the Constitution whose fame as an eloquent orator-preacher is highlighted in the inscription: 'Ḥājī Malek-al-Motakallemīn, the preacher, who gave particularly many agitating speeches in support of the constitution, and showed people their rights.' He was executed on 23 June, 1908 during the Lesser Autocracy, together with Mīrzā Jahāngīr Khan, the editor of the newspaper *Ṣur-e Esrāfil*, and further constitutionalists, in Bagh-e Shah in front of Moḥammad ʿAli Shah. This postcard with its informative inscription effectively illustrates how the makers of history are remembered even years later. Even more so, the additional handwritten message adds an emotional, ideological layer: 'he was murdered by order of absolutism'.

Photographs were purposefully invoked for political ends to evoke certain sentiments, as is exemplified by this postcard of Joseph Naus (Fig. 16). It is a reproduction of a photograph of Joseph Naus, dressed as a cleric at a fancy-dress party at the New Year ball in 1902. Only three years later in 1905 it was widely disseminated, enjoying great publicity. The *Tārikh-e bidāri-e Irāniān* describes the manner in which activists gained possession of this photograph and how they employed it in pursuit of their ends to enter a political alliance with the clergy, and, generally, in fuelling resentments.[49] The protests of merchants, supported by clerics, between 1900 and 1905 emerged out of the customs, trade and tariff reforms that Joseph Naus had introduced to Iran. Indeed, this was increasingly directed against Naus himself, who came to hold key positions in the service of Qajar administration. In 1905 these protests culminated in the *bast* in the British legation, where a general public pushed for reforms, one of which was the dismissal of Joseph Naus.[50] Purposefully torn out of its original context, the image was taken as evidence for the nation's political misfortunes, national resistance,

49 See Nāẓem-al-Eslām Kermāni, *Tārikh-e bidāri-e Irāniān*, p. 285–286.

50 See for example: Browne, E. G., *The Persian Revolution of 1905–1909*, (New Ed. ed. by Amanat A.), Washington, 2006, pp. 109–110, p. 112, pp. 136–138.

victories and the constitution. It thus obtained an integral role as an affective symbol in the imagined discourse of a nation.

The medium of the postcard, though appearing in Iran at the end of the Nasiri era, only enjoyed its golden age during the Constitutional Revolution and the years thereafter. The popularity of the medium can be traced back to three elements: reproduction, cost, and dispersion. Postcards could be produced at low cost – significantly cheaper than photographic productions – and thus in great quantities. Aside from that, postcards were better suited than photographs to be dispersed amongst a broader audience.[51] The eminent bearing and role of the press during the Constitutional Revolution led to a blossoming of printing and gravure techniques in Iran. Nevertheless, photographs could not yet be published in newspapers, leaving a gaping demand for images. While this was partly alleviated through caricatures and hand-made lithographs,[52] the aforementioned technological advances set the stage for the low-cost, quantitative reproduction of postcards that could ultimately satisfy the entire extent of the demand for images. Many of these postcards reveal valuable information regarding their production and distribution, making them invaluable historical documents.

According to contemporaneous memoirs, a local market for photographs and postcards had already been established, enabling common people to purchase images of nobilities and celebrities, views of holy places and archaeological sites, historical and official events, even the European journey of the Qajar rulers.[53] Nevertheless, most of the photographs that were circulating in the public space had been ordered either by the king himself, by local elites, diplomatic circles or had been produced for European markets. During the Constitutional Revolution, however, the local market started to respond directly to the demands of common people for those images that soon were to be the symbols and icons of the Constitutional Revolution. Indeed, such interplay of demand and supply became so significant to the proliferation of Constitutional ideas and thoughts that photographic studios, print shops and ordinary purchasers were subjected to considerable reprisals, especially during the Lesser Autocracy, photographic

51 The golden age of the postcard medium in Iran is chronologically similar to Europe. Hagenow provides an overview of the reasons why the postcard had become a mass medium, as well as its meaning as a political medium: von Hagenow, E., 'Propaganda per Hand. Politische Gesten auf Postkarten', in Warnke, M. (ed.), *Politische Kunst. Gebärden und Gebaren*, Berlin, 2004, pp. 53–72.

52 Sheikh, 'National identity and photographs of the Constitutional Revolution', p. 265.

53 Tahmasbpour, *Of Silver & Light*, p. 50.

studios in Tehran were closed, barred and sealed. Many photographers were forced to vow not to sell photographs, while others were arrested, tortured and publicly humiliated. Contemporaneous memoirs report how the heroic deeds of Sattār Khan reached Tehran at a time when Tabriz had turned into the core of resistance. Sattār Khan became a national icon, his image emblematic of a nation's hopes and aspirations. His photographs, moving from hand to hand, evoked a sense of belonging and identification with the resistance so much so that, for fear of their power, they were forbidden.[54] This postcard (Fig. 17), an example of such an iconic image, portrays Satār Khan, *sardār-e melli*. Printed in Tehran by the print house of ʿAbbās Kāshāhni and his brothers, it states 'leader of the revolutionaries in Azerbaijan' in four different languages.

Many of the postcards were reprinted with informative texts, political statements and poems. Handwritten comments were retrospectively added to numerous postcards. With reference to some unique examples, Reza Sheikh inquires into the reasons for such textual additions. They constitute 'micro-historical records', through which the events of the Constitutional Revolution are once again revisited and retraced. The inscriptions commonly reveal a sense of chaos, loss, despair, and nostalgia.[55] In discussing the practice of supplementing photographs with inscriptions, Carmen Pérez González points to a long and established tradition in Iran: that of placing inscriptions on all types of media, independent of size and function, of the visual arts. While she classifies the contents of the inscriptions and the way in which inscriptions have been used within the photographic space, Pérez González also analyses some postcards of the Constitutional Revolution.[56] A popular postcard is one of the prisoners of Bagh-e Shāh, which has been numerously reprinted in various ways and with differing textual arrangements (Fig. 18). Having become a paradigm of atrocities, the postcard shows twenty-two prisoners held captive after a number of Constitutionalists had been pursued, arrested and executed by order of Moḥammad ʿAli Mīrzā.[57] The caption reads 'a row of nobles

54 Zokā', *Tarikh-e ʿakkāsi va ʿaākkāsaān-e pishgām dar Īran*, pp. 284–285.

55 Sheikh, 'National identity and photographs of the Constitutional Revolution', pp. 260–265.

56 Pérez González, C., 'Written Images: Poems on Early Iranian Portrait Studio Photography (1864–1930) and Constitutional Revolution Postcards (1905–1911)', in Ritter, M. and Scheiwiller, S. (eds.), *The Indigenous Lens: Early Photography in the Near and Middle East*, Berlin, 2016 (forthcoming). I am greatly thankful to Pérez González for the access to her as yet unpublished article.

57 Browne extensively describes the preliminaries to this event. Interestingly, Browne prints a different image of the prisoners, presumably a photograph that differs both in textual arrangement and in the printed poem. Browne, *The Persian Revolution of 1905–1909*, pp. 199–210, Fig. 211.

of the constitution, put in chains by order of absolutism in Bagh-e Shāh,' while the bottom of the postcard contains their names, together with a poem.

It was common for images to be retrospectively coloured and reprinted as postcards, just like this image of members of the first parliament in Tehran (Fig. 19). The whole artistic value of the postcard is revealed in the careful colouring of some individuals and in creating an ensemble between the group and the background through the colour composition. In addition to being coloured and textually supplemented, many of the circulating postcards were further adorned with ornaments, popular symbols and decorative elements. Sometimes photo assemblages arose as well. This postcard, one of the many displaying the public execution in Tabriz, is an extraordinary example of such assemblage (Fig. 20). After occupying Tabriz, Russian troops executed a group of constitutionalists, amongst them the famous cleric Seqat al-Islam Tabrīzi (1861–1911) on 31 December, 1911. There are many assemblages, coloured and supplemented with drawings of hanged freedom fighters, of this photograph, which became a way of remembering the atrocities incurred by the Russian troops. It exemplifies how such popular practices ranging from textual supplements all the way to photo assemblages transformed photographs into 'commemorative image-objects'. The photograph in itself recedes into the background to let its social function as commemorative object gain precedence. In being interwoven into these cultural practices, the postcards of the Constitutional Revolution release themselves as social objects that are embedded in personal stories, oral traditions and individual memories. Reciprocally, they are agents in (re)interpreting and (re)defining the narratives of the Constitutional Revolution. Far from being passive containers of history, these 'commemorative image-objects' have become performative by conjoining history and the social realm, in (re)negotiating the former.[58]

Concluding Remark: Imagery of a Nation

The tremendous body of photographs of the Constitutional Revolution raises many pressing questions: How did photography narrate the Constitutional Revolution; for whom and to what end? How were images recalled and revisited in the

58 Compare Joshua Bell, who examines a photograph taken in 1922 by the government anthropologist F.E. Williams in the Purari Delta in what now is Papua New Guinea. He argues for image-objects as ways of materialising history, and encouraging source communities to think about their social relations. Bell, J., 'Out of the Mouths of Crocodiles: Eliciting Histories in Photographs and String-Figures', in *History and Anthropology*, vol. 21, no.4, 2010, pp. 351–373.

aftermath of the Constitutional Revolution; by whom, in what way, and with what intention? This paper has addressed this plethora of questions, which range from the narration of history to the construction of memory. To this effect, it is inevitable to put the photographs of the Constitutional Revolution in their ideological context, encompassing their generation, circulation, and perception. This constitutes the historical framework that endowed them with meaning. The images of the Constitutional Revolution were examined in the interplay between their ambiguous duality, for which Mitchell so forcefully argues, and the idea of a nation as an 'imagined community' that has become so pervasive. Against this theoretical background, their function as visual facts and also animated by emotions in the process of nation-building was discussed. Photographs (re)define, construct, and popularise national iconographies, symbols and metaphors, but they also evoke an emotional legitimacy and a sense of belonging, making for both their affectivity and effectiveness in nation-building. As Joan Schwartz reasonably explains in general terms, 'such thinking about "photography and experience" encourages us to press beyond visual facts and surface appearance, to discover how photographs have played – and continue to play – a role in constructing, legitimizing, and maintaining the idea of nation.'[59]

In the aftermath of the Constitutional Revolution, its visual legacy was revisited, and recalled in various ways. Photographs became an integral component of the historiography of the Constitutional Revolution to reinforce and consolidate national narratives. Reciprocally, national narratives, social testimonies, oral traditions, and even individual stories embedded photographs, and thus gave them a further layer of meaning. In light of this, images and popular practices surrounding them became acts of commemoration and remembrance of the Constitutional Revolution, requiring the active agency of individuals and the collective. Taking the idea of memory as a performative act, memory needs a medium in order to be trained, shared and transmitted, as discussed by Liedeke Plate and Anneke Smelik.[60] They further state that 'Memory is always re-call and re-collection [...], and, consequently, it implies re-turn, re-vision, re-enactment, re-presentation: making experiences from the past present again in the form of narratives, images, sensations, performances.'[61] Following the Constitutional Revolution, photographs

59 Schwartz, J. M., 'Photographic Archives and the Idea of Nation: Images, Imaginings, and Imagined Community', in Caraffa, C. and Serena, T. (eds.), *Photo Archives and the Idea of Nation*, Berlin, 2015, p. 25.

60 Plate and Smelik, *Performing Memory in Art and Popular Culture*, p. 2.

61 Plate and Smelik, *Performing Memory in Art and Popular Culture*, p. 6.

and the cultural practices surrounding them, which range from the production of postcards all the way to 'commemorative image-objects', offered a residue of the lived present and the remembered past. They selectively retain memories of the past in the service of propagating a self-conception in the present. Photographs and cultural practices surrounding them have the power to materialise and authenticate national history and construct a collective memory through which people can presently conceive and identify themselves as a cohesive nation.

Bibliography

Ansari, A., *The Politics of Nationalism in Modern Iran*, New York, 2012.

Amanat, A., *Pivot of the Universe: Nasir-al-Din Shah Qajar and the Iranian Monarchy, 1831–1896*. Berkeley and Los Angeles, 2004.

Amanat, A., 'Bāqer Kkan Sālār-e Melli', in *Encyclopaedia Iranica,* vol. III, fasc. 7, 1988, pp. 726–728.

Anderson, B., *Imagined Communities,* (Rev. Ed.), London and New York, 1991.

Behdad, A., 'The Powerful Art of Qajar Photography: Orientalism and (Self)-Orientalizing in Nineteenth-Century Iran', in *Journal of Iranian Studies*, vol. 34, no. 1–4, 2001, pp. 141–152.

Bell, J., 'Out of the Mouths of Crocodiles: Eliciting Histories in Photographs and String-Figures', in *History and Anthropology*, vol. 21, no.4, 2010, pp. 351–373.

Browne, E. G., *The Persian Revolution of 1905–1909*, (New Edition, ed. by Amanat A.), Washington, 2006.

Derrida, J., *Memories for Paul de Man*, (Rev. Ed., transl. by Lindsay, C., Culler, J., and Cadava, E.), New York, 1986.

Diba, L. S., 'Images of Power and the Power of Images: Intention and response in early Qajar painting (1785–1834)', in Diba, L. S. and Ekhtiar, M. (eds.), *Royal Persian Paintings: The Qajar Epoch, 1785–1925*, London, 1998, pp. 30–49.

Edwards, E., 'Photographs as Strong History?', in Caraffa, C. and Serena T. (eds.), *Photo Archives and the Idea of Nation*, 2015, pp. 321–329.

von Hagenow, E., 'Propaganda per Hand. Politische Gesten auf Postkarten', in Warnke, M. (ed.), *Politische Kunst. Gebärden und Gebaren*, Berlin, 2004, pp. 53–72.

Halbwachs, M., *Das Gedächtnis und seine sozialen Bedingungen*, (transl. by Geldsetzer, L.), Frankfurt am Main, 1985.

Helbig, E., 'Geographies Traced and Histories Told: Photographic Documentation of Land and People by ʿAbdullah Mirza Qajar, 1880s–1890s', in Ritter, M. and Scheiwiller, S. (eds.), *The Indigenous Lens: Early Photography in the Near and Middle East*, Berlin, 2016 (forthcoming).

Jäger, J., 'Picturing Nations: Landscape Photography and National Identity in Britain and Germany in the Mid-Nineteenth Century', in Schwartz, J. M. and Ryan, J. R., *Picturing Place: Photography and the Geographical Imagination*, London, 2006, pp. 117–141.

Kasravi, A., *Tarikh-e Mashrute-ye Iran* [History of the Iranian Constitutional Revolution], vol. 2, (16th Ed.), Tehran, 1363(1984).

Kasravi, A., *Tārikh-e hejdah sāla-ye Āẕarbāijān: bāzmānda-ye Tārikh-e mashruṭa-ye Irān* [Eighteen-year History of Āẕarbāijān: The Rest of the History of the Iranian Constitutional Revolution], (2nd Ed.), Tehran, 1333(1954).

Kasravi, A., *History of the Iranian Constitutional Revolution*, (transl. by Siegel, E.), Tehran, 2006.

Mraz, J., 'Archives and Icons: Constructing Post-Revolutionary Identities in Mexico', in Caraffa, C. and Serena, T. (eds.), *Photo Archives and the Idea of Nation*, Berlin, 2015, pp. 239–261.

Manafzadeh, A., 'Aḥmad Kasravi as Historian', in *Encyclopaedia Iranica,* vol. XVI, fasc. 1, 2012, pp. 94–97.

Martin, V., 'Constitutional Revolution', in *Encyclopaedia Iranica*, vol. VI, fasc. 2, 1992, pp. 176–187.

Mitchell, W. J. T., *What Do Pictures Want?: The Lives and Loves of Images*, Chicago, 2005.

Nabavi, N., 'Readership, the Press and the Public Sphere in the First Constitutional Era', in Chehabi, H. and Martin, V. (eds.), *Iran's Constitutional Revolution: Popular Politics, Cultural Transformations and Transnational Connections*, London, 2010, pp. 213–223.

Nāẓem-al-Eslām Kermāni, *Tārikh-e bidāri-e Irāniān* [History of the Awakening of Iranians], vol. 2, (7th Ed., ed. by Saʿidi Sirjāni, A.), Tehran, 2005.

Nora, P., 'Between Memory and History: Les Lieux de Mémoire' [1984], in *Representations* no. 26, 1989, pp. 7–27.

Pérez González, C., 'Written Images: Poems on Early Iranian Portrait Studio Photography (1864–1930) and Constitutional Revolution Postcards (1905–1911)', in Ritter, M. and Scheiwiller, S. (eds.), *The Indigenous Lens: Early Photography in the Near and Middle East,* Berlin, 2016 (forthcoming).

Pistor-Hatam, A., 'The Iranian Constitutional Revolution as *lieu(x) de mémoire*: Sattar Khan', in Chehabi, H. and Martin, V. (eds.), *Iran's Constitutional Revolution: Popular Politics, Cultural Transformations and Transnational Connections*, London, 2010, pp. 33–44.

Plate, L. and Smelik, A. (eds.), *Technologies of Memory in the Arts*, London, 2009.

Plate, L. and Smelik, A. (eds.), *Performing Memory in Art and Popular Culture,* New York and London, 2013.

Renan, E., 'What is a Nation', (transl. by Thom, M.), in Bhabha, H. (ed.), *Nation and Narration*, London, 1990, pp. 8–22.

Schwartz, J. M., 'Photographic Archives and the Idea of Nation: Images, Imaginings, and Imagined Community', in Caraffa, C. and Serena, T. (eds.), *Photo Archives and the Idea of Nation*, Berlin, 2015, pp. 17–40.

Sheikh, R., 'National identity and photographs of the Constitutional Revolution', in Chehabi, H. and Martin, V. (eds.), *Iran's Constitutional Revolution: Popular Politics, Cultural Transformations and Transnational Connections*, London, 2010, pp. 249–276.

Tahmasbpour, M., 'Photography in Iran: A Chronology', in *History of Photography* no. 37, 2013, pp. 7–13.

Tahmasbpour, M., *Of Silver & Light*, Tehran, 2012.

Zokā', Y., *Tarikh-e 'akkāsi va 'aākkāsaān-e pishgām dar Īran* [History of Photography and Pioneer Photographers in Iran], Tehran, 1376(1997).

Acknowlegment: I wish to express my gratitude to the collector Naser Hasanzaadeh, who so generously provided me with a large number of postcards from his collection and for allowing me to publish them. Further, I am deeply indebted to the Kimia Foundation, in specific to Houman Sarshar, for granting me access to its exceptional photographic archive so as to examine it and publish some of their images. Lastly, my sincere thanks go to Mehrdad Oskouei and the Visual Heritage Centre in Tehran for providing me with very rare postcards of the Constitutional Revolution. I am grateful to Somaye Amiri and Shahriar Rakhshanizadeh for their support in practical matters.

3

The Enlightenment and Historical Difference: The Case of Iran's Constitutional Revolution

Kamran Matin

This chapter challenges the Enlightenment's key idea of historical 'progress' through a critical interrogation of the application of the classical Marxist concept of 'bourgeois revolution' to Iran's Constitutional Revolution. It shows that this concept, and the wider Enlightenment paradigm, predicts, and is predicated on, developmental 'sameness' by extrapolating from a specific European experience of (capitalist) modernity, which accords no causal significance to 'the international', i.e., the ontological fact of the social world's numerical multiplicity and developmental difference. Following a critical reading of the concept of bourgeois revolution the chapter introduces the concept of 'revolution of backwardness' – a derivative of Leon Trotsky's idea of 'uneven and combined development' – to produce an alternative, internationally sensitive account of the Constitutional Revolution.

Introduction

Canonical theories of history are arguably rooted in the Enlightenment idea of 'progress', that is, the assumption that all societies move, albeit with different tempos and from different starting points, along a similar developmental path, and arrive in essentially similar end-points of western style modernity. The notions of 'reason' and 'freedom' – fundamentalised by Kant and Hegel – are central to this 'progressive' conception of history.

The enlightenment paradigm and its mono-linear and progressive conception of history have come under sustained and mounting critiques since at least the end of the Second World War. A consistent theme in the more recent critiques has been this intellectual enterprise's Eurocentric constitution, which simultaneously internalises the sources of modernity into Europe, and universalises its normative scope to the entire world depriving non-European societies and actors from historical agency and significance.[1]

However, beyond this powerful normative critique the Enlightenment's idea of progress has also been shown to be analytically deficient. Central to this line of critique is the argument, most forcefully made by postcolonialists, that the progressive and unilinear constitution of the Enlightenment's conception of modernity, and history more generally, fails to theoretically digest the evidently differentiated outcomes of modern development, particularly in non-European societies. Failing to theorise non-European experiences of modernity most varieties of classical social theory, the legatees of the Enlightenment, pacify the theoretical challenge of these experiences by expunging them as extra-theoretical anomalies or exceptions.[2] This manoeuvre reinforces the cultural-essentialist modes of explanation, which have, in different guises, outlived Edward Said's seminal critique of 'orientalism'.[3] Thus, social theories grounded in the European Enlightenment reduce the phenomenon of historical difference – an evidently persistent feature of inter-societal life – to a merely empirical problem eliding its theoretical comprehension.

A common way in which this intellectual act is performed is what I describe as 'negative explanation' whereby non-European experiences of modernity are

1 Bhambra, G., 'The possibilities of, and for, global sociology', in Go, J. (ed.), *Postcolonial Sociology: Political Power and Social Theory*, Bingley, 2015, pp. 295–314; Matin, K., 'Redeeming the Universal: Postcolonialism and the Inner Life of Eurocentrism', *European Journal of International Relations*, vol. 19, no. 2, 2013, pp. 353–377; Matin, K., *Recasting Iranian Modernity: International Relations and Social Change*, London, 2013.

2 Matin, *Recasting Iranian Modernity*, p. 2.

3 Said, E., *Orientalism: Western Conceptions of the Orient*, London, 1978.

defined in terms of what they are not, and then explained in terms of the absence of certain historical conditions, social agents, or cultural forms that are assumed to have been causal to the 'original' European instance of the phenomenon or experience in question – an exercise that Dipesh Chakrabarty has called 'narrative of lack'.[4]

An illuminating example in this regard is the notion of 'failed bourgeois revolution' used to describe 'incomplete' versions of the 'original' cases of the English, and especially French, bourgeois revolutions. This notion has been applied to, *inter alia*, 1905, 1906, and 1911 revolutions in Russia, Iran, and China, respectively.[5] But it has also been used to describe revolutions of 1848 in Europe.[6] In this sense the study of the classical concept of bourgeois revolution, of which the idea of 'failed bourgeois revolution' is a negative derivation, reveals more clearly the intellectual flaws of the enlightenment discourse of universal and progressive history in which the concept is ultimately rooted.

In what follows I will therefore attempt a critical study of the concept of the bourgeois revolution by reference to Iran's 1906 Constitutional Revolution. For, in a clear divergence from the causal premises of the concept of 'bourgeois revolution' deployed by most Marxian accounts of the modern Iranian history[7], the Constitutional Revolution occurred in the absence of any substantive domestic

---

4 Chakrabarty, D., *Provincializing Europe: Postcolonial Thought and Historical Difference*, Princeton, 2008.

5 Skocpol, T., *States and Social Revolution: A Comparative Analysis of France, Russia and China*, Cambridge, 1979; Ivanov, M. S., *The Iranian Constitutional Revolution*, Tehran, 1978.

6 Marx, K., *The Revolutions of 1848: Political Writings Volume 1*, London, 2010.

7 See *inter alia* Abrahamian, E., 'The Causes of the Constitutional Revolution in Iran', in *International Journal of Middle Eastern Studies*, vol. 10, no. 3, 1979, pp. 381–414; Ashraf, H., 'Historical Obstacles to the Development of a Bourgeoisie in Iran', in Cook M. A. (ed.), *Studies in the Economic History of the Middle East: From the Rise of Islam to the Present Day*, Oxford, 1970, pp. 308–32. There are two other recent and important accounts by John Foran (Foran, J., *Fragile Resistance: Social Transformation in Iran from 1500 to the Revolution*, San Francisco, 1993) and Janet Afary (Afary, J., *The Iranian Constitutional Revolution: 1906–1911: Grassroots Democracy, Social Democracy, and the Origins of Feminism*, New York, 1996), which are based, in the case of Afary partially, on the concept of 'dependent development'. I do not deal with these accounts separately since their theoretical frameworks involve problems similar to those entailed in the use of the classical Marxist concept of bourgeois revolution (e.g. Eurocentrism, the marginality of the state and geopolitics, an exchange-based and therefore ahistorical conception of capitalism). Robert Brenner (Brenner, R., 'The Origins of Capitalist Development: A Critique of Neo-Smithian Marxism', in *New Left Review*, no. 104, 1977, pp. 25–92) provides a penetrating critique of dependency approach.

development of capitalist relations and classes. At the time of the revolution Iran did not have any mentionable level of capitalist development.[8]

To be sure, by the time of the revolution Iran had been incorporated into the world capitalist system as a raw material supplying, peripheral economy through a twofold process of colonial and dependent development. But neither this incorporation nor the Constitutional Revolution subsequent to it involved or introduced any significant change into Iran's non-capitalist social relations and economic structure. Overall, Iran remained a collection of self-sufficient peasant and tribal communities whose relations with each other and the Qajar rulers were mediated through their subordination to local magnates and power-holders such as notables, nobles, land-lords, senior clerics and tribal chiefs, who were themselves only nominally subject to the Qajars.[9]

Given that no centres of competitive capital accumulation – the *sine qua non* of a capitalist economy – preceded or followed the Constitutional Revolution and monarchic autocracy was eventually restored Marxist accounts of the Constitutional Revolution describe the revolution as an 'unfinished' or a 'failed' bourgeois revolution. But in so doing, as mentioned above, they essentially describe what the revolution was not, instead of explaining what it actually was.[10] Such moves leave an intellectual gap that has traditionally been, and continues to be, the ideal space for the operation of orientalist approaches and their highly essentialist, often pathologising, accounts of the purported incongruence between Muslim culture and modern democracy.[11]

In order to resolve the apparent paradox of a bourgeois-democratic revolution in a precapitalist society we need to interrogate Marx's account of the rise of capitalism.

---

8 See *inter alia* Dabashi, H., 'Early Propagation of Wilayati-I Faqih and Mulla Ahmad Naraqi', in Nasr, S. H., Dabashi, H. and Nasr, S. V. R. (eds.), *Expectations of the Millennium: Shi'ism in History*, New York, 1989, pp. 288–300; Foran, *Fragile Resistance*.

9 Bakhash, S., 'Center-Periphery Relations in Nineteenth-Century Iran', in *Iranian Studies*, vol. XIV, no. 1–2; Lambton, A. S., 'Land Tenure and Revenue Administration in the Nineteenth Century', in Avery, E. *et al* (eds.), *The Cambridge History of Iran*, (vol. 7), Cambridge, 1991, pp. 459–505.

10 Afshari, M. R., 'The Pishivaran and Merchants in Precapitalist Iranian Society: An Essay on the Background and Causes of the Constitutional Revolution', in *International Journal of Middle East Studies*, vol. 15, no. 2, 1983, pp. 133–155.

11 E.g. Kedourie, E., *Democracy and Arab Political Culture*, Washington, 1992.

Marx, Capitalist Development, and the International[12]

There are essentially two rather different accounts of the rise of capitalism in Marx's work. One quantitative, found in *The German Ideology*, based on the expansion and complexification of the 'division of labour'.[13] And a later, qualitative account, found in *Grundrisse* and *Capital*, based on the separation of the direct producers from their means of reproduction and the formation and generalisation of the wage labour through the process of 'the so called primitive accumulation'.[14] The introduction of an anterior political moment, that is, the violent expropriation of the direct producers, supplies Marx's later account with a new historical and political dynamic that was absent from his earlier account based on the progression of a purely technical-internal process of division of labour.

The crucial corollary of this later, qualitative account of the rise of capitalism is, according to Marx, the fact that the expropriated direct producers are under an impersonal and systemic compulsion to sell their labour-power in the market in order to gain their subsistence. As a result, an apparently separate and autonomous sphere of economy comes into being in which the operation of purely economic, exchange relations obviates the necessity for the threat or exercise of brute force and political coercion in the immediate relations and processes of production and exploitation, the hallmark of all precapitalist formations.

Crucially, this capitalist form of consensual-contractual exploitation based on exchange relations presupposes the juridical equality of the parties to the exchange. In other words, unlike precapitalist modes of production, in capitalism 'political inequality is not inscribed in the relations of production …'[15] This specifically capitalist phenomenon of the formal 'separation of the economic and the political'[16] was the fundamental pre-condition for, and expression of, the rise of a bourgeois-democratic state. And it is precisely this causal complex that the orthodox concept of bourgeois revolution correctly captures. But what the concept fails to register is that this process could not be, and has not been, repeated in the same sequence of

12 The rest of this chapter heavily draws on Matin, *Recasting Iranian Modernity*, Chapter 3.

13 Most accounts of the Constitutional Revolution as a (failed) bourgeois revolution implicitly rely on this conception of capitalism in which trade plays a key role.

14 Marx, K., *Grundrisse*, London, 1993, pp. 497–498; Marx, K., *Capital* (vol. 1), London, 1990, p. 874.

15 Rosenberg, J., *The Empire of Civil Society: A Critique of Realist Theory of International Relations*, London, 1994, p. 84.

16 Wood, E., 'The Separation of the Economic and the Political in Capitalism', in *New Left Review*, no. 127, 1981, p. 82.

the English case, the key empirical referent in the formation of the concept, where the rise of representative government followed a protracted and organic process of primitive accumulation and class struggle.[17]

Why and how? A brief consideration of the archetypical case of the French Revolution can provide the crucial clue.[18]

The rise of capitalism in England occasioned a gradual but definite shift in the traditional Anglo-French geopolitical rivalry in favour of Britain. A series of French military defeats by Britain threw into sharp relief the limits of the economic and (geo)political power of the comparatively backward France. Financing costly external wars against the rising British Empire precipitated a chronic and deteriorating fiscal crisis. The state's fiscal crisis in turn progressively loosened the political and ideological cohesion of the French ruling classes and fuelled the discontent of the peasantry. French peasants had traditionally borne the brunt of multiple forms of taxation by the government, feudal *signeurs*, and the church. The latter two groups evaded the absolutist state's highly unequal and inefficient taxation regime. As a result the intensified taxation by the crisis-struck Bourbons placed an unbearable burden on the peasants more than any other social class.[19] The conjunction of the aristocratic recalcitrance, peasant unrest, and the urban bourgeoisie's discontent culminated in a revolutionary crisis that imploded in 1789.

The French revolution occurred in a fashion markedly different from the English revolution: a broad-based and convulsive democratic political revolution preceded a much more gradual but deeper capitalist social revolution. 'There was', as George Comninel points out, 'no 'class struggle' related to the growth of modern forms of capitalism before, or indeed during, the revolution; there was, instead, conflict within a ruling elite'.[20] Through the destruction of 'all separate local, territorial, urban and provincial powers in order to create the civil unity of the nation'.[21] the revolution however set the stage for an incrementally but irreversible reconstitution of precapitalist communal peasant property into capitalist private property. By the middle of the nineteenth century a significant basis of industrial capitalism

17 Brenner, *The Origins of Capitalist Development*.

18 The following three paragraphs are based on: Skocpol, *States and Social Revolution*, pp. 60–67; Comninel, G., *Rethinking the French Revolution*, London, 1990; Teschke, B., 'Bourgeois Revolution, State Formation and the Absence of the International', in *Historical Materialism*, vol. 13, no. 2, 2005, pp. 3–26.

19 Lewis, G., *The French Revolution: Rethinking the Debate*, London, 1999, p. 60.

20 Cited in: Lewis, *The French Revolution*, p. 110.

21 Marx cited in: Comninel, *Rethinking the French Revolution*, p. 203.

was established in France. Yet, even after its full consolidation, capitalist France was considerably different from its English *agent provocateur*. Étatism and a much stronger and institutionally and culturally articulated nationalism marked capitalist France. Wars of revolutionary and Napoleonic years were pivotal in this process.

In comparison to England there was, therefore, a clear reversal in the sequence of the socio-economic and political revolutionary change in France. This was, I contend, due to the specifically international dimension of the impact of English capitalism: external capitalist pressure, transmitted geopolitically, over-determined the internal pattern of capitalist development in France. A capitalist social revolution could not have occurred because a direct and immediate transformation of non-capitalist social property relations would have meant the dispossession of the very social class that was the main victim of the fiscal crisis of the state and hence was the principal agent of the revolution, i.e., the 'third estate' and its largest section, the peasantry.

But France is by no means the exception. The same goes for Germany, Japan, Russia, China, and, of course, Iran. All processes of capitalist transformation that followed the development of capitalism in England began as defensive nationalist or democratic projects, often combining both. In other words, they began with *political* revolutions that formally abolished precapitalist political hierarchies enshrined in feudal, tributary, and royal special rights and privileges. The reason is that initially the creation of political equality within a society subordinate, or susceptible, to a centralised and bureaucratic national-state was the most effective mechanism for the mobilisation of precapitalist social energy and resources against the threat or actual subjugation by foreign industrialised or industrialising countries.

Thus, in the original case of England, bourgeois-democratic politics and institutions were consequent upon, and increasingly functional to, capitalist development. But the multi-layered international mediation of English capitalism's expansion meant that in all subsequent instances nationalist-democratic reconstruction of precapitalist states preceded and co-determined wider processes of capitalist development, and industrialisation more generally. In this sense, 'every revolution [after the English revolution]', to rephrase an interesting remark by Albert Camus, is 'a foreign revolution'.[22] And herein lies the basic tension in the application of the classical concept of the bourgeois revolution to post-1688 modern revolutions. For such an application involves the impossible task of comprehending an

---

22 Camus' original phrase was 'every future revolution will be a foreign revolution' (cited in Kumar, K., *Revolution: The Theory and Practice of a European Idea*, London, 1971, p. 302) where 'future' referred to the period after the Russian revolution and the onset of the Cold War.

internationally induced political revolution in terms of an absent process of internal capitalist development.

Uneven and Combined Development and the Revolution of Backwardness

The apparent mismatch between history and theory that we identified in the case of revolutions traditionally conceptualised as 'bourgeois', including Iran's Constitutional Revolution, marked Russia's 1917 revolution in an even more acute form. For in a clear rebuke to Marx's predictions the predominantly semi-feudal Tsarist Russia became the site of the world's first proletarian revolution. Needless to say this circumstance posed a huge intellectual challenge to Marxist theory, which foresaw socialist revolutions to occur in most advanced capitalist countries. A highly innovative and compelling solution was offered by Leon Trotsky who went against the grain of classical Marxism and showed, in conceptual terms, why Russia, a backwater in capitalist world, could actually produce a socialist revolution. And his argumentation contained the basic intellectual ingredients for a non-Eurocentric social theory that unlike Enlightenment-rooted theories of history conceptually digested the ontological phenomenon of historical difference.

In his magisterial book *The History of the Russian Revolution* Trotsky begins with a strategic emphasis on social reality's differentiated constitution. 'Unevenness', he argues, '[is] the most general law of the historic process …'.[23] The social world has always consisted of the coexistence of social formations different in their social, cultural, and political forms and developmental capacities. This ontological condition of developmentally uneven inter-societal multiplicity *ipso facto* entails the interactive co-existence of the constitutive elements or what Trotsky describes as 'combined development' – 'a drawing together of the different stages of the journey, a combin[ation] of separate steps, an amalgam[ation] of archaic with more contemporary forms'. In short, through the idea of 'uneven and combined development' Trotsky provides the 'conceptual comprehension and expression of the ontological condition of the interrelation of societies' patterns of development, such that their interactive coexistence is constitutive of their individual existence and vice versa'.[24] Unevenness and combination therefore render history always already interactive and multi-linear and hence developmental difference its organic feature.

23 Trotsky, L., *The History of the Russian Revolution*, London, 1985, p. 27. Unless stated otherwise all citations from Trotsky in this section are from this source.

24 Matin, *Recasting Iranian Modernity*, pp. 16–17.

Processes of uneven and combined development take on an intensified form under capitalism which, once fully crystallised in England, as we saw, generated an inescapable dynamic of developmental contrasts and geopolitical pressures that transformed the erstwhile inter-societal developmental difference into a problematic condition for all non-capitalist polities. For now developmental capacities of the non-capitalist societies prove qualitatively and fundamentally inferior and self-restricting compared with far vaster productive potentialities of capitalism. Thus, capitalism generated 'backwardness.'

In Trotsky's works the concept of backwardness captures a specific condition of developmental agility generated by the belated entanglement of a premodern country into the internationally driven process of capitalist transformation. One of the key consequences of the condition of backwardness is that the state becomes the strategic receiver of, and the immediate responder to, external capitalist pressures. In their fierce existential struggle backward states have two broad kinds of strategy: 'defensive accumulation' and 'defensive modernisation'; by the former I refer to an intensification of the modes of quantitative amassing of material and human resources in order to maintain an embattled or threatened backward state. These modes include elements of practices that Robert Brenner places under the rubric of 'political accumulation', i.e., 'build up of larger, more effective military organization and/or the construction of stronger surplus–extracting machinery'.[25] But defensive accumulation can also take the form of the domestic sale of state property, land and offices, and external sale of economic concessions and privileges. The French monarchy, for example, had created 70,000 venal offices by the eighteenth century.[26]

Defensive accumulation is a developmentally conservative strategy insofar as it does not involve any immediate change in the backward country's basic social property regime and reproductive relations. But more importantly, it is also politically highly contradictory in three main ways. First, it violates pre-existing practices of the sustainable, and more or less legitimate, levels of fiscal claims that the state can make on the subject population. Second, it tends to fragment state authority and administrative efficacy. And third, it involves varying degrees of the cession of economic, and by implication political, sovereignty to foreign states and subjects, which is diametrically opposed to the strategic goal of the political reproduction

---

25 Brenner, R., 'The Agrarian Roots of European Capitalism', in Aston, T. H. and Philpin, C. H. E. (eds.), *The Brenner Debate: Agrarian Class Structure and Economic Development in Pre-Industrial Europe*, Cambridge, 1988, p. 238.

26 Doyle, W., *Venality: The Sale of Offices in Eighteenth-Century France*, London, 1996.

of the backward state. It therefore simultaneously and paradoxically weakens the state *and* antagonises both the dominant and subaltern classes, thereby undermining socio-political order as a whole. *Ancien regime* France, imperial China, and Ottoman, Tsarist and Qajar states all displayed various levels of the operation and outcomes of defensive accumulation.

Defensive accumulation is therefore neither a viable nor sustainable strategy for protection against the growing pressures of the more advanced states whose geopolitical power originates from a qualitatively different source, i.e., the capitalist mode of production. In fact, all single-track strategies of defensive accumulation have invariably led to military defeats followed by radical restructuring of the state and a subsequent or concomitant project of 'defensive moderniation'.[27] Eighteenth-century France and mid-nineteenth-century Russia are paradigmatic examples.

Defensive modernisation involves the importation of modern industrial, technological and organisational products, which are deployed primarily, though not exclusively, for military and security purposes. In embarking on defensive modernisation, backward states utilise what Trotsky describes as the 'privilege of historic backwardness' whereby they can import end products of very long processes of development in other countries. Backward states therefore become substitutes for their indigenous possessing classes, which had been the main agency of capitalist transformation in the classic English case.

Defensive modernisation also entails potentially explosive contradictions. Some of these contradictions are generated by backward states' simultaneous adoption of defensive accumulation strategy in financing their defensive modernisation efforts. The Ottoman *tanzimat* reforms project is a classic example. But there is also a qualitatively different kind of contradiction involved in defensive modernisation, which I call the 'contradictions of adaptation'. The contradictions of adaptation emerge in the aftermath of the backward state's successful importation of capitalist products and forms. For these modern forms and products are, as mentioned above, results of a prior and protracted transformation of precapitalist social property regime and reproductive relations that cannot be re-enacted. If it were, it would dissolve, or considerably erode, the material and cultural bases of the power of precapitalist ruling elites themselves. As a result, defensive modernisation, particularly at early stages, assumes a highly selective character: modern economic and technological forms are imported but social and political forms are excluded. Thus, modern imported forms and their premodern environment lack historical synchrony and

27 Curtin, P., *The World and the West: the European Challenge and the Overseas Response in the Age of Empire*, Cambridge, 2000, p. 150.

developmental affinity and therefore have no organic connexion. As a result, in the course of defensive modernisation backward states, as Trotsky points out, 'debase the achievements borrowed from outside'[28] and create a contradictory and unstable form that I shall call 'asymmetric amalgamation'. Paradoxically, the reproduction of asymmetric amalgamations tends to elicit further self-contradictory responses. For example, during the latter parts of the nineteenth century defensive modernisation projects of the backward states of Germany and Japan created socio-political tensions, which these states subsequently sought to contain through foreign wars and imperialist chauvinism. These in turn provoked intervention by other western capitalist states that led to their destruction.

Asymmetric amalgamation is not limited to the combination of modern and premodern economic products and relations alone. It can also involve the combination of modern political products and organisations and premodern socio-economic relations and forms. These often result from defensive strategies of indigenous classes that in their attempts to contain the arbitrary encroachments of the backward state on their property and prestige adopt and adapt modern political forms that are out of sync with the level of backward country's socio-economic development. Late imperial China and late Qajar Iran are important cases in point. Whatever their precise configuration, asymmetric amalgamations tend to explode into political revolutions that set the backward states on the path of transformation into broadly centralised, territorialised and formally bourgeois-democratic *nation-states*. Important examples include 1848 Germany, 1905 Russia, 1906 Iran, and 1908 Turkey.

Now, my key argument here is that such revolutions, which have their origins in the contradictions of defensive accumulation and defensive modernisation, which are in turn generated by the condition of backwardness in the specific sense I described above, cannot be adequately explained in terms of the concept of bourgeois revolution. The reason is simply that the concept has an internalist constitution while these contradictions are, as we just saw, international in origin and operation. This means that such political revolutions cannot be fully derived from the internal developmental patterns and socio-political structures of the countries experiencing them.[29]

---

28 Trotsky, *The History of The Russian Revolution*, p. 27.

29 For a partially similar argument see Robert Tucker's thesis that successful 'communist revolutions' are better understood as instances of 'revolutions of underdevelopment' (Tucker, R. C., 'The fate of the Marxian revolutionary idea: the revolution of underdevelopment', in Kumar, K. (ed.), *Revolution: The Theory and Practice of a European Idea*, London, 1971, pp. 313–315).

Revolutions of backwardness therefore always involve 'historical reshuffling'.[30] More specifically, they include a reversal in the order of modern social and political changes as they first occurred in England; an order that is central to the classical concept of the bourgeois revolution.[31] However, it should be noted that this reversal only takes place within the specific country in which the revolution of backwardness takes place. From a global perspective the sequence of social and political transformations remains the same: (political) revolutions of backwardness follow capitalist social transformation in England, which was itself the product of wider processes of uneven and combined development.

Moreover, the revolution of backwardness frequently involves the mutation of the forms and functions of the modern European political and juridical forms and institutions imported by backward states, a process which, as we saw, Trotsky described as 'debasment'. For example, the 1848 German revolution gave rise to the formula of the 'king *over* the parliament' (as opposed to the English formula of the 'king *in* the parliament). And Iran's Constitutional Revolution, as we shall see below, involved the mutation of the German formula through the imposition of a religious stricture on secular legislations of the parliament.

The Constitutional Revolution as a Revolution of Backwardness

Early Qajar Iran was marked by comparative economic backwardness, a weak state, and a small but relatively strong and autonomous native merchant class.[32] There also existed the peculiar system of 'dual sovereignty'[33] whereby the Shiʿa quasi-hierocracy shared power with Qajar monarchy. The Shiʿa ulama had acquired significant power and wealth during the late Safavi period and long post-Safavi interregnum. In the absence of an operational central state, they increasingly became local arbiters in various judicial, social and commercial matters.[34] This increased and solidified their social prestige and influence. The ulama's ownership of vast swaths of *waqf* (charitable) lands, which were cus-

30 Matin, *Recasting Iranian Modernity*, p. 19.

31 Cf. Davidson, N., *Discovering the Scottish Revolution, 1692–1746*, London, 2003.

32 Issawi, C., 'European Economic Penetration, 1872–1921', in Avery, E. *et al*, *The Cambridge History of Iran*, (vol. 7), p. 590.

33 Arjomand, S A., 'Shiism, Authority, and Political Culture', in Arjomand, S. A. (ed.), *Authority and Political Culture in Shiism*, New York, 1988, p. 192.

34 Algar, H., 'Religious forces in Eighteenth- and Nineteenth-Century Iran', in Avery, E., *et al*, *The Cambridge History of Iran*, (vol. 7), pp. 705–732.

tomarily exempted from taxation, reinforced their power and status. Moreover, the wealthier ulama also accumulated significant amount of wealth through commercial activities. These activities reinforced their traditionally close relationship with the bazaar merchants. Furthermore, the Qajars lacked prophetic descent and hence religiously legitimate authority. As a result they were dependent on the Shi'a ulama for ideological legitimation and popular mobilisation in times of war.

The international context of Qajar state formation was also inauspicious. The Safavids established their empire at a time when the Russian state was still in gestation and the Ottomans engaged major European powers, which as a result had very little presence in, or influence on, West Asia and Iran. The Qajars by contrast formed and ruled their tribal state in the era of the supremacy of European great powers of which Russia posed the greatest challenge. With the end of the Napoleonic wars Tsarist Russia had resumed its southward expansion in the Caucasus and Central Asia towards the 'warm waters of the Persian Gulf', which Russian tsars had seen as vital to the empire and sought to access since the time of Peter the Great. The Qajars on the other hand saw the Caucasus as their traditional domain. In fact, the khanates of the Caucasus had been tributary principalities of Iran since the time of the Safavids. War with Russia was therefore inevitable. But the Qajars' small ragtag tribal army was no match for the Russian imperial army seasoned in the Napoleonic wars. Iran suffered two major defeats in 1812 and 1826 and lost all of its territories north of the Aras River including Azerbaijan, Georgia and Daghestan. Iran's recognition of Russian sovereignty over the entire South Caucasus was formalised in the humiliating treaties of Gulistan (1812) and Turkmanchai (1828). At the same time, Russian advances alarmed the British who saw Iran as a key component of their overall strategy of protecting India against Russian expansion. This meant that they would consider tactical support to the Qajars but not to the extent that it could enable Iran to pose similar threats to India right at its southeastern frontiers. For the British Iran was therefore a buffer state.

The Qajars reacted to their rapidly declining power by taking *ad hoc* measures that in their logic, though not necessarily in their conception and execution, amounted to an abortive project of defensive modernisation. Thus, in the immediate aftermath of the Russo-Iranian wars, crown prince Abbas Mirza (1789–1833) launched the *nizami jadid* (New Order) reforms to modernise their tribal army. The reforms were a half-hearted emulation of the Ottoman modernisation project of *tanzimat*, which similarly had been a defensive project of modernisation undertaken, as Albert Hourani correctly argues, due to the 'fear of Europe, and pressure from Europe'.[35] Financing the reforms necessitated increased spending. But state revenues had drastically plummeted following the large loss of territory in the north, which had been traditionally supplying a significant part of the Qajars' tax-revenue. The Qajars therefore turned to the strategy of defensive accumulation to finance their defensive modernisation. Thus, Prime Minister Amir Kabir (1848–1852) launched a reform programme that included administrative centralisation and reducing state-pensions to courtiers, provincial elites and the ulama. However, the latter groups resisted the reforms, which they saw as a breach of their *de facto*, traditionally observed, rights and privileges. They succeeded in persuading Naser-al-din Shah (1831–1896) to dismiss and execute Amir Kabir. Consequently, the Qajar monarchy intensified the sale of government offices, crown and state lands, titles, and tax-farms.

These measures, however, failed to halt the decline of Qajar monarchy. From the mid-nineteenth century onward, the Qajars therefore adopted a second form of defensive accumulation. They started to sell commercial and economic concessions to foreign capitalists, primarily British and Russian.[36] Apart from meeting the immediate dire fiscal needs of the state these sales can also been as a strategy of 'positive equilibrium' whereby the co-presence of significant economic interests of competing imperial powers would protect Iran from being formally colonised or annexed by individual imperial powers. As such it therefore represented a desperate attempt by the Qajars to create an external base for their increasingly uncertain domestic rule. Moreover, the concessions facilitated a limited import of Western technological and administrative products. However, positive equilibrium had a self-propelling dynamic. Any concession made to one imperial power would trigger a demand for a similar concession from the other imperial power or the cancellation of the original concession. Increasingly, such demands could not be resisted or rejected as Anglo-Russian relations increasingly were influenced by the exigencies of dealing with the German threat in Europe, which tended to dilute their rivalry over Iran. The strategy of positive equilibrium culminated in 1907 secret partitioning of Iran into two northern and southern spheres of influence for Russian and Britain, respectively, and a neutral central sphere.

The Qajars' defensive accumulation based on granting economic concessions to Anglo-Russian imperial powers had other unintended consequences. Firstly, and most importantly, commercial concessions to Russian and British capital had a disastrous impact on the bazaar, which was already in a dire situation unable

35 Hourani, A., *The Emergence of the Modern Middle East*, London, 1981, p. 14.

36 Keddie, N., *Religion and Rebellion in Iran: The Tobacco Protest of 1891–1892*, London, p. 7.

to compete with cheaper Western manufactured goods. The new concessions, coupled with the Qajars' growing arbitrary exactions, increasingly led the bazaar merchants to invest in land. This amounted to a process of the feudalisation of the mercantile bourgeoisie that was accelerated by the growing trade in cash crops, cotton and opium in particular. The world-market price of cotton increased significantly during the American Civil War (1861–1865) while Britain displayed a growing demand for cheap opium imported to India where it was re-exported to China to pay for Chinese tea. Iran was therefore indirectly implicated in the 'Opium Wars' between Britain and China. The growth of cash-crop farming also reduced the country's food self-sufficiency and thus increased the likelihood of famine, which actually struck the country in 1869–1872. It structurally exposed the Iranian economy to the fluctuations of commodity prices in the world market. It also drastically deteriorated the living conditions of the artisans, craftsmen, peddlers and the urban poor who engaged in the traditional handcraft industries closely related to the rapidly declining bazaar.

Secondly, the ulama were also affected by the judicial and educational reforms that defensive modernisation entailed. The proliferation of civil courts, partly to facilitate the smoother function of foreign capital and partly merely to emulate Western institutions, undermined the ulama's influence and prestige associated with their erstwhile control over the judicial system.[37] Similarly, education traditionally was concentrated in the ulama-run *madrasa*s (religious schools), which now faced competition from new secular schools teaching modern sciences and foreign languages.[38] However, the ulama's opposition to the Qajars or support for the constitutional movement was neither universal nor consistent.[39] The constitutionalists' attempt to regulate *waqf* (charitable) lands especially antagonised richer sections of the ulama. Others who had royal appointments and patronage were in fact staunch anti-constitutionalists. Sheikh Fazlollah Nuri is a famous example. Nuri articulated his opposition to constitutionalism through the notion of *mashrutey-e mashru'eh* (the Shariʿa conforming constitutionalism).[40] His persistent opposition

37 The judicial system was *de facto* divided into the Shariʿa courts run by the ulama and administrative or customary (*'urf*) courts managed by the state (Keddie, N., *Modern Iran: Roots and Results of Revolution*, Yale, 2003, p. 29.

38 Keddie, *Modern Iran*, pp. 26–27.

39 Bayat, M., *Iran's First Revolution: Shiʿism and the Constitutional Revolution of 1905–1909*, Oxford, 1991.

40 Martin, V. A., 'Shaikh Fazlallah and the Iranian Revolution, 1905–9', in *Middle Eastern Studies*, vol. 23, no. 1, 1987, pp. 39–53.

to the secular tone of the new constitution was instrumental in the inclusion in the draft of the Supplementary Fundamental Law of a controversial article that subjected all parliamentary legislations to the approval of a committee of five leading Shi'a clerics. Nuri's elitist and restrictive conception of popular sovereignty drew on the work of the early *Usuli* jurists such as Mulla Ahmad Naraqi and anticipated the institution of The Council of Guardians of the Constitution as a key element in the political structure of the Islamic Republic following the 1979 revolution.

Thirdly, the Qajar's concessions to European powers entailed increasing contacts with the West. This gave rise to a small but influential stratum of Western-influenced intelligentsia. Impressed by Western development, they entirely attributed Iran's 'backwardness' to the Qajars' arbitrary rule. This placed them at the forefront of the anti-Qajar constitutional movement. It is noteworthy that despite their own secular leanings, many members of this modern intelligentsia presented their political views in a religious idiom in order to communicate better with an audience whose vast majority was still illiterate and deeply imbued with religious ideology and discourse. This process itself represented a form of combined intellectual development that produced a host of vocabulary and terms whose Western etymological veneer did not always conform to their mutated conceptual substance.

Finally, the dire economic situation and the increasingly intensified exactions of the government had forced hundreds of thousands of peasants and the urban poor to migrate to Russia's Caucasus region where they were employed in the oil and mining industries in Azerbaijan and Armenia and exposed to the revolutionary politics of Russian social democracy.[41] Elements of this 'proletariat in exile' played an important role in the constitutional movement. For instance, the radicalism of the first *majles* was to a great extent due to the influence of the Azeri delegates many of whom had close association with both Russian social democracy and the Iranian immigrant worker communities in Russia.

By the early twentieth century, dynamics of backwardness had created a deep politico-economic and ideological crisis in Qajar Iran. The traditional balance of class forces had been radically disturbed. The mercantile bourgeoisie and the ulama, two propertied but non-capitalist classes, sought to preserve their power and interests by limiting the legislative powers of the monarchy through modern political institutions, parliament in particular. New subaltern classes and the secular intelligentsia, generated by the wider process of uneven and combined development, pursued more radical socio-political change.

41 For relevant statistics see Afary, *The Iranian Constitutional Revolution*, p. 22.

The ulama-bazaar alliance had already had the 'dress rehearsal' of the Tobacco Boycott Movement of 1891–92. The international conjuncture was also conducive to nationalist-democratic movements in the region. Russia's defeat by Japan and its subsequent 1905 revolution had intensified anti-imperialist and anti-monarchical sentiments in Iran. The customs reforms under Mozaffar-ad-Din Shah (1896–1907) fuelled the discontent among the bazaaris. In addition, the decline of the price of silver in the world market had a drastic effect on the Iranian economy, whose currency, the *qiran*, was pegged to silver. The effect was particularly severe since the currency of Iran's main trading partners, e.g., Russia, Britain and India, were pegged to gold.[42] A few consecutive bad harvests exacerbated the situation, as the price of bread and other basic items soared and led to widespread, urban 'bread riots'. The government's response was a heavy-handed punishment of the bazaar merchants who were accused of hoarding and artificially increasing the prices. This last episode caused popular protests that rapidly developed into a large urban movement against the monarchy.

In July 1906, tens of thousands of people staged two large sit-ins in the holy shrines of Qum and the vast gardens of the British legation in Tehran. The demonstrators came from all walks of urban life: guild members, artisans, shop-keepers, petty bazaaris, junior clerics and religious seminary (*hawza*) students. They demanded the establishment of a National Consultative Assembly (*majles*). Their action was supported and financed by Tehran's prominent merchants, some leading Shiʿa clerics, and discontented senior technocrats, princes and courtiers. The reigning Qajar shah, Muzaffar al-Din Shah, eventually succumbed and on 5 August 1906 issued an edict for the convening of Iran's first parliament and the drafting of Iran's Fundamental Laws. These events were followed by five years of intensive struggle between the constitutionalists and the royalists, including two years of bloody civil war. The royalists received both overt and covert support of Tsarist Russia. Britain also supported the royalists, albeit intermittently. Royalists also benefited from growing tensions between the reformist and radical social-democratic tendencies within the constitutional movement, which paved the way for the temporary return of the Qajar monarchy to power during 1908–1909, a period known as the 'lesser despotism' (*estebdad-e saghir*).

In mid 1911 royalist forces staged another attack on the constitutional government, which was defeated thanks to the military support of the powerful southern

42 Avery, P. W. and Simmons, J. B., 'Persia on A Cross of Silver, 1880–90', in Kedourie, E. and Haim, S. G. (eds.), *Towards a Modern Iran: Studies in Thought, Politics and Society*, London, 1980, pp. 1–37.

Bakhtiyari tribe. The period 1909–1911 saw the growing radicalisation of the constitutional movement (1909–1911) and the collapse of all effective nationwide authority. As part of their attempt at reforming state finances and obtaining the necessary revenue for establishing control over the provinces, the constitutional government employed Morgan Shuster, an American citizen, as treasurer general. The appointment angered Russia, which managed to rally the British against it. In November 1911 Russia demanded the dismissal of Shuster in an ultimatum. The ultimatum was rejected by the majles. As the Russian troops advanced on Tehran the conservative Bakhtiari-dominated cabinet dissolved the majles. Although the constitution was never abrogated the Constitutional Revolution was pacified.

Conclusion

Interpretations of the Constitutional Revolution based on the concept of bourgeois revolution involve two basic problems: the material conditions the concept identifies as necessary (relatively advanced levels of capitalist development and class formation) are lacking; and, relatedly, they are fashioned in a negative fashion insofar as they have to qualify the revolution as a 'failed bourgeois revolution', which means they explain the revolution in terms of what it was not rather than what it actually was.

I have tried to address these problems by introducing the idea of 'revolution of backwardness', which is a derivative of the idea of 'uneven and combined development', where backwardness is itself an inherently international phenomenon. Accordingly, I have re-theorised the Constitutional Revolution as a revolution of backwardness in the following general sense. The Constitutional Revolution was not the political aftershock of an *internally* generated capitalist transformation superseding a feudal *ancien régime*. It did not follow or involve 'primitive accumulation' as the fundamental basis of capitalist relations, which as Marx points out is 'the basis of the whole process' of the formation of a capitalist class and capitalism.[43] Rather, it was essentially an attempt by *non*-capitalist bazaar merchants and their allies to circumscribe the arbitrary power of autocratic Qajar state which under mounting *international* pressures had been increasingly forced to resort to a strategy of defensive accumulation that involved the penetration and operation of foreign capital in Iran. The Qajars' defensive accumulation therefore entailed the growing violation of the traditional privileges of the propertied classes, who responded by demanding radical reforms that placed them on a bourgeois revolutionary road.

43 Marx, *Capital*, p.876.

Nevertheless, the Constitutional Revolution was indeed generated by the impact of capitalist socio-economic relations, which were objectively absent from Qajar Iran but existed at the international level and affected it geopolitically. It is in this general sense that both nineteenth-century European revolutions and Iran's Constitutional Revolution defy a simple analogy with the English bourgeois revolution of seventeenth century. They relate to capitalism and each other as specific instances of 'the revolution of backwardness' integral to the world-wide process of modern uneven and combined development. This argument also applies to the revolutions of 1905 and 1911 in Russia and China, respectively.

The Constitutional Revolution thus represented the explosion of the tensions generated by the combination of qualitatively different capitalist and precapitalist dynamics at the international and internal levels; a combination which concretely manifested itself in a reversal in the *social* and the *political* moments of the classic case of capitalist transformation in England, which was the main referent in the construction of the concept of the bourgeois revolution.

However, beyond the specific case of Iran's constitutional revolution my analysis here contributes to a growing body of literature informed by the idea of uneven and combined development that not only, *à la* postcolonial approaches, critiques the eurocentric constitution of the enlightenment and modern European social thought and its false pretentions to universalism, but also provides a positive non-ethnocentric social theory that foregrounds, at the deepest ontological level, the plural and interactive character of social world and developmental multilinearity that it necessarily generates.[44] Equally importantly, the idea of uneven and combined development does not simply discard the basic ideas of the Enlightenment due to their Eurocentric constitution. Rather, it shows that the problems of those ideas, their false universalism in particular, are not necessarily inherent to the ideas themselves but to their internalist construction and therefore can be overcome through their interactive reconstruction. In this manner uneven and combined development supplants and preserves (*Aufhebung*) the emancipatory ideals of the enlightenment.

44 For a list of classical and contemporary literature on uneven and combined development see www.unevenandcombined.com

Bibliography

Abrahamian, E. 'The Causes of the Constitutional Revolution in Iran', in *International Journal of Middle Eastern Studies*, vol. 10, no. 3, 1979, pp. 381–414.

Afary, J., *The Iranian Constitutional Revolution: 1906–1911: Grassroots Democracy, Social Democracy, and the Origins of Feminism*, New York, 1996.

Afshari, M. R., 'The Pishivaran and Merchants in Precapitalist Iranian Society: An Essay on the Background and Causes of the Constitutional Revolution', in *International Journal of Middle East Studies*, vol. 15, no. 2, 1983, pp. 133–155.

Algar, H., 'Religious forces in Eighteenth- and Nineteenth Century Iran', in Avery, E. *et al* (eds.), *The Cambridge History of Iran,* (vol. 7), Cambridge, 1991, pp. 705–732.

Arjomand, S A., 'Shiism, Authority, and Political Culture', in Arjomand, S. A. (ed.), *Authority and Political Culture in Shiism*, New York, 1988.

Ashraf, H., 'Historical Obstacles to the Development of a Bourgeoisie in Iran', in Cook M. A. (ed.), *Studies in the Economic History of the Middle East: From the Rise of Islam to the Present Day*, Oxford, 1970, pp. 308–332.

Avery, P. W. and Simmons, J. B., 'Persia on A Cross of Silver, 1880–90', in Kedourie, E. and Haim, S. G. (eds.), *Towards a Modern Iran: Studies in Thought, Politics and Society*, London, 1980, pp. 1–37.

Bakhash, S., 'Center-Periphery Relations in Nineteenth-Century Iran', in *Iranian Studies,* vol: XIV, no. 1–2.

Bayat, M., *Iran's First Revolution: Shi'ism and the Constitutional Revolution of 1905–1909*, Oxford, 1991.

Bhambra, G., 'The possibilities of, and for, global sociology', in Go, J., (ed.), *Postcolonial Sociology: Political Power and Social Theory*, Bingley, 2015, pp. 295–314.

Brenner, R., 'The Agrarian Roots of European Capitalism', in Aston, T. H. and Philpin, C. H. E. (eds.), *The Brenner Debate: Agrarian Class Structure and Economic Development in Pre-Industrial Europe*, Cambridge, 1988.

Brenner, R., 'The Origins of Capitalist Development: A Critique of Neo-Smithian Marxism', in *New Left Review*, issue: 104, 1977, pp. 25–92.

Chakrabarty, D., *Provincializing Europe: Postcolonial Thought and Historical Difference*, Princeton, 2008.

Comninel, G., *Rethinking the French Revolution*, London, 1990.

Curtin, P., *The World and the West: The European Challenge and the Overseas Response in the Age of Empire*, Cambridge, 2000.

Dabashi, H., 'Early Propagation of Wilayati-I Faqih and Mulla Ahmad Naraqi', in Nasr, S. H., Dabashi, H., and Nasr, S. V. R. (eds.), *Expectations of the Millennium: Shi'ism in History*, New York, 1989, pp. 288–300.

Davidson, N., *Discovering the Scottish Revolution, 1692–1746*, London, 2003.

Doyle, W., *Venality: The Sale of Offices in Eighteenth-Century France*, London, 1996.

Foran, J., *Fragile Resistance: Social Transformation in Iran from 1500 to the Revolution*, San Francisco, 1993.

Hournai, A., *The Emergence of the Modern Middle East*, London, 1981.

Issawi, C., 'European Economic Penetration, 1872–1921', in Avery, E. *et al.* (eds.), *The Cambridge History of Iran*, (vol. 7), Cambridge, 1990.

Ivanov, M. S., *The Iranian Constitutional Revolution*, Tehran, 1978.

Keddie, N., *Modern Iran: Roots and Results of Revolution*, Yale, 2003.

Keddie, N., *Religion and Rebellion in Iran: The Tobacco Protest of 1891–1892*, London, 1966.

Kedourie, E., *Democracy and Arab Political Culture*, Washington, 1992.

Lambton, A. S., 'Land Tenure and Revenue Administration in the Nineteenth Century', in Avery, E. *et al* (eds.), *The Cambridge History of Iran*, (vol. 7), Cambridge, 1991, pp. 459–505.

Kumar, K., *Revolution: The Theory and Practice of a European Idea*, London, 1971.

Lewis, G., *The French Revolution: Rethinking the Debate*, London, 1999.

Marx, K., *The Revolutions of 1848: Political Writings Volume 1*, London, 2010.

Marx, K., *Grundrisse*, London, 1993.

Marx, K., *Capital* (vol. 1), London, 1990.

Martin, V. A., 'Shaikh Fazlallah and the Iranian Revolution, 1905–9', in *Middle Eastern Studies*, vol. 23, no. 1, 1987.

Matin, K., 'Redeeming the Universal: Postcolonialism and the Inner Life of Eurocentrism', *European Journal of International Relations*, vol. 19, no. 2, 2013.

Matin, K., *Recasting Iranian Modernity: International Relations and Social Change*, London, 2013.

Rosenberg, J., *The Empire of Civil Society: A Critique of Realist Theory of International Relations*, London, 1994.

Said, E., *Orientalism: Western Conceptions of the Orient*, London, 1978.

Skocpol, T., *States and Social Revolution: A Comparative Analysis of France, Russia and China*, Cambridge, 1979.

Teschke, B., 'Bourgeois Revolution, State Formation and the Absence of the International', in *Historical Materialism*, vol. 13, no. 2, 2005, pp. 3–26.

Trotsky, L., *The History of the Russian Revolution*, London, 1985.

Tucker, R. C., 'The fate of the Marxian revolutionary idea: the revolution of underdevelopment', in K. Kumar (ed.) *Revolution: The Theory and Practice of a European Idea*, London, 1971, pp. 313–15.

Wood, E., 'The Separation of the Economic and the Political in Capitalism', in *New Left Review*, no. 127, 1981.

4

Shrinking Borders and Expanding Vocabularies: Translation and the Iranian Constitutional Revolution of 1906

Milad Odabaei

This essay explores the movement of concepts from European political culture, and the historical and political order of things of the Enlightenment, to Iran in the nineteenth century. It elaborates translation as a process that brings together Iranian contact with European culture, and the changes in the language and practice of politics around the 1906 Iranian Constitutional Revolution. While tracing the translation of European thought to a paradigmatic piece of Qajar travel writing by Mirza Saleh Shirazi, it relates translation to the epistemic shifts that give form to 'the modern' in Iran. It demonstrates that Mirza Saleh Shirazi's travelogue is marked by an 'epistemic confusion' that reflect the changing order of Iranian things and shape the novel religious and political discourses of the Constitutional Revolution. As a result, and in contrast to the conventional narrative that attribute the Constitutional Revolution to the emulation of Europe as a site of difference, it argues that the 1906 Revolution was made possible through a transferential relation with the difference internal to Iranian history and cultural traditions.

New Words of an Unsettled Order

Shortly after the 1906 Constitutional Revolution in Iran, Ayn al-Saltaneh, a somewhat peripheral member of the royal family, took note in his journal that new terms had come to dominate the political culture of Iran. His list includes, and I translate: *mashruta,* 'constitutionalism'; *mustabeda,* 'despotic'; *azadi,* 'liberty'; *baradari,* 'fraternity'; *barabari* and *mosavat,* the Persian and Arabic words for 'equality' with different epistemic resonances; *jalase,* 'meeting', 'congregation'; *janan malan,* an Arabic phrase denoting radical devotion to a cause, literally: 'with my life and possessions'; *ba tamam ghova,* 'with all power'; *zendeh bad,* 'long-live'; *past bad,* 'down-with'; *ghoveyeh mojriyeh,* 'executive power'; *ghoveyeh moghananeh,* 'legislative power'; *ekhtar,* 'warning'; *tozih* 'justification'; *vojdan,* 'conscience'; *anjoman,* 'assembly'; *meliyat,* 'nationality'; *ghomiyat,* 'ethnicity'; *mojahed,* someone who struggles for a cause, or embarks on *jahad; fadaye-e majles,* 'devote of the parliament'; *alani,* 'public'; *serri,* 'secret'; and lastly, 'commission', 'cabinet', 'archive', and 'party,' which were transliterated in Persian and thus require no translation.[1]

This essay explores the movement of concepts from European political culture, and the historical and political order of things of the Enlightenment, to Iran in the nineteenth century. How did the terms such as those recounted by Ayn al-Saltaneh emerge in the linguistic frames of Iranian history and come to dominate Iranian political culture at the turn of the twentieth century?

Many studies of Iran have acknowledged the significance of the country's intellectual and cultural contacts with Europe in the nineteenth century and the subsequent formation of various registers of *modern* Iran. Few, however, have developed an adequate methodology for correlating the cultural exchange between Iran and Europe to the concrete transformations of Iran's culture that ground its modernity. In the conventional narrative, the Iranians who encountered European culture in the nineteenth century promoted reformist ideologies and centralised projects of reform that animated Iranian modernity. As part of this narrative of reform and modernisation, scholars have studied intellectual and diplomatic exchanges, travels and travel writing, and the contribution of Iran's diasporic communities in generating historical transformations. Although this narrative is not without its merits, not all instances of cultural and intellectual exchange engender epochal transformations.

The narrative of modernisation, moreover, risks stabilising various registers

1 Tabatabaei, J., *Ta'amoli darbareh-ye Iran, Nazariyeh-ye Hokomat-e Ghanoon dar Iran, Mabaniye Nazarieh-ye Mashruteh-khahi*, Tehran, 2012, p. 87.

of 'the modern' in relation to Europe and the vicissitudes of European cultural traditions by suggesting that it only arrives in Iran through contact with Europe. If Iran's encounter with Europe in the nineteenth century is a catalyst of changes that prompt a new periodisation in its history, these encounters will need to be grounded in more profound conditions and transformations within nineteenth century Iran. The periodisation of 'modern' Iran, as well as respective historiographical categories such as 'reform' and 'revolution', acquire their distinct meaning only when they are defined in relation to Iranian traditions, their dynamics and developments. For example, the paradigmatic political event of modern Iran, the Constitutional 'Revolution' of 1906, cannot be defined independently from the debates of the Shiʿa *ulama* (scholars), and the novel and unique 'reform' within the Shiʿa jurisprudential discourses, in relation to the nature of modern political rule.[2] While the internal dynamisms and the specificity of the various traditions that animate Iran do not prohibit drawing parallels with other traditions and cultures, they do place constraints on sociological and historiographical studies that treat 'the modern' and relevant concepts as universal categories of analysis.

In order to render visible the relation between Iran's encounter with Europe and the formation of 'modern' Iran, this essay theorises the rise and grounding of European social and political concepts in the epistemic terrain of Iranian history. It does so by foregrounding *translation* as a process that brings together Iranian contact with European culture, and the changes in the language and practice of Iranian social and political traditions. Through elaborating the various dimension of the translation of European culture, I hope to make clear how otherwise 'European' concepts secure their meaning on the terrain of history in Iran. In this task, I draw insights from anthropology and historical epistemology as they converge in the early work of Michel Foucault and his elaboration of 'episteme' in *The Order of Things*.[3] Foucault's elaboration of the episteme elucidates the fundamental role of order in the constitution of human culture.[4] He does so by elaborating

---

2 For a thorough discussion of this debate in Persian, see: Tabatabai, J., *Ta'amoli darbareh-ye Iran, Nazariyeh-ye Hokomat-e Ghanoon dar Iran, Maktab-e Tabriz va Mabani-ye Tajadod-khahi*, Tehran, 2012, pp. 373–526. In English, see: Hairi, A., *Shiʿism and Constitutionalism in Iran: A Study of the Role Played by the Persian Residents of Iraq in Iranian Politics*, Leiden, 1977.

3 Foucault, M., *The Order of Things: An Archeology of Human Sciences*, New York, 1970.

4 Foucault's attention to order recalls Claude Lévi-Strauss' *La Pensée sauvage* that just a few years earlier, had posited 'drive to order' as a constituent, as opposed to 'super-structural', role of 'culture'. Drawing on the linguistic anthropology of Franz Boas and the linguist Roman Jacobson, Lévi-Strauss demonstrated that all forms of cultural production are ordering practices that are predicated upon a process of de-semanticisation. What he articulated as the 'work of culture'

how discursive regularities, rationalities and cosmologies make possible not only knowledge, but also various dimensions of inter-subjectivity. While foregrounding the constitutive role of order, Foucault emphasises the role of contingency by elaborating historical breaks that separate the past from the present and coincide with distinct organisation of knowledge and sociality.[5] In so doing, he correlates the modality of order that foregrounds the identity of an episteme to the periodisation of a culture in space and time. What defines a period in the long development of a culture is the period's particular modality of order.[6]

Translation provides a basis to acknowledge the contemporaneous relation that Iran and Europe have to one another in the nineteenth century while remaining attentive to internal movements unfolding in Iran relative to its own historical and cultural development. In the plane of simultaneity, translation first appears as a simple transposition of words and texts across two languages. For example, the English phrase 'Constitutional Revolution' is often used in order to translate from Persian *inqilab-i mashruta*.[7] This translation takes for granted the translatability

consists in formulation of a particular relationship with concrete historical experience. This original insight, which is his contribution to twentieth century European thought, renders culture not only as a marker of difference but a site of generation of an ordered relation with the materiality of history. Lévi-Strauss and Foucault's elaboration of 'culture' informs my use of the concept in this essay. See Lévi-Strauss, C., *The Savage Mind*, Chicago, 1966.

5 Foucault's conceptualisation of epistemic shift is indebted to the work of historians of science Gaston Bachelard and Georges Canguilhem. The two French epistemologists ushered a novel historical approach to the formation of knowledge that emphasised the constitutive role of contingency, context and milieu in the historical formation of universal rationalities. See Foucault, *The Order of Things*, p. xx.

6 Foucault writes: 'In any given culture and at any given moment, there is always only one episteme that defines the conditions of possibility of all knowledge, whether expressed in theory or silently invested in a practice.' What concerns me here is not this totalising quality of episteme as it is put forth in *The Order of Things*, or the absence of synchronic relations of the West and the non-West as studied by thinkers such as Edward Said and Ann Stoler. I am primarily interested in the anonymous or elusive character and the conditioning power of the episteme. The episteme works in the background and conditions how we perceive and cognise, what we can know, who we are, and what we can become. While Foucault will revise the totalising quality of the episteme starting in the *Archeology of Knowledge* and his subsequent elaboration of discursive formations, the anonymity and conditioning qualities assigned to episteme are only further elaborated in his subsequent works. See Said, E., *Orientalism*, New York, 1978; Stoler, A., L., *Race and the Education of Desire: Foucault's History of Sexuality and the Colonial Order of Things*, Durham, 1995; Foucault, M., *Archeology of Knowledge*, London, 1972.

7 Historian Abbas Amanat traces the first use of the terms 'Constitutional Revolution' for

of the Persian and English concepts and the phrase as a whole and makes possible a discourse on the event and the developments of modern Iran. Translation, however, also concerns the historicity of a language and a culture. The Persian terms of *inqilab-i mashruta,* as well as the concepts 'constitutional' and 'revolution', are only meaningful within their respective and distinct historical and political culture and diverging epistemic constellations. Without recognition of the background that makes their meaning and the grammar of their use possible, we risk rendering these concepts as historically meaningless. Translation thus concerns moving between historically divergent orders of things – however disorderly they might be – and traversing distinct epistemic conditions. Somewhat independent from cross-linguistic and cross-cultural differences, translation mediates the relation of a language and culture with itself. It emerges between its 'now' and its future. Here, translation comes up against the historical possibilities and limitations of languages and cultures and becomes part of historical development. In its terrain, translation emerges as part of Iranian forms of life – and death. *Life and death*, I write, because following Foucault and anthropological elaborations of language and conceptuality, I understand the discursive use of language and concepts, with or without self-reflection, to constitute the possibilities and limitations of forms of life.[8] In this terrain, translation relates to the exteriority that language mediates and against which discourses form, deform and reform.

Drawing on Foucault, I show how translation enters the epistemic shifts of Iranian political and religious culture, and gives words to the changing Iranian order. In contrast to the West, where 'the modern' is a genesis of 'tradition', albeit a discontinuous and genealogical genesis, this study demonstrates that modern Iran is marked by a temporal disharmony of contemporaneous and indeterminable concepts and practices. Translation, in this historical conjuncture, performs

---

inqilab-i mashruta. For Brown consequential naming, see Amanat, A., 'Memory and Amnesia in the Historiography of the Constitutional Revolution', in Atabaki, T. (ed.), *Iran in the 20th Century: Historiography and Political Culture*, New York, 2009.

8 Among others, I have in mind the work of anthropologists such as Talal Asad and William Hank who respectively draw on the philosophical discourses of Ludwig Wittgenstein and Pierre Bourdieu and elaborate the role of language and grammar in relation to historical formation, transformation and disintegration of forms of life and its various registers. See Asad, T., *Formations of the Secular: Christianity, Islam, Modernity*, Stanford, 2003 and 'The Trouble of Thinking', in Scott D. and Hirschkind, C., (eds.), *Powers of the Secular Modern: Talal Asad and His Interlocutors*, Stanford, 2006. See also Hanks, W., *Converting Words: Maya in the Age of the Cross*, Berkeley, 2010.

a unique and crucial task of giving linguistic and cultural expression to incommensurabilities that are contemporaneous. Translation does so by introducing new vocabularies and expanding the potentialities of available concepts and conceptual traditions. In so doing, translation makes possible a transferential relation within Iranian cultural traditions. I analyse this conceptual transference by elaborating a productive 'epistemic confusion' that corresponds to the changing order of Iranian things and provides the grounds of novel religious and political debates of the nineteenth century. In conclusion, I point to the religious debate on Constitutionalism to exemplify the work of translation in a generative encounter with historical difference. This analysis shows that in Iran translation emerges as an historical and cultural practice that extends beyond the linguistic transposition of texts and animates the potentiality of linguistic and cultural traditions to open to and articulate difference and thereby re-encounter and regenerate themselves.

Pathogenesis of Translation in the Nineteenth Century

The systematic translation of European thought in Iran emerged in the second half of the nineteenth century during the rule of Naser al-Din Shah of Qajar (1848–1896). However, the first translations of European thought can be traced to Qajar travelogues earlier in the century, in the aftermath of Iran's defeats in the first episode of the Perso-Russian War (1804–13). In *Taken for Wonder*, a recent study of nineteenth-century travel writing, Naghmeh Sohrabi recalls 283 journeys to Europe from Iran between 1809 and 1897 that are equally divided across the two halves of the century.[9] Abdulhosein Azerang's recent history of translation in Iran describes the gradual rise of interest in translation in the nineteenth century and its culmination in the systematic translations of the Naseri period.[10] In Azerang's account, and that of many others, the Iranian losses in the war with the Russian Empire provided a significant boost in the Iranian efforts to learn about Europe and translate European discourses. Qajar travel writings, their underlying inspirations, and their particular form, set the stage for the subsequent intellectual, political and courtly interest in translation of various categories of European thought. They mark the renewal of travel writing in Persian, and usher other literary genres and practices including writing journals such as the one which brings us Ayn al-Saltaneh's observation in the opening lines of this essay.

9 Sohrabi, N., *Taken For Wonder: Nineteenth-Century Travel Accounts from Iran to Europe*, New York, 2012, pp. 3–4.

10 In Azerang, A., *Tarikh-i Tarjomeh dar Iran*, Tehran, 2014, p. 245.

Tracing the discourse of the translation to the event of the Perso-Russian War on the one hand, and the ensuing Iranian political discourse on the other, allows us to discern the particular external and internal political articulation of translation in modern Iran. Therefore, I trace the translation of European political culture to the first episode of the Perso-Russian War and a paradigmatic piece of Qajar travel writings: *Safarnameh,* or 'travelogue', of Mirza Saleh Shirazi.[11] Iran's devastating losses in the war made manifest both Iranian's domestic turmoil and its weak position in the global distribution of power. This prompted the Qajars to send their first ambassadors and students to Europe and to commission the translation of European texts. Mirza Saleh Shirazi headed the first group of students sent to Europe and was tasked with the study of English, French and Latin. Although, to my knowledge, there are no monographs on the life and works of Mirza Saleh Shirazi, almost all studies of the Qajar era recall him and note his significance as a scholar and a statesman.[12] Mirza Saleh's text introduces some key terms to Iranian political discourse, some of which subsequently appear in the religious and political debates of the 1906 Constitutional Revolution. Through the analysis of his text, we can see how translation enters the epistemic shifts of Iranian political and religious culture that constitutes 'the modern' in Iran. Moreover, we can see the contribution of translation to the expansion of potentialities and possibilities of concepts and their transformations. I analyse this conceptual transformation by elaborating an emergence of a productive 'epistemic confusion' that corresponds to the limits of political practice and debate in modern Iran. This analysis shows that in Iran translation emerges as historical and cultural practice that reaches beyond the linguistic transposition of texts and concerns the potentiality of linguistic and cultural traditions to open to and articulate difference and thereby re-encounter and regenerate themselves. In conclusion, I will highlight an example of such a movement of renewal in the Shiʿa tradition that contributed to the Revolution of 1906.

11 Shirazi, M. S., *Safarnameh*, Tehran, 1968.

12 In addition to Tavakoli-Targhi and Naghmeh Sohrabi's studies of Qajar Iran discussed earlier, see: Tabatabai, J., *Ta'amoli darbareh-ye Iran, Nazariyeh-ye Hokomat-e Ghanoon dar Iran, Maktab-e Tabriz va Mabani-ye Tajadod-khahi*, Tehran, 2012, p. 211. Monica Ringer has devoted an article length examination of Safarnameh that remains in the framework of modernisation and reform described earlier: Ringer, M., 'The Quest for the Secret of Strength in Iranian Nineteenth-Century Travel Literature: Rethinking Tradition in the Safarnameh', in Keddie N. and Matthee, R. (eds.), *Iran and the Surrounding World: Interactions in Culture and Cultural Politics*, Seattle, 2002.

Mirza Saleh Shirazi's *Safarnameh*

Mirza Saleh Shirazi leaves Tabriz in northwestern Iran for England on April 19, 1815.[13] He travels there through the Russian Empire and returns over three years later by way of the Ottoman Empire. A Qajar statesman, and a member of what Mojtaba Minavi characterised as *avalin karevan ma'refat,* 'the first caravan of knowledge', Mirza is sent as an elder to four other students and in order to learn the European languages of English, French and Latin.[14] He comes across and writes about a diverse array of things. His travelogue is not just a journal. It includes, for example, translation of a text on the Napoleonic fate in Russia from the French as well as a conscious and systematic attempt at a political historiography of Britain. Needless to say, his text is rich in depth and breadth. My interest is limited to the dynamics of translation that unfolds within the text, and the history that encapsulates its author.

Consider, for example, how Mirza introduces the British Museum:

> In London there is a house named 'the British Museum.' It's an expansive and regal house that first belonged to Duke Montagu and was rendered a museum in 1753. Henri [*sic*] Salone Baronet, the Royal physician, had a museum – that is, a collection of the marvels of the land and the sea as well as various subterranean elements that are worth one hundred thousand British tomans. He had willed his collection for the British nation. It's been placed in the British Museum for all to see. The parliament, that is *mashverat khane-ye Engelizi*, 'the British house of council,' allocated one hundred thousand tomans to complete the museum and display the marvels for the people of the city.[15]

Note that he keeps 'museum' in the original and treats it as a concept demanding an explanation. He explains it in terms that I loosely translate as: 'a collection of the marvels of the land and the sea as well as various subterranean elements'. Note the process and the conceptual background that he mobilises to traverse the incommensurability of the term and to make it commensurate within his own

---

13 For alternative discussions of Mirza's text and other travelogues from the same period see Abdulhosein Azerang's *History of Translation in Iran* (2015), Naghmeh Sohrabi's *Taken For Wonder* (2012), Javad Tabatabai's *A Meditation on Iran* (2012) and Mohamad Tavakoli-Taragh's *Refashioning Iran* (2012).

14 Minavi, M., 'Avalin Karevan-e Ma'refat', in *Tarikh va Farhang*, Tehran, 1990.

15 Shirazi, *Safarnameh*, Tehran, 1968, p. 314.

conceptual categories. The 'marvels of the lands and the sea', in this process, acquire a relationship with state-funded public education. With no immediate reference for museums – the ways in which they come together, in terms of how they are ordered and enframed, within modern government, in relation to funding processes and different forms of public education – he is shocked at the government's interest in funding the project and for allowing the freedom of access necessary for the creation of museums. He nonetheless grasps that the logic of the museum has something to do with modern government as well as the education of the British public, and their freedoms.

The modern concept of 'freedom', part of liberal political thought and legal practice, is novel and wondrous for him. This concept underlies Mirza's description of the 'freedom' of the public to use the British Library; of the jury to decide on guilt or innocence in a trial; of men – and only men at this point – to choose parliamentary representatives; and of the parliament to refuse funding for a war decided upon by the British monarch and thus effectively placing a limit on his sovereignty. Freedom, he writes, protects men, however poor they might be, from the will of the sovereign. His description makes clear that freedom, defined independently from the sovereign right of the King, does not mean lack of order. On the contrary, he points to freedom as the defining feature of the British political order:

> A country with this kind of security and freedom is called the land of freedom. In freedom, there is an order! The King and the homeless both consent to this order and respect it; whichever disrespect this order will be subject to punishment.[16]

Mirza Saleh finds the British synthesis of freedom and order so noteworthy that he describes it as the reason for devoting nearly one third of his travelogue to explain its historical genesis.[17] What is noteworthy, if not bewildering, is how the translation of the term freedom as a 'mere description' of freedom of access to a library, leads to open-ended questions of British history and modern political order that, despite translation, remain unassailable to the epistemic grounds of Mirza's being and understanding. What his translation achieves, however, is to introduce some of the first articulations of the modern conception of freedom in Persian and within Qajar political culture.[18] In Mirza's language, and subsequently in the

16 Shirazi, *Safarnameh*, p. 207.

17 Shirazi, *Safarnameh*, p. 207.

18 For a different discussion of the emergence of modern conception of freedom in Qajar travel

epistemic and political culture of Persia, the modern concept of 'freedom' runs up against Mirza's presupposed understanding of freedom as the absence of subjection. A layman can freely access books in the library or choose representatives, Mirza explains, because he does not owe anyone anything. Similarly, the legal culture that sustains modern 'freedom' comes up against, among other things, the Shiʿa articulation of *shariʿa* as it was deployed in Qajar Iran. British judges cannot deliver a *fatwa*, he writes, because judgment belongs to the reasoning of the twelve sworn men who witness the procession of the trial.

Notice the incommensurabilities traversed and made commensurate in what I call a space of 'epistemic confusion'. In this space, the concept of the *fatwa*, for example, is severed from its epistemic context and commensurated in relation to a liberal legal tradition. The legal conception of the right to choose representatives is put in relation to freedom as *hurriat,* the state of being free from the will of others, a state of answering to nobody except, perhaps, to God. One possible explanation of Mirza's translation here is that offered by Mateo Mohammad Farzaneh in his recent text on the Constitutional Revolution. Writing in relation to Mirza's writing on France, Farzaneh writes and I quote:

> Mirza Saleh's interchangeable use of the term *fatwa* with decisions made by the French parliament attest to his ignorance that the Catholic establishment was only partially responsible for such decisions… Mirza Saleh mistook the French making secular laws in a parliament with an Islamic decree that is issued by a single high-ranking Shiʿite cleric independent of council. This significant error attest that Iranians seldom fully appreciated how parliament in France and England functioned, and I argue that this superficial understanding of affairs outside Iran created expectations in the minds of political activists later on that were beyond delivery at that point in Iranian history. [19]

An analysis based on the subjective judgment of the translator as well as identification of 'ignorance', 'mistakes' or 'superficial understanding', presupposes the availability of a framework of judgment and an established discourse as the grounds of understanding. Only within an established discourse true and false statements

writing see Tabatabai J., *Ta'amoli darbareh-ye Iran, Nazariyeh-ye Hokomat-e Ghanoon dar Iran, Maktab-e Tabriz va Mabani-ye Tajadod-khahi*, pp. 231–4.

19 Frazaneh, M. M., *The Iranian Constitutional Revolution and the Clerical Leadership of Khurasani*, Syracuse, 2015, pp. 32–3.

and judgments of right and wrong can be discerned. Translation puts into question the availability and stability of such a framework and discourse. Translation affects the pre-subjective condition of the possibility of such a framework or discourse. In contradistinctions to the analyses that reference the understanding, intention or the agenda of a translator, what I call 'epistemic confusion' is not a 'mistake' in translation or the lack of a translator's lucidity or rigor. It does not entail collapsing the difference between European traditions, on the one hand, and Iranian and Islamic ones on the other. Epistemic confusion is the mark of an Iranian historical and cultural state as it emerges in the writing of Mirza Saleh. It reveals the emergence of a historical rupture in the Iranian order of things and the formation of nascent historical discourses. Epistemic confusion is the mirror of the historical crises that propelled the Iranian translation effort underway and engendered innovations such as the Constitutional Revolution.

Michel Foucault, who elaborated the concept of episteme, did so in relation to the condition of possibility of inter-subjectivity that constitutes a culture and allows men to be at home.[20] Our man is not at home when traveling, and as it turns out, he is traveling because home is – or might be – no longer. Mirza was sent to London in the midst of the Perso-Russian wars. The first war (1805–1813) culminated in the Treaty of Gulestan in which Iran ceded most of modern day Azerbaijan, Daghestan, eastern Georgia and northern Armenia to the Russian Empire. The second war broke out in 1826 and concluded in the infamous Turkmenchay Treaty and the secession of the southern Caucasus, an area roughly equivalent to modern day Armenia and Azerbaijan. The humiliation caused by the defeat was felt in what was emerging as a 'national consciousness', and a corresponding 'public', and was symptomatically captured in the massacre of the Russian diplomatic mission by a mob in Tehran just a year after the 'peace treaty'. As Qajar historian Abbas Amanat observes:

> In the following decades with varying intensity Russia held the implicit threat of military occupation as a Damoclean sword over the Qajar state in order to accomplish diplomatic and other objectives.[21]

At this moment, the submission to Russia went hand in hand with Iran's dependence on Great Britain, which held substantial influence in Iran's southern and eastern borders with India. Iran, desperately in need of containing Russia,

---

20 Foucault, *The Order of Things*, p. xx.

21 Amanat, A., *Pivot of the Universe: Nasir al-Din Shah Qajar and the Iranian Monarchy, 1831–1896*, Berkeley, 1997, p. 16.

acquiring military training, and instigating reform, developed a highly ambivalent relationship with Britain. The British, of course, proceeded based on their imperial interest in India, Herat, and the containment of Napoleonic expansions east. The Anglo-Persian relation included treaties in 1801 and 1857. The first promised support for Iran against the Russian Empire's southern expansion and the French movement east in exchange for Iranian support against the Napoleon campaign of Egypt. The second was a culmination of a war between the two countries in 1856–7 over Herat. Iran, which was weakened from the earlier treaty, abandoned its sovereign claims to Herat and the other lands of Afghanistan.

Notice how amidst these global historical changes translation erupts: during the reign of Fath-Ali Shah when Iran lost its northern territories to Russia, Napoleon, who was advancing east in the Russian territory and had his eyes on the British India, wrote a letter to the Persian monarch.[22] The letter was in French. No one could be found in Iran to translate the letter, which was subsequently sent to Baghdad for translation. This is the background that prompted the crown prince Abbas Mirza to commission Mirza Saleh to learn English, French and Latin and led to translation in the travelogue. Mirza's mission was part of larger translation effort that involved selection of French, Russian and British texts, including *Encyclopedia Britannica*, which the prince had reportedly studied closely. Edward Gibbon's *The History of the Decline and Fall of the Roman Empire* was one of the first English-Persian translations that the prince had ordered.[23]

These translations were part of a military and political campaign of the prince and his advisors and confidants, Ghaem Magham Farahanis. Javad Tabatabaei, among others, has argued that Tabriz's proximity to the war front and its distance from the royal palace in Tehran, the capital, allowed for the development of a distinct political ethos and the revival of the Persian tradition of *vezarat,* or 'the ministerial office' as somewhat autonomous from *saltanat,* or 'the royal office'.[24] For this reason, among others, Tabatabaei points to the developments in Tabriz as the pre-history of Iranian Constitutionalism. Given that in the ensuing decades two important Qajar prime minsters, Mirza Abul Ghasem Ghaem Magham Farahani who was one of the principle figures of the Tabriz effort and Mirza Taghi Khan Amir Kabir, were murdered during the internal struggles of the court, it is

22 In Azerang, A., *Tarikh-i Tarjomeh dar Iran: Az Doran-e Bastan ta Payan-e Asr Qajar*, Tehran, 2014, p. 218.

23 Adamiyat, F., *Amir Kabir va Iran*, Tehran, 1983, p. 163.

24 Tabatabai, J., *darbareh-ye Iran, Nazariyeh-ye Hokomat-e Ghanoon dar Iran, Maktab-e Tabriz va Mabani-ye Tajadod-khahi*, pp. 133–210.

certainly plausible to consider their efforts as the pre-history of the Constitutional Revolution.

Translation and the Religious Debates on Constitutionalism

The epistemic confusion that is the mark of the first translations of the Enlightenment in Iran and characterises the Iranian political culture of the time reflects and refracts the changing order of Iranian things. Signaling 'uncertainty', 'a breakdown of order', and sometimes 'a disorderly jumble', confusion bears witness to the redrawing of the spatial borders of empires and nations and the temporal boundaries of epochs and traditions. It reflects an ossification of things such as *saltanat-e mostaghel,* or the 'independent', or 'absolute monarchy' and their lapse into 'untimeliness', And at the same time, however, epistemic confusion corresponds to the condition of possibility of novel discourses such as *tajadod* and events such as the Constitutional Revolution. In conclusion, I want to note one of the most significant religious debates around the Constitutional Revolution which proceeds in the epistemic grounds indebted to the Qajar translations of European political culture such as the one analysed here.

Mirza Saleh's description of British politics in the travelogue, among other contemporary travelogues of his time, introduced a concept of 'legal representation' that was unprecedented in the nineteenth-century Iranian legal discourses of Islam and the court. In so doing, it set the stage for the political and religious debate that reached its climax in the Constitutional Revolution and continues to the present day albeit in a transformed fashion. Mirza Saleh translated the nineteenth-century British liberal conception of 'legal representation' and the term 'representative', into the Shiʿa, jurisprudential understanding of *vakalat*, 'representation', and *vakil,* 'representative', as it was deployed in the Persian political culture of the time. In its genealogy and conception, however, the underlying grammar of Shiʿa 'representation' radically differed from the nineteenth-century British one. *Vakalat,* in its Shiʿa conception concerns matters of personal status in the discourse of *fiqh* or 'Islamic jurisprudence' grounded in *Shariʿa*. The Shiʿa jurists oversaw *vekalat* as the contracts through which private persons would bestow their will provisionally and temporarily to another private person. Gradually, and through translation, however, there emerged a double valance and hence a generative 'confusion' regarding the terms *vekalat*, 'representation' and *vakil,* 'representative' in the Persian political discourse.

The instability and the indeterminacy of *vekalat* and *vakil* made divergent political and religious judgments and practices in the subsequent Iranian developments possible. The divergence reached its height in the debates and disagreements around the Constitutional Revolution. Against the monarch who understood the throne as his divine right, there emerged a new genre of Iranian political practitioner known as *monavar al-fekr,* 'enlightened thinker' who demanded legal representation by insisting on what, in modern Iranian discourse, can be identified as 'the modern European' meaning of the term. More importantly, however, the confusion engendered unprecedented disagreements among the Shiʿa *ulama,* 'scholars', and promoted an unprecedented execution of a leading *mujtahid* of Tehran, Sheikh Fazl-allah Nouri, in the aftermath of the 1906 Revolution. The religious debate among the *ulama* was conducted on the grounds of the Shiʿa tradition of jurisprudence. On one side of the polarisation, Sheikh Fazl-allah Nouri rejected the newly valorised meaning of representation. At the moment of its disruption, he sought to mobilise the authority invested in him in the Shiʿa discourse and justify the absolute power of the monarch. In the Shiʿa discourse, the source of power of the state was understood to reside in the divine will that during the Great Occultation of the Twelfth Imam, resides with the Shiʿa *mujtaheds*, 'jurists'. In other words, amidst the occultation of the Twelfth Imam, the practices of the jurists justified the rule of the monarch provisionally.[25] In Nouri's authoritative judgment:

> Speaking in public affairs and public good is the prerogative of the Imam or his *nawab* [Muslim prince sitting in place of the Imam] and is none of the business of others whose interference is *haram* and usurping the seat of the Prophet and the Imam...Representing and leading during the occultation of the 12th Imam is with the *faqihs* and *mujtahids*, and not with the grocer, the tailor. Reliance on the majority of opinion is wrong in the religion of the Imams. Writing the law is meaningless. The law of us Muslims is Islam.

Although Nouri was insisting on a traditional Shiʿa position that is usually described as 'quietist' in relation to the state, he was doing so by rejecting the

25 For an examination of Shaikh Fazlallah Nuri's argument against the constitution, as well as Ayatollah Na'ini counter view see: Martin. V., A., 'The Anti Constitutionalist Arguments of Shaikh Fazlallah Nuri', in *Middle Eastern Studies*, vol. 22, no. 2, 1986, pp. 181–196. For a thorough discussion of this debate in Persian, see: Tabatabai, J., *Ta'amoli darbareh-ye Iran, Nazariyeh-ye Hokomat-e Ghanoon dar Iran, Maktab-e Tabriz va Mabani-ye Tajadod-khahi*, Tehran, 2012, pp. 373–526. In English, see: Hairi, A., *Shiʿism and Constitutionalism in Iran: A Study of the Role Played by the Persian Residents of Iraq in Iranian Politics*, Leiden, 1977.

newly elaborated meaning of representation. Consequently, in the political struggle between the monarch and the constitutionalists, Nouri's 'traditional' and 'quietist' position came to signify something quite new: anti-constitutionalism. In other words, it ceased to be traditional or quietist. Other leading *mujtahids* of the time such as Ayatollah Khorasani and Ayatollah Na'ini were opposed to the absolute power of the monarch which they judged to be related to the poor political and existential conditions of life in Iran. These Iranian residents of Najaf seminaries emerged opposed to Nouri's religious adjudication of the absolute legitimacy of the monarchy.[26] Unlike Nouri, these jurists confronted the historical changes that were underway and included the changes that correspond to the transformation of the term 'representation' in Iranian political culture of the time. Against Nouri, but importantly mobilising the same Shiʿa discourse used by Nouri, they offered an *ijtehad,* 'learned judgment', on the confusion within the term 'representation'. Na'ini, for example, drew on the conception of equality before *shari'a* and rejected the exceptional position of the monarch in relation to rights, commandments and punishments as understood within the *shari'a*. Representation as understood within the constitutionalist discourse, he thus argued, was continuous with *shari'a*. At a time when despotic sovereignty had become unquestionably untimely, Na'ini's insistence on the equality of all subjects before the *shari'a*, disentangled the seat of the monarch from the customary religious justifications of the likes of Nouri. Consequently, it provided a religiously sanctioned conception of legal representation. Some scholars of Islam and Iran have interpreted the *ijtehad* of Na'ini and Khorasani as the emergence of the rule of law from the *shari'a* and as the most significant political development within the Islamic tradition in the modern period.[27]

I briefly recall the emergence of the unprecedented clerical disagreements over political representation and the Constitution to point out how translation interacts

26 For a recent examination of Ayatollah Khorasani in relation to the Constitutional Revolution see: Frazaneh, *The Iranian Constitutional Revolution and the Clerical Leadership of Khurasani*, Syracuse, 2015. For a history of the *ulama* in Qajar Iran see: Hamid, A., *Religion and State in Iran 1785–1906: The Role of the Ulama in the Qajar Period*, Berkeley, 1980.

27 Among thinkers writing in Persian and in Iran, Javad Tabatabaei is the strongest proponent of this view. Writing in the last three decades, in the aftermath of the Islamic politics of revolution and the state in Iran, his work has produced a rich intellectual discourse, particularly among Shiʿi seminarians, which considers the possibilities and limitations of the *fiqh* discourse in authorising the modern state and all that goes along with it. Within this discourse, the religious debates of the Constitutional Revolution have been considered as a fundamental development of modern Islamic politics.

with the languages and practices of religion and politics in Iran. Through introducing new terms and expanding the possibilities of existing ones, in this case *vekalat,* translation gives words to the novel political practices of 'enlightened thinkers', and more importantly, engenders a generative debate within the discourse of the Shiʿa *ulama* on the nature of modern law and government. This example demonstrates that the anchor of the Constitutional Revolution was not the simple introduction of liberal ideas and ideologies from Europe, but the novel Iranian discourses on history and the potentiality of Shiʿa tradition, among others, to offer an *ijtehad* on Iranian historical transformations.

Europe was, and continues to be, a site of difference for Iran. However, innovations such as the Constitutional Revolution are not the result of emulation of Europe as a locus of difference, but of remaining open to the difference internal to Iran's history and traditions.

In contrast to European modernity, the 'modern' in Iran is not defined as a spatiotemporal continuum rendered discontinuous by epistemic transformations, but as a doubled discontinuity in which it is both separated from its past and its present. The present, in Iran, is constituted by 'past' discourses that remain untransformed and which no longer represent the order of the present. Their confusion is epistemic since the present is not marked apart from its past. In this condition, modern discourses from Europe, which have emerged through the practice of translation, appear as more meaningful and representative than Iran's past discourses. Translation is herein at once the realisation of a condition of crisis and the regeneration of past discourses in the present. By holding together the discontinuity between past and present, translation, alternatively, is capable of providing a language for engaging the present and making possible the encounter with confusion. Translation is a way of relating the past to the present towards an open future.

Acknowledgements

The author would like to thank Christopher Cochran, William Callison, Hooman Ghasemi, and Naveed Mansoori for their engagements on the ideas and drafts of this essay.

Bibliography

Adamiyat, F., *Amir Kabir va Iran*, Tehran, 1983.

Amanat, A., 'Memory and Amnesia in the Historiography of the Constitutional Revolution', in Atabaki, T. (ed.), *Iran in the 20th Century: Historiography and Political Culture*, New York, 2009.

Amanat, A., *Pivot of the Universe: Nasir al-Din Shah Qajar and the Iranian Monarchy, 1831–1896*, Berkeley, 1997.

Azerang, A., *Tarikh-i Tarjomeh dar Iran: Az Doran-e Bastan ta Payan-e Asr Qajar*, Tehran, 2014.

Foucault, M., *Archeology of Knowledge*, London, 1995[1972].

Foucault, M., *The Order of Things: An Archeology of Human Sciences*, New York, 1994.

Frazaneh, M. M., *The Iranian Constitutional Revolution and the Clerical Leadership of Khurasani*, Syracuse, 2015.

Hairi, A., *Shi'ism and Constitutionalism in Iran: A Study of the Role Played by the Persian Residents of Iraq in Iranian Politics*, Leiden, 1977.

Hamid, A., *Religion and State in Iran 1785–1906: The Role of the Ulama in the Qajar Period*, Berkeley, 1980.

Hanks, W., *Converting Words: Maya in the Age of the Cross*, Berkeley, 2010.

Lévi-Strauss, C., *The Savage Mind*, Chicago, 1966.

Martin. V., A., 'The Anti Constitutionalist Arguments of Shaikh Fazlallah Nuri', in *Middle Eastern Studies*, vol. 22, no. 2, 1986.

Minavi, M., 'Avalin Karevan-e Ma'refat', in *Tarikh va Farhang*, Tehran, 1990.

Ringer, M., 'The Quest for the Secret of Strength in Iranian Nineteenth-Century Travel Literature: Rethinking Tradition in the Safarnameh', in Keddie N. and Matthee, R. (eds.), *Iran and the Surrounding World: Interactions in Culture and Cultural Politics*, Seattle, 2002.

Said, E., *Orientalism*, New York, 1978.

Scott D. and Talal Asad, 'Appendix: The Trouble of Thinking', in Scott D. and Hirschkind, C., (eds.), *Powers of the Secular Modern: Talal Asad and His Interlocutors*, Stanford, 2006.

Shirazi, M., S., *Safarnameh*, Tehran, 1968.

Sohrabi, N., *Taken For Wonder: Nineteenth-Century Travel Accounts from Iran to Europe*, New York, 2012.

Stoler, A., L., *Race and the Education of Desire: Foucault's History of Sexuality and the Colonial Order of Things*, Durham, 1995.

Tabatabaei, J., *Ta'amoli darbareh-ye Iran, Nazariyeh-ye Hokomat-e Ghanoon dar Iran, Mabaniye Nazarieh-ye Mashruteh-khahi*, Tehran, 2012.

Tabatabai, J., *Ta'amoli darbareh-ye Iran, Nazariyeh-ye Hokomat-e Ghanoon dar Iran, Maktab-e Tabriz va Mabani-ye Tajadod-khahi* , Tehran, 2012.
Talal Asad, T., *Formations of the Secular: Christianity, Islam, Modernity*, Stanford, 2003.

5

The Iranian Constitutional Revolution and the influence of Mirza Aqa Khan Kermani's Political Thought

Pejman Abdolmohammadi

This article analyses the influence of Mirza Aqa Khan Kermani's political thought on the Iranian Constitutional Revolution. Kermani is one of the most relevant intellectuals of the nineteenth century in Iran. His thought regarding the rule of law, the separation between religion and politics, and freedom of expression exercised particular influence on the Persian constitutionalism. Kermani's thought, based on secularism and nationalism, has influenced the ideological basis for the Iranian constitutional movement of 1906 and for the first attempt at secularisation of Iranian society.

Mirza Abdolhossein Bardsiri (1853–1896), known as Mirza Aqa Khan Kermani, was one of the most significant secular political thinkers of the nineteenth century in Persia. His intellectual life[1] can be divided into two main phases: he spent the first part of his life – from 1853 to 1886 – in Persia; then, at the age of 33 years old, he went in Istanbul, where he lived until 1896. In that year, in fact, following his extradition in Persia, in the city of Tabriz, Kermani was executed on the orders of the heir to the throne, Mohammad Ali Mirza.[2] Kermani spent the first phase of his intellectual life mainly in the cities of Bardsir, Kerman, Isfahan and Tehran (he lived for a few weeks in Mashad and Rasht also); the Persian thinker developed, during this period, his critical view of conservative Imamite Shiʿite Islam approaching the Babi[3] religious movement. The second phase of his life will be concentrated in Istanbul,[4] where Kermani will become a secular and nationalist intellectual, abandoning his religious views.

Kermani was one of the first Iranian political thinkers who, after being in contact with the liberal and constitutional ideas of western thinkers, particularly British and French, and also after a new revision of Persian history and philosophy, was able to work out a new way of thinking which was based on secularism, nationalism and constitutionalism. Kermani's thought has certainly influenced the ideological basis for the Iranian constitutional movement of 1906 and for the first attempt at secularisation of Iranian society. He was one of the first Iranian intellectuals who understood Western, Islamic and Iranian thought. This led him to a unique synthesis, which incorporated on the one hand, the Western Enlightenment and, on the other hand, the myth of the 'good government' of Cyrus and Zoroastrian philosophy. His political views became increasingly troublesome not only for

1 On Kermani's political biography see Adamyyat, F., *Andisheha-iye Mirza Aqa Khan Kermani*, Tehran, 1978, pp. 13–48; Bayat, P.M., 'The Concepts of Religion and Government in the Thought of Mirza Aqa Khan Kermani, A Nineteenth-Century Persian Revolutionary', in *International Journal of Middle East Studies*, vol. 5, no. 4, 1974, pp. 381–400; Nateq, H., *Nameha-ye Tab'id*, Köln, 1989, pp. 13–43; Kermāni, M. A., *Se Maktub be-kushesh va virayesh-e Bahram Chubineh*, Essen, 2000, pp. 3–92; Kermāni, M. A., *Sad Kehtabeh ba virastar-e Mohammad Ja'far Mahjub,* Tehran, 1990, pp. I–XXXIII.

2 On the reasons of Kermani's execution and its historical reconstruction see: Nateq, H., *Nameha-ye Tab'id*, pp. 35–42.

3 On the Babi's movement and thoughts see: Browne, E. G., 'Catalogue and Description of 27 Bábí Manuscripts', in *The Journal of the Royal Asiatic Society of Great Britain and Ireland*, 1892, pp. 433–499; Momen, M., *The Babi and Baha'i Religions, 1844–1944: Some Contemporary Western Accounts*, Oxford, 1981.

4 During the second phase of his life he spent some times in Cyprus and in today's Syria.

the Persian dynasty but also for the Ottoman Empire. Kermani also calls for the establishment of a constitutional monarchy in Persia, considering the Qajar despotism one of its biggest problems; he believed in an elite group of intellectuals, who would have led the population to revolt against the ruling dynasty. The role of enlightened elite should not have been limited only to the revolutionary stage, but it would have to be a determining factor in the establishment of a constitutional form of government based on human rights and that would limit the power of the monarch.

There are three main elements which characterise his thought: Kermani is the first Iranian intellectual whose political thought, in a brief period of about ten years (1886–1896), evolved from Islamism to secularism. He underwent a series of intellectual steps that led him first of all to criticise Islamism and thus brought him closer to the reformist religious movement of that time, guided by Seyyed Ali Mohammad Bab. The next step, however, made him critical not only towards Babi faith, but towards all the monotheistic Abrahamic religions. In fact, Kermani adopted Descartes' rationalism and began to develop his thinking on the basis of the principle of rationality and not on the divine. After that, influenced by Western thinkers – especially those belonging to the French Enlightenment – he further elaborated his thought, moving towards the political sphere and highlighting the need for the institution of a secular, constitutional state in which civil and penal rights are based on human sciences and not on religious laws such as shari'a. Kermani then became one of the most important secular thinkers from Persia whose political ideas were also strengthened by the principle of Iranian nationalism. Kermani, in his theory of a secular state in Persia, recalls the importance of Iranian national identity, considering it as a symbolic resource indispensable to achieving civil progress in Persia. Therefore, the singularity of his thought is formulated having experienced a deep transformation, step by step, from a religious base to reach a secularist interpretation. The second peculiarity of his thought is the ability to elaborate a harmonious combination between Western Enlightenment and Persian nationalism. Kermani managed to draw the most salient aspects of eighteenth- and nineteenth-century Western thought, combining it with Persian Renaissance, recalling the good governance of Cyrus the Great, of Zoroastrian philosophy and the mythology narrated by the famous Iranian poet, Ferdowsi.[5]

---

5 On the role of myth of nationalism in the Iranian modern political thought and political movements consult Ansari, A. M., *The Politics of Nationalism in Modern Iran*, Cambridge, 2012, pp. 13–24.

The third distinguishing feature of his thought lies in his vision of constitutional and anti-despotic politics. Kermani, who was particularly influenced by Montesquieu, sees in despotism the true source of Persia's backwardness and he identifies the monarchy and the clergy as the main culprits responsible for Iranian obscurantism. In this sense Kermani overcomes the two greatest ideological models of Persia and the Middle East: nationalism[6] and Islamism, encouraging the establishment of a constitutional state based on the rule of law.

Some remarks on the historical and social context

Historical, social and cultural contexts remain the main factors for the analysis of a political thinker. The socio-political context in which Kermani developed his thought played an important role in the formation of his ideas. In the first instance the main events which exerted an important influence on the formation of Kermani's ideas, particularly during the first phase of his intellectual life in Iran, will be examined. Some of these events are the following: a) The rise of the religious movement of the Bab. The execution of Seyyed Ali Mohammad Bab (1850) took place just a few years before the birth of Kermani. This means that Kermani grew up in a cultural environment in which the Babi faith was still important in a section of Persian society, particularly among those Islamic scholars who had left Islam to follow the Babi faith. Babi ideas attracted him when he was young: Kermani wrote two of his most significant works on the political and religious level (Rezvan and Hasht Behesht) inspired by Babi faith; b) The Persian defeats by Russia during the first three decades of the nineteenth century, when Persia lost an important part of its territories in the Caucasus (see Gulistan and Turkmenchay Treaties). Kermani's birth is almost 30 years after the last severe defeat against the Tsarist Empire. Despite the major territorial losses for Persia, these historical events presented an opportunity in terms of the evolution of Iranian political thought: some Persian intellectuals were able to learn Russian, and thus they could have access to several texts by Russian intellectuals or other Western thinkers whose works had been translated into Russian. Mirza Fathali Akhundzadeh, for example, is one of the most important intellectuals whose political thought was shaped in particular by the consequences of the Persian defeat by Russia. Kermani was particularly influenced in the development of his nationalism, of his criticism

6 Although Kermani was also one of the fathers of modern Persian nationalism, in the final part of the evolution of his political thought, he suggests the overcoming of religious and nationalist ideology in order to achieve a secular and pluralistic political system.

of Islam and of his secular proposal for Persia by Akhundzadeh's ideas; c) Amir Kabir's progressive policies. The founding of the first university Dar al-Funun and a series of policies aimed at opening the country, decided by Amir Kabir, had slightly contributed to a cultural openness in the Qajar's Persia. Amir Kabir was assassinated in 1852, one year before Kermani's birth; d) The domestic Ottoman Empire crisis and the assassination of Naser al-Din Shah in 1896 played also an important role on his extradition to Persia and on his execution in Tabriz under the order of Mohammad Ali Mirza in 1896.

Kermani in Iran and his Babism orientation

The period from the time that Kermani still lived in Iran until the first three years of his stay in Istanbul (1880–1889) was a phase during which Kermani is still religiously oriented and closed-off to Babi religion and the Azali movement. Even though he is critical towards the Shiʿite Islamic clergy, he still has some sympathy towards Islam. However, according to Kermani, Islam is not anymore adapted to regulate modern social life and therefore it is time for the people to accept the new Babi religion which, according to him, *has* adapted to the modern era. His two first works *Rezvan* and *Hasht Behesht* are inspired with his Babi orientation.

Kermani in Istanbul: the role of rationalism and the critique of Abrahamic religions

Kermani then began to develop his rationalism, increasingly moving away from the religious education he had experienced for over thirty years in Persia. In fact Kermani, in his two most philosophical texts, *Hekmat-e Nazari* and *Takvin va Tashrih*, formulates his discourse around the idea of the importance of science in the Creation, affirming that the universe is governed by a series of natural laws, based on rational intelligence and not on divine intervention.

During the first years of his life in Istanbul, philosophy gradually held an important place in his thought, and religion became more and more marginalised. Kermani, influenced by Plato and Descartes, defines philosophy as a science that enables man to attain knowledge of the origins of things and of living beings. The ultimate goal of philosophy is to remove the darkness of ignorance and to reach the light of reason. In other words, Kermani, as Descartes does, explains how the use of reason and common sense is fundamental to humans in order to distinguish the truth from the false.

Nationalism and the myth of Cyrus

Kermani, much like his predecessor Akhundzadeh, in the second phase of his intellectual life in Istanbul and especially in the last six years of his life (1890–1896), began to further develop his thinking by focusing on the concepts of nation and nationalism. Kermani pursues two important goals through the development of Persian nationalism: the first is to overcome the political and cultural backwardness in Persia and to achieve social and institutional progress; the second is a desire to fight Western colonialism. In other words, with the development of nationalism, Kermani wants to achieve political development, such as the Western Enlightenment, in Persia and actually stop Western interference in the country.

Kermani, as Akhundzadeh did, rebuilds a romantic idea of the Persian homeland. His thinking re-evaluates pre-Islamic Iranian civilisation, well distinct from the Arab-Islamic one. The re-evaluations of the ancient history of Persia, along with the criticism of all forms of foreign domination, characterise the nationalism theorised by Kermani. He admires pre-Islamic Persia, while he disapproves of Islamic Iran, considering the former element as the symbol of Persian imperial power and the latter as the representation of its weakness and instability. Kermani also sees in the myth of Cyrus's 'ideal government' a possible way to introduce liberal political concepts and principles in the Iranian traditional society of the time.

Tarikh-e Iran-e Bastan (A'iney-e Sekandari) and *Name-ye Bastan* (Salarname) are particularly focused on his nationalism orientation.

Confrontation with Islamic reformism and Middle Eastern unity

During his stint in Istanbul, particularly between 1892 and 1895, Kermani had to also deal with Jamaleddin Afghani's Islamic project. This brought him some reflections regarding the Islamic Unity of the Middle Eastern people and the relation between religion and politics. Indeed Afghani's Islamic ideology was distant from that of Kermani in those years. Nevertheless Kermani, who had already overcome the Islamic ideology, adhering firstly to Babi faith, most likely became a follower of Afghani because he was attracted by his political goal of uniting the Muslim peoples against the colonial powers. Therefore, from 1892 until 1893, Kermani was politically committed to the project of the unification of the Islamic world. The writing of the work *Haftad va do Mellat* represents this stage of his thought. In this book Kermani, through a short story, tries to represent a cosmopolitan world in which religious believers belonging to different faiths come together and discuss all manner of things in a cafe.

After about two years of working with Afghani, Kermani, who had a revolutionary spirit and was sensitive to the issue of justice and freedom, begin to notice several critical elements in Afghani and in his project, and they gradually began to drift apart. Kermani accuses Afghani of not caring about the welfare of the population, being, in fact, just a pragmatic politician concerned with his own interests.

Secularism and the rule of law

The series of disillusionments related to Islamism, Babism and Azalism leads Kermani to permanently embrace a new phase of his political thought. Kermani in the last three years withdrew into himself as he wanted to ponder all the intense political activities he experienced in his short period spent in Istanbul. The disappointment with Afghani's project convinces him that the main problem of the Persian people has been their superstitious devotion to Islam or the so-called 'Islam-zadeqi'. He then maintains that the true medicine for the Persian people is not Islamic religion, nor the Babi faith, nor the Islamic reformist project of Afghani, but that a solution can be found by referring to Persian Renaissance (characterised by a return to the pre-Islamic Persian origins) on the one hand, and to Western Enlightenment on the other.

This last phase of his life represents his most important contribution to the Persian constitutionalism: Kermani elaborated an important reflection for the Middle East, marked by modernism, secularism and nationalism. Two of his most significant political works, *Sad Khetabeh* and *Se Maktub*, express exhaustively this latest stage of his political thought. In the nineteenth century Kermani was already aware of the importance for Persia, but also for other Eastern countries, of limiting the role of religion in the public sphere and of focusing on secular ideology in order to achieve progress.

The relation between religion and politics, anti-despotism, pluralism and the relativity of religion are the most important elements of his thought, which contributed later on in influencing the Iranian constitutional revolution intellectuals in 1906. In the elaboration of this part of his thought, Montesquieu, Hobbes, Rousseau and John Stuart Mill play an important role.

Kermani and anti-despotism: Montesquieu – Voltaire

According to Kermani despotism is the worst of evil with two tyrannical symbols that cause evil and injustice in Persian society: the clergy and the monarchy.[7] The former continues to leave the people in ignorance and spreads a sense of fear among the population against God's power, while the latter keeps the people in poverty by creating terror through the use of violence against men.[8] The influence of Montesquieu's thought seems obvious. Identifying terror as a principle of despotism has its origin in Montesquieu's classification of the various forms of government, with their principles and their different characteristics.[9] Kermani, like Montesquieu, is also very sensitive to despotism, which he considers the worst evil for a society and thus it must be fought. In one of his last two political works, *Sad Khetabeh*, he states: 'When religion and politics are subjected to the despotism of the rulers and to religious fanaticism, the breath will be taken away from that people, now subjugated. Its evolution will be suspended and its future annihilated'.[10]

The religious fanaticism of the clergy or of those who take interest in the spiritual sphere of society, together with the despotism of the rulers, are considered by Kermani to be the two worst of evils of human society.[11] In his argument on the origin of despotism and its relationship with religion, Kermani, influenced by Voltaire and Rousseau, makes a distinction between polytheistic and monotheistic religions.[12]

According to Kermani, oriental peoples (referring to the Chinese, Mongolians, Semitics and Aryans) in their religious history have often built an absolute and unique idea of their God: 'they recognized in their sovereign a divine figure descended from the sky or they widened their fantasies, believing in one God gifted with all the existing positive attributes'.[13]

In front of such a power there is no possibility for any criticism or protest. This type of behavior, according to Kermani, leads to the establishment of despotic governments in the world. The followers of monotheistic religions, therefore, need a shepherd to guide them to the truth: this leader is infallible and his word is indisputable. The people seek in their sovereign 'a political shepherd' who wants

7 Kermani, *Se Maktub* , p. 129.

8 Kermani, *Sad Khetabeh* , speech n. 41; Kermani, *Se Maktub* , p. 207.

9 Montesquieu outlined his classification of governments in *L'esprit des lois*, Genève, 1748, vol. II, chap. II–V.

10 Kermani, *Sad Khetabeh*, speech n. 13.

11 Kermani, *Sad Khetabeh*, speech n. 27.

12 In his reasoning on Oriental religions Kermani includes also Judaism and Christianity

13 Kermani, *Sad Khetabeh*, speech n. 13.

to guide them in an absolute way to the material bliss. As a consequence, the sovereign becomes infallible: his policies, although absolutist, cannot be called into question.[14]

'The idea of an absolute mono that appears mainly in Eastern religions', according to Kermani, 'has led these communities to develop the idea of despotic political power and to not be able to develop a real critical consciousness'.[15] The Persian thinker maintains that 'the people of the West had, in Greek and Carthage civilizations, a polytheistic religious tradition in which there were several Gods with different powers. Each of them enjoyed a fairly wide sphere of power, but at the same time this sphere found its limit in the presence of the other Gods'.

This allowed Western religious thought to develop the idea of non-omnipotence of the divine, an idea that has moved from the religious sphere to the political one, bringing the Greeks, for example, to not being subjected to the will of a single entity without the opportunity to discuss and criticise. 'The polytheistic roots of the West', according to Kermani, 'helped the enlightened Western thinkers, once freed from the Abrahamic monotheistic thought, to lay the foundations for a rational thinking, pluralistic and not absolute'.[16]

Kermani believes that this basic difference between the philosophy of religions of the East and of the West has been significant in the development of Western thought in the direction of a republican form of government and constitution, while in the East the growth of despotism was due to the monotheistic shepherd mentality.

Kermani's political thought focused also on the idea of a popular revolution led by intellectuals who will be able to overthrow the tyranny and establish a constitutional monarchy. This will be possible 'only through the revolution of educated people' – so it will be the man, through his will, strength, and courage to depose the oppressor. Kermani considered the French constitution as a good model for Persia in order to establish a fundamental law based on secular principles, which would guarantee the political and civil liberties and institute a clear separation between religion and politics. According to this intellectual, an irreproachable constitution could not coexist with Islamic principles, because the latter is opposed to a free and modern government based on men's wisdom. To support the thesis of the incompatibility between Islam and a parliamentary system Kermani, following the methodology of Akhundzadeh, lists some of the precepts within the shari'a,

14 Adamyyat, *Andisheha*-iye *Mirza Aqa Khan Kermani,* p. 117.

15 Kermani, M. A., *Tarikh-e Iran-e Bastan* (A'iney-e Eskandari), Tehran, 1947, p. 196.

16 Cited in: Adamyyat, *Andisheha*-iye *Mirza Aqa Khan Kermani,* p. 116.

including the inequality between men and women, the lack of adequate protection of the rights of religious minorities, the possibility of the sale of slaves and the harsh punishments laid down in Islamic criminal law. The ideal constitution for Kermani, therefore, consists of a *corpus* of laws based on the principle of a secular state, without any interference of religion in politics.

Kermani is one of the first Middle Eastern thinkers to openly criticise the ideals of Islamic Reformism, which were in full bloom during the nineteenth century. In a critical observation, the Iranian intellectual points out the contradiction between Western political philosophy and Islamic Shari'a, claiming that as a matter of fact it was not possible to Islamise modernity or to modernise Islam. It should be underlined that Kermani follows Akhundzadeh who addresses directly the father of Islamic reformism Sayyid Jamal al-Din Asadabadi (al-Afganī),[17] advancing the following critical analysis:

> These religious intellectuals equate the parliamentary system to the Islamic principle of *Šūra*; they associate 'the contract that establishes a society' to the bey'at, besides considering a Republican State in conformity with *šarīʿa* precepts. All these considerations and speculations are meaningless for the following reasons: in a parliamentary system, the positive laws are based on human rationality, while in the Islamic state, the *šarīʿa* laws follows the principles of the divine creator. The foundations of Western parliamentarism are Philosophy and a clear separation between politics and religion. In an Islamic government, instead, religion and politics are intertwined. Justice in Islam assumes a religious value, while in Western philosophy justice is based on the principle of rationality and on the rule of nature. In reality, the category of Islamic intellectuals (so-called Islamic reformers) knew very well Islamic principles, whereas their knowledge of Western philosophy remained superficial. Therefore, despite their general understanding of European political institutions, they had significant gaps in the knowledge of Western modern political thought. The basis of modern European institutions are founded on the natural right of the individual and on the will of the people, while the *šarīʿa* does recognize in its origins neither the law of nature nor

17 Sayyid Jamāl al-Dīn Asadābādī (al-Afġānī) was one of the most notable members of the so called religious intellectuals who believed that ideas of modern state are compatible with Islam and equated constitutionalism with consultation and social contract with bey'at (allegiance). See Rahnema, S., 'Retreat and Return of the Secular in Iran', in *Comparative Studies of South Asia, Africa and the Middle East,* vol. 31, no. 1, 2011, p 38.

> the will of the people. Even in Islamic philosophy these concepts cannot find expression and space for reflection. [18]

Kermani anticipates the complicated legal issue that, a few years later, would emerge within several modern states with a Muslim majority which were established following the end of the First World War and then the fall of the Ottoman and Persian empires. He highlights how a modern national State, in the event that the Shari'a had to be fully implemented, would face some constitutional limits that would damage some sectors of society, such as the non-Muslim citizens. In a modern constitutional state, the issue of belonging to the *umma* should not exist, according to Kermani but instead a modern concept of rights should be developed. A concept that would then be included under the principle of citizenship rights: the idea of belonging to the nation should thus prevail over being affiliated with a particular faith. These ideas would certainly influence the first draft of the Iranian constitution in 1906.

The political thought of Kermani is based on natural law as the foundation of modern political philosophy. Concerning the right to freedom Kermani argues that all individuals, since their birth, enjoy absolute freedom that encompasses both moral and physical freedom. Moral freedom – according to Kermani – has been long subjected on the Persian people by the clergy, while physical freedom has been subjected for centuries to the rule of the despotic monarchy of that time.

Then Kermani takes into consideration the freedom of thought and expression, reaffirming how the social evolution of man is deeply connected to the principle of freedom: '*There is no development without freedom*'. Development emerges under the idea of a modern civilisation in which progress and stability are both present. Such a virtuous system can only be achieved if each individual has freedom of speech and action without fearing the rulers. Therefore we must encourage the people to develop a critical awareness towards their rulers in order to freely express their opinions within a society[19]. Regarding freedom of thought he points out:

> In terms of civil rights, Kermani demonstrates the inadequacy of the shari'a in the context of a modern parliamentary state. Unlike the reformists, who want to Islamize modernity, Kermani wants to separate Islam from modernity. At the same time he recognizes that Islam ascribes an important

18 Cited in Adamyyat, F., *Andishha*-iye *Fatḥ'ali Akhundzadeh* (The Political Thoughts of Fatḥ'ali Akhundzade), Tehran, 1970, pp. 157–158.

19 Adamyyat, *Andishha*-iye *Fatḥ'ali Akhundzadeh*., p. 400.

role in the community of believers. Therefore he urges the experts of Islamic law to modernize Islam in order to make this religion suited to the modern era, while still maintaining the separation of religion from the political arena.

Kermani's political thought exerted a major influence on the political and institutional evolution of Persia, both during the Constitutional Revolution of 1906 and during the reign of Reza Shah Pahlavi, based on modernism, nationalism and secularism. Kermani, following his notable predecessor Akhundzadeh, elaborates, on the one hand, Persian nationalism and, on the other hand, examines the issue of the secular state, laying the foundations of constitutionalism in Iran.[20] In other words Kermani succeeded in spreading Akhundzadeh's ideas, also adding his own personal reflections, thus acting as a bridge between his thought and those politicians and intellectuals who were the protagonists of constitutional revolution years, from 1892 until 1909. Furthermore Kermani and Akhundzadeh's thought on nationalism finds its political realization, at least on a cultural level, under the reign of Reza Shah Pahlavi (1925–1941)[21], who founded the Pahlavi's dynasty on the principle of Persian nationalism.

---

20 'Kirmānī was first and foremost a Persian nationalist. His struggle was in the name of Iran and not Islam, which he came to blame for the political downfall of the Persians'. See Bayat, 'The Concepts of Religion and Government', p. 382.

21 The adoption of the surname Pahlavī by Rezā Shah already clearly demonstrated the political ideology of the new king, an ideology based mainly on the Iranian revival of patriotism and on the opposition to the Arab-Islamic culture that the Ṣafavids and Qājār dynasties had imposed in Persia. His reign is characterised by the revival of an Iranism based on the reference to the pre-Islamic Persian civilisation of Cyrus and Darius, and the values and principles related to the Arab-Islamic culture were put aside and even opposed. See Wilber, *Iran: Past and Present,* Princeton, 1950, pp. 97–98; Katouzian, H., *State and Society in Iran: The Eclipse of the Qajars and the Emergence of the Pahlavis,* London, 2000, pp. 294–299.

Bibliography

Adamyyat, F., *Andisheha-iye Mirza Aqa Khan Kermani*, Tehran, 1978.

Ansari, A. M., *The Politics of Nationalism in Modern Iran*, Cambridge, 2012.

Bayat, P.M., 'The Concepts of Religion and Government in the Thought of Mirza Aqa Khan Kermani, A Nineteenth-Century Persian Revolutionary', in *International Journal of Middle East Studies*, vol. 5, no. 4, 1974, pp. 381–400.

Browne, E. G., 'Catalogue and Description of 27 Bábí Manuscripts', in *The Journal of the Royal Asiatic Society of Great Britain and Ireland*, 1892, pp. 433–499.

Katouzian, H., *State and Society in Iran: The Eclipse of the Qajars and the Emergence of the Pahlavis,* London, 2000.

Kermãni, M. A., *Sad Kehtabeh ba virastar-e Mohammad Ja'far Mahjub,* Tehran, 1990.

Kermãni, M. A., *Se Maktub be-kushesh va virayesh-e Bahram Chubineh*, Essen, 2000.

Kermani, M. A., *Tarikh-e Iran-e Bastan* (A'iney-e Eskandari), Tehran, 1947.

Momen, M., *The Babi and Baha'i Religions, 1844–1944: Some Contemporary Western Accounts*, Oxford, 198.

Montesquieu, *L'esprit des lois*, Genève, 1748, vol. II.

Nateq, H., *Nameha-ye Tab'id*, Köln, 1989.

Rahnema, S., 'Retreat and Return of the Secular in Iran', in *Comparative Studies of South Asia, Africa and the Middle East,* vol. 31, no. 1, 2011, pp. 34–45.

Wilber, D., *Iran: Past and Present,* Princeton, 1950.

6

Iranian Enlightenment and Literary Self-consciousness: A Discussion about Modernity and Philosophy of Literature with Regards to the Works of Mirza Fatali Akhundzade

Salour Evaz Malayeri

This article aims to investigate the thought of Mirza Fatali Akhundzade about literature and his contribution to Persian literary criticism in the context of the Persian modernisation movement by applying the Hegelian notion of 'Self-consciousness'. I use the term 'literary self-consciousness' to explain the reciprocal relation between the literary text and the text which seeks to define and analyse literature and literary text through philosophical or multi-disciplinary discourses. In this regard, Akhundzade, I argue, was the first Iranian proto-modernist who asked about the nature of literature as an independent concept in the context of materialist – idealist philosophical discourse. To elaborate his contribution in a wider critical perspective, I will give a short critical argument about rhetoric as the dominant form of literary self-consciousness before Akhundzade in pre-modern Iran, as well as the state of 'translational dialogue' in the Persian modernist works, Akhundzade in particular. In the end, having studied the concept of 'criticism', nationalism and realism in Akhundzade's literary views, I will propose the question that to what extent Akhundzade's argument about the nature and function of literature, breaks away from that of rhetoric in the traditional context.

Introduction

During the nineteenth century, a ground-breaking social movement encompassed Iran, which resulted in fundamental changes in the ways of Iranians' socio-political thought and their attitude towards general issues – from politics and civil rights, to education, literature, and social institutions. Throughout this period Iran was in a complex but major transitive stage from reformist efforts to radical and revolutionary positions. The last attempts of Iranian political elites to find a way for 'progress' and 'progressive politics' inside the Qajar monarchy was about to fail in favour of 'modernisation' and fundamental change, as the long-standing despotic system along with its relevant ideological superstructure was gradually losing its legitimacy and function under the Qajar rule. The increasing political and economic crises served to intensify the historical antagonism between social classes and the state as anger and public dissatisfaction among the general populous coincided with emerging radical, revolutionary ideas among elites and intellectuals.[1]

Little by little, as state repression on intellectuals and individuals increased, Persian modernists were forced to leave their country and emigrate to places such as Istanbul and the Caucasus region which had a proximity that not only allowed them to express and implement their new idealism without fear, but also to keep a watchful eye on developments within Iran. These 'cultural crossroads', had vibrant cultural environments and had an enormous effect on the intellectual progress of Persian modernists, helped them to experience new cultural and technological manifestations of modern civilisation elsewhere, as well as exposure to some of the contemporary philosophical debates on issues such as, secularism, materialism, nationalism, democracy, human rights, etc. Indeed, time spent among other modernist intellectuals from Russia, Armenia, and the Ottoman Empire in public places, like cafes and libraries, or in business enterprises, such as newspapers and journals, influenced both the form and content of Persian modernist discourse.

---

1 For a thorough historical analysis of the transition from the traditional socio-political order to the formation of the ideal of 'progress' and reformist politics see: Adamiyat, F., *The Idea of progress and the rule of law (Andishe-ye Taraghi-o Hokoomat-e Ghanoon Asr-e Sepahsalar)*, Tehran, 1972, pp. 13–53; Adamiyat, F., *The Idea of Freedom and the Start of the Constitutional Movement (Fekr-e Azadi- o Moghaddame-ye Nehzat-e Mashroutiyat)*, Tehran, 1961.
A brief but highly enlightening account of the critical situation of Iran's politics and society during the nineteenth century which led to the constitutional revolution of 1906 can be found in: Keddie, N., 'The Iranian Power Structure and Social Change 1800–1969: An Overview', in *International Journal of Middle East Studies*, vol. 2, no. 1, 1971, pp.3–20.

Fig. 1: Nāder Shah Afshār, Karīm Khan Zand, Mīrza Taqī Khan Amīr Kabīr, and all Shahs of Qajar, Tehran around 1910, postcard from the collection of Naser Hassanzadeh.

Fig. 2: Members of the Iranian national assembly of the first legislature in Tehran, and two high clerics propagating the Iranian Constitution, Tehran 1906, postcard from the collection of Naser Hassanzadeh.

Fig. 3: Moḥammad-Walī Khan, *Sepah-sālār* (Supreme Commander), the first leader of the revolutionaries in Gīlān and Qazvīn, from the series 'Souvenir of the Iranian Revolution', Tehran 1909, postcard from the collection of Naser Hassanzadeh.

Fig. 4: Māshāllāh Khan, son of Naīeb Hossein-e Kāshī, and Ḥājī Mīr Panj (as prisoners), postcard from the collection of Naser Hassanzadeh.

عکس سادات و طلاب متحصنین سفارت انگلیس برای مشروطیت
Les curés et les moines réfugiés à la légation d'Angleterre pour exiger la constitution

Fig. 5: Theology students taking refuge in the British legation, from a photograph taken 1906 in Tehran, postcard from the collection of Mehrdad Oskouei, Visual Heritage Centre, Tehran.

Fig. 6: The kitchen during the *bast* in the British legation, from a photograph taken 1906 in Tehran, postcard from the collection of Mehrdad Oskouei, Visual Heritage Centre, Tehran.

Fig. 7: Representatives of the guild of mercers taking refuge in the British legation in Tehran, 1906, postcard from the archive of Kimia Foundation.

Fig. 8: The guild of traders of tea, sugar, and pepper taking refuge in the British legation in Tehran, 1906, from the collection of Mehrdad Oskouei, Visual Heritage Centre, Tehran.

Fig. 9: Bāqer Khan *sālār-e melli* (national chieftain) – Azerbaijan, postcard from the collection of Mehrdad Oskouei, Visual Heritage Centre, Tehran.

Fig. 10: National army in Tabriz, postcard from the collection of Mehrdad Oskouei, Visual Heritage Centre, Tehran.

Fig. 11: Barricade in the court of the citadel in Tabriz with Khalīl Khan, the leader of this group of *mojāhedīn*, most likely taken by Estepān Estepāniān, postcard from the collection of Mehrdad Oskouei, Visual Heritage Centre, Tehran.

Fig. 12: Sattār Khan and Bāqer Khan in the mid of a group of *mojāhedīn*, postcard from the collection of Mehrdād Oskoueī.

Fig. 13: Bāqer Khan among groups of *mojāhedīn* in the Blue Mosque in Tabriz, postcard from the archive of Kimia Foundation.

Fig. 14: Staged photograph, from the collection of City Photo Museum in Tehran.

Fig. 15: Ḥājī Malek-al-Motakallemīn, orator-preacher for the Constitution, postcard from the collection of Naser Hassanzadeh.

مسیو نوز فرنگیهایی که در روز عید میان تقلید لباس و دره لباس های ایران

Monsieur Nose, chef de la douane de la Perse et les personnes étrangères pendant une fête à Téhéran en divers vêtements de turbans et coiffées à la perse.

Fig. 16: Monsieur Naus, Head of Customs, dressed as a cleric during a celebration with other foreigners, postcard from the collection of Naser Hassanzadeh.

ستارخان سردار ملی
Sattar Khan, Führer der Aufständigen von Azarbayedjan.
Саттар-Хан, Вожак революционеров в Азербейджане.

Fig. 17: Satār Khan, *sardār-e melli*, postcard from the collection of Naser Hassanzsdeh.

Fig. 18: Political prisoners of Bagh-e Shāh, postcard from the collection of Naser Hassanzsdeh.

Fig. 19: Members of the first parliament in Tehran, 1906, postcard from the collection of Mehrdad Oskouei, Visual Heritage Centre, Tehran.

Fig. 20: Public execution in Tabriz, postcard from the collection of Naser Hassanzadeh

The demand for progress and reformation that had long been voiced by reformists and political elites, could now articulate itself through reading the philosophical and cultural heritage of European enlightenment. Persian intellectuals began to enlighten their readership in Iran through their monographs, pamphlets and books with radical criticism on a great number of subjects that the 'Iranian people' had to acknowledge if they were to 'know' in what 'decedent' historical situation they were living, so that they could find the road to 'salvation' and 'prosperity'.

Towards a new form of critical writing

Focusing on all the issues that have been discussed by Persian intellectuals regarding the reformation and modernisation would be outside of the scope of this article, which will concentrate on one in particular: a key element of Iranian culture that modernist Iranian thinkers thought of as a large part of Iran's decadence: literature. However, before I open the discussion on the subject of literature in particular, I would like to address a few points about the form and discursive structure of the Iranian modernist writings.

The writings of the Iranian modernists on numerous occasions are vocative texts in which the 'people' are considered as the 'implied reader',[2] to the extent that one might say the public consciousness was more of a problem than the despotic rule. At this time, there are the ordinary people whom intellectuals find it necessary to address as there is no use in advising the king any longer. If there is any criticism of the king, which surely there is, it will not be in the traditional form of the 'Mirror for Princes' or '*Siyasatname*', but in the radical and direct form of criticism which aims at the despotic and arbitrary kingship in general; such radical knowledge is for the people, not the king, and moreover, it should be written in a language that the people should understand.

Having the people as the implied reader in the Persian modernist writings also refers to a new knowledge, a new form of thought, which the people 'do not know'

2 'A term used by Wolfgang Iser and some other theorists of reader-response criticism to denote the hypothetical figure of the reader to whom a given work is designed to address itself. Any text may be said to presuppose an 'ideal' reader who has the particular attitudes (moral, cultural, etc.) appropriate to that text in order for it to achieve its full effect. This implied reader is to be distinguished from actual readers, who may be unable or unwilling to occupy the position of the implied reader'- Baldick, C., *The Oxford Dictionary of Literary Terms*, (3rd Edition), Oxford, 2008, available online: http://www.oxfordreference.com/view/10.1093/acref/9780199208272.001.0001/acref-9780199208272-e-586 (last accessed August 30, 2016).

since they have been accustomed to the traditional, decayed and useless system of thought that has made them ignorant and unaware. Religious superstitions, solid and irrational traditions, social depression as well as lack of knowledge and education were among the main reasons through which, according to intellectuals, the despotic rule had held its position throughout history over the people. But since the people must be the ones to perform the uprising against the arbitrary political system, they must be first enlightened and 'awakened'. Such a discursive attitude puts the modernist intellectuals in a high and privileged position of the required knowledge – those who know 'what is to be done' and can also create the enlightening knowledge formed of pure and abstract ideas – a set of concepts, terms, statements and solutions. It also made the writers use a simplified and inartificial form of communication and, most importantly, to repeatedly advise young writers with it, sometimes with strong language. In fact, the most spoken and criticised issue about literature proposed by Persian modernists is undoubtedly one addressing the prevalence of an over-sophisticated and grandiloquent style of writing utilising rhetoric devices. Encouraging young writers to write in a simple style and avoid any superfluous, clichéd rhetoric techniques was the main discourse of Persian modernists.

In Akhundzade's case, however, it is rather different from those who were mostly under strong influence of Akhundzade, such as Malkam Khan or Mirza Agha Khan-e Kermani. There are signs of some theoretical potentials and epistemological breaks in Akhundzade's discourse which, as a proto-modernist, make him exceptional, though unfortunately these potentials were never elaborated on by others, only repeated and rephrased. Even Akhundzade himself, as we shall see later, was not successful enough to expand and go deeper into what he had once proposed, as a result, the theoretical formation of the modern approach towards Persian literature remained focused on generalities and failed to offer a new episteme, a new logic of literary thought.

The primary aspect of Akhundzade's ideas on literature are his philosophical/theoretical enquiries on the subject of literature and poetry as an independent concept. Poetry, according to Akhundzade, has a definition in itself which separates it from other disciplines such as philosophy, theology or ethics. For Akhundzade, any criticism of classical poetry or style of writing must be based on the philosophical understanding of poetry and prose. Considering the fact that literature in the Persian cultural tradition has always been regarded only as a secondary device for a sublime truth. Whether that truth belongs to the realm of theology, philosophy or even science, this aspect of Akhundzade's opinions, in my view, is very important. A further aspect of Akhundzade's literary discussion which separates him from other Iranian modernists is his view about drama and the novel as two literary genres that have unique capabilities of representing the reality of the human condition, and the complexity of its behaviours and relations. It is important to note, however, that this view may have been formulated by his own discovery of drama and the novel, and a desire to introduce them to a new readership, given that these forms of creative writing were totally new to Iranians at that time. Nevertheless, his emphasis on the formal and technical aspects of the novel and drama is indeed considerable, as if he is consciously trying to draw attention to the nature of these new forms of writing and the necessity of understanding them as a novelist or playwright might. The final aspect of Akhundzade's significant role in modern literary criticism in Iran is his idealist view of literary realism through which his influence from Russian literary criticism at that time is extremely evident. For Akhundzade, realism has more philosophical and historical significance as, being the essential feature of criticism, has more to do with the historical truth of a nation. So, for Akhundzade, any criticism necessarily follows a historical narrative by which the general reality/truth of a nation is constructed in a form of totalised identity, while the realist literature must represent such reality/truth through creating particular and concrete human conditions, even through metaphors, symbols and forms of imagination. Therefore, we can see in Akhundzade's works how realism and realist literature is tied with nationalism.

The aim of this chapter is to analyse these three features of Akhundzade's views about criticism and literature, with more focus on the philosophical and theoretical aspects, given the fact that both Akhundzade's comments on realism and drama (as the new genres of writing) are related to the philosophical capacity of Akhundzade's view about the concept of literature.

Critique, Criticism, *Critika*

The first Russian poet to complain about the absence of a Russian term for the French word 'critique', was Antiokh Kantemir (1709–1744)[3] in 1739, but it did not result in any attempt to start a critical tradition. Thus, nine decades later in 1825 Alexander Pushkin (1799–1837), one of the greatest figures of Russian literature whom Akhundzade wrote an elegy for[4], would still complain in a letter that: 'we have no criticism… we have not a single commentary, not a single book of

3 Wellek, R., *A History of Modern Criticism: 1750–1950, vol. 3. The Age of Transition*, London, 1966, p. 241.

4 Adamiyat, F., *The Thoughts of Mirza Fatali Akhundzade (Andisheha-ye Mirza Fatali Akhundzade)*, Tehran, 1970, p. 28.

criticism'.[5] A few decades later, Mirza Fatali Akhundzade, spoke of a specific form of writing 'the art of *Critika* (critique), which he argued, was new to the Muslim world. He did not propose any Persian equivalent for the word 'critique' or 'criticism'; like many of the new political terms that he discussed, Akhundzadeh used the original word pronounced and written to correspond with *Azari* phonetics. He even named his seminal essay, which was later celebrated as the first modern work of literary criticism in the history of Persian literature, 'Critika' (رساله قرطیکا).[6]

I began my discussion with two quotations from Russian literary figures, to highlight their important historical link to Akhundzade's critical ideas and to propose the main argument and approach of this chapter. I interpret the above-mentioned quotations as preliminary articulations of two kinds of literary thought. In my view, Kantemir's argument about the absence of a Russian equivalent for the term 'critique' refers to the lack of a philosophical discourse about literature and literary criticism, while Pushkin's objection shows the lack of practical examples of literary criticism based on a theoretical approach and a philosophical context. It seems the same consciousness about the absence of the concept 'Criticism', as well as the critical 'writing' among Iranians was one of the main intellectual contemplations of Akhundzade. For Akhundzade, as a radical thinker, the term has a much wider meaning. In addition to both of these concepts of literary thought, Akhundzade uses the term 'Critika' for critical debates in modern journalism as well as satirical pieces.[7]

To analyse the particular dimensions of Akhundzade's contribution to literary criticism, I will first explain my theoretical terms and arguments which construct my approach. My key term in these contexts is 'literary self-consciousness'. Then I will discuss how the Iranian enlightenment was in translational dialogue with Western thought, and by 'translational dialogue' I mean the process of reading and interpretation of 'the other' which is usually based on 'the self', or the indigenous cultural context and, in the case of Persian enlightenment, such a process was embedded in the context of Iranian/Islamic traditional thoughts. I will conclude through Iranian interpretation of Western thought during the nineteenth and early twentieth century, a kind of 'linguistic confusion' occurred. The pre-modern conception of literary text in Iran is my next discussion in which I examine the theory

5 Wellek, R., *A History of Modern Criticism: 1750–1950*, p. 242.

6 Parsinejad, I., *Persian Enlightenment and Literary Criticism (Roshangaran-e Irani va Naghd-e Adabi)*, Tehran, 2001, p. 35.

7 For the meanings of the '*Critica*' in Akhundzade's works see: Parsinejad, *Persian Enlightenment and Literary Criticism*, pp. 27–28.

of rhetoric as the form of literary self-consciousness in medieval Persia to give an analytical account as to the nature of literary criticism before Akhundzade. Finally, I will make a brief argument about the influence that Russian critics in the nineteenth century had on Akhundzade and conclude with a viewpoint regarding the contradictions in Akhundzade's view about form and content as well as his failure in constructing a proper and well-articulated theoretical argument relevant to his modern approach.

Literary self-consciousness

The rich, creative and ground-breaking literary traditions in each historical period and among each nation, apart from producing amazing artistic creativity, often articulates a sort of 'literary self-consciousness'[8] by which the literary creativity, owing to its powerful and history-making effects, recognises itself through philosophy and theory. Literary creativity, at its highest stage of development, realises itself not merely as a text which 'belongs' to a sublime truth or specific from of knowledge (the literature of/for the other), but as an independent text, belonging to a specific mode of creativity (the literature as an institution for itself). At this stage, the literary text confirms its 'literariness', identifies its institutional nature, and sets its own rules and principles by its own; the literary text accepts its reality as 'literature' and starts to construct a discourse based on such self-consciousness.

From this point of view, one can conclude that any philosophy of literature as well as literary theory is first initiated from a preliminary form of literary self-consciousness, since both of these developed disciplines recognise literature as an independent and self-referential institution. While philosophy of literature is searching for an answer to the question 'what is literature?', presupposing the fact that literature is an existing and distinctive medium which has particular functions and specific qualifications, literary theory tries to establish a set of statements and instructions as to how to read and criticise the literary text relying on philosophical traditions or other disciplines in humanities.[9]

---

8 By 'self-consciousness' I refer to the Hegelian notion, in which the consciousness in its particular moment of its historical dynamism, looks back and recognises its historical 'self'. Such developed stage for consciousness occurs after objective perception in which consciousness is alienated with / limited to its object. See: Singer, P., *Hegel*, Oxford, p.74. Also: Hegel, G.W.F., *The phenomenology of Spirit,* (transl. by Miller, A. V.), Oxford, 1977, pp. 110–119.

9 Lamarque, P., *The Philosophy of Literature*, Oxford, 2009, p. 2.

The forms of literary self-consciousness develop throughout history with correspondence to dominant discourse as well as the political-economic infrastructure in each period and therefore, like the Hegelian notion of 'self-consciousness', literary self-consciousness must be considered historically. In pre-modern societies, a cultural sphere was based mostly on myth and religion with poetry as the dominant form of literature, thus literary self-consciousness was mainly about defining poetry as an appropriate tool for divine truth or sublime values and meanings. Nonetheless, the case of Aristotle shows a unique moment in the history of literary self-consciousness. It is indeed the most significant and philosophically developed example of such self-consciousness in which poetry was recognised not simply as a secondary device to elaborate the pre-existing sublime truth, but rather as an independent medium, which has its own particular mode of producing meaning within different categories and genres.[10] But in Iran, as I will discuss later, the literary self-consciousness had a different logic; the belongingness of poetry to the sublime meaning was the subject of Persian literary self-consciousness. This does not suggest that literature was not recognised as an independent medium in Persian medieval culture, in fact, it was the sublime and precious truth or wisdom (*hekmat*) that determined the nature of literature (*adab*) and its importance. Literature, from the perspective of such cultural logic, recognised and acknowledged itself in the form of rhetoric.[11]

Western terms and indigenous explanations: the process of 'translational dialogue' and the problem of 'linguistic confusion'

It would be too simplistic to assume that Iranian enlightenment in the nineteenth century emerged in imitation of Western enlightenment. Such an abstract view ignores the context in which Western enlightenment was understood and interpreted. In fact, as I will try to show in Akhundzade's case, Iranian enlightenment was the result of a dialogue between the indigenous cultural heritage and the

---

10 Ford, A., *The Origins of Criticism*, Princeton, 2002, pp. 286–296. The book also contains a very thoughtful and thorough discussion about the formation of literary criticism and philosophy of literature among Greek philosophers. Also a brief but comprehensive account of Aristotle literary views can be found in: Habib, M.A.R., *A History of Literary Criticism*, Oxford, 2005, pp. 41–61.

11 For a Historical overview of the concept of 'Adab' in the Perso-Islamic tradition and its relation with ethics, politics and aesthetics see: Pellat, Ch., 'Adab ii. Adab in Arabic Literature', in *Encyclopædia Iranica*, vol. I, fasc.. 4, pp. 439–444, available online: http://www.iranicaonline.org/articles/adab-ii-arabic-lit (last accessed: August 31, 2016).

modern Western culture and philosophy. This interaction occurred within the complex socio-political conditions of nineteenth-century Iran in which conflicts between progressive ideas and reactionary politics had already shaped and transformed the discursive and political life of Iran.[12]

On the one hand, the constant presence of indigenous, cultural unconsciousness influenced the perception of the western culture; Persian thought was not only a receiver of Western civilisation but also reconstructed its own progressive potentials and ideas through understanding and observing the West. It is important to emphasis on the discursive level of the Persian enlightenment at this point, the moment when the will of change and progress in the form of native perceptions has to articulate itself through discursive disciplines such as philosophy and science in order to textualise and identify itself, so it can produce a power to mobilise the social classes. Therefore, for analytical intention, one must separate the indigenous perception of modernity based on the will and demand for progress, and those philosophical texts and commentaries that tries to articulate and formulate such 'will' and 'demand' for reformation and modernisation. It is during the latter process that Iranian enlightenment had to read and interpret the European enlightenment to find the power of expression and to conceptualise its indigenous perception of modernity that was formed during decades before interpreting the Western enlightenment.[13] It is important to see both parts interrelated and interacting, rather than two separated, even antagonistic aspects of Iranian modernisation movement.[14]

---

12 Ajand, J., *Literary Modernism During Persian Constitutional Revolution* (*Tajaddod-e Adabi dar Dowreye Mashrouteh)*, Tehran, 2006, pp.17–35.

13 For the indigenous aspects of Iranian modernity see: Tavakkoli-Targhi, M., *The indigenous modernity and rethinking of history (Tajaddod-e Boomi- o Bazandishi-ye Tarikh)*, Tehran, 2003, pp. 9–120.

14 Such 'ideological separation' between the indigenous and European aspects of Iranian modernity has caused reductionist and sometimes abstract conclusions from both sides of the debate: the post-colonial approach and the so called 'orientalist' approach. While the first ignores the importance of Iranian reading from the European enlightenment, the latter ignores the indigenous attempts towards modernity and over-estimates the role of western ideas in the Iranian project of modernity. As a result of the post-colonial approach, the concept of modernity or *Tajaddod* loses any concrete and distinctive quality, turns into a mere 'concept' or a hollow 'idea' upon which any interpretation of the 'indigenous culture', regardless of its historical context, can be considered as an attempt to modernity, while on the other side, the orientalist approach cannot trace the impacts and interruptions of the indigenous perception of modernity during the process of translating the western thought.

Cultural dialogue as such, however one-sided in might seem, inevitably comes with interventions and interpretations from the receiving side and that brings the active presence of indigenous culture. Moreover, the historical moment in which such translational dialogue is forming has its own influence on the process of interpreting 'the other' – it puts forward the necessities, which results in the superior position of the other being accepted and affirmed.

On the other hand, given the fact that interpretation of the western 'progressive' culture was made possible by the indigenous perception and awareness of the idea of progress, the absence of an established discourse about such progressive ideas made Iranian modernists use the original words for philosophical categories and some sociopolitical terms. In a Hegelian context, there was consciousness to progressive ideas, but not self-consciousness towards them. The 'consciousness towards' idea is one with an absence of a relevant discursive and institutional establishment, formulated without knowing and understanding itself and therefore, without any influential social function. One of the reasons for this inability or 'stutter' in articulation can be the lack of historical and practical experience of the idea, the most vital and determining fact of modernity. However, when the socio-political contradictions are at their highest state of antagonism, the progressive idea needs to find appropriate words to express itself. In such a situation, by looking at the 'other' culture standing in a dominant position, the indigenous idea recognises its inability to articulate itself and tries to overcome by reading and interpreting 'the other' cultural text. As a result, the terms and expressions of the other culture that have come from a different socio-economic context are explained with traditional indigenous literature.

The process of forming self-consciousness through reading the hegemonic culture of 'the other' resulted in what I would call 'the linguistic confusion'. In the condition of linguistic confusion that appeared in the Persian modernist movement, the Western philosophical and sociological terms are explained in a literature with different cultural context that does not correspond with their Western historical background. Most of the essays and writings of Persian modernists illustrate linguistic confusion in expressing the modern ideas; while the terms and expressions of Western modern philosophy and science are articulated in different socio-economic contexts, the explanations of each term are made in a more traditional and indigenous language. For instance, Akhundzade's most important book *The Letters of Kamal al-Dawla* (مکتوبات کمال الدوله) begins with categories and expressions in which he mentions the original word for each term and then brings his Persian explanations for each of them. Terms such as 'despot', 'philosophe', 'revolution', 'literature', 'poesy' and 'progress' are some of the words that Akhundzade starts his radical and philosophical book with.[15] From one point of view, for a prominent thinker like Akhundzade, choosing the original words is done consciously, to address the significant difference between the Persian equivalent and the original term, not letting the traditional meaning of the Persian word shadow the European meaning.[16] However, one of the results of such translational dialogue, was the immature, idealist perception of modernity that occurred among Persian modernists, including Akhundzade. Focusing on Western progressive ideas without making any argument as to the historical background or the material conditions of those ideas, made the modernists perception of modernity too abstract and ideal, spoken from an elitist position, and hardly able to provide any practical or social potentiality.

The theory of rhetoric, from philosophy to ideology

The common form of literary self-consciousness in pre-modern Iran was the theory of rhetoric.[17] Rhetoric, in the original Greco-Roman context is generally regarded as the embellishment of speech, while in the Persian context, rhetoric has been one of the most developed literary traditions, deeply rooted in Persian philosophy with various aesthetic and social functions. Being essentially dependent on Persian philosophical traditions, literary practice was mostly based on rhetorical techniques such as allegory, ambiguity and metaphor to serve the artistic articulation of the Persian philosophical worldview. Three types of rhetorical science in Arabic-Persian literary tradition exist: *Badi'* (the study of rhetorical embellishments based on phonetic characteristics); *Ma'ani* (the study of semantic aspects of syntax); and *Bayan* (the study of tropes) show the highly-developed and complicated state of the science of rhetoric in Iran.

From one aspect, rhetoric was a device – a secondary tool to speak effectively and differently from ordinary speech according to the subject and to the condition of audience;[18] from another, its function was to transfer from an ordinary,

15 Akhundzade, M., *Maktoobat (The Letters)*, (ed. by Sobhdam, M.), Tehran, 1985, pp. 9–14.

16 The example of 'politic' interestingly can show such association. While its Persian equivalent, *Siyasat*, refers to authoritative and autocratic rule of the king over the people (*ra'iyat*), its modern meaning in the context that Akhundzade is trying to situate his argument, signifies to rational mechanism of governing in which the social interest is considered as the priority.

17 Parsinejad, *Persian Enlightenment and Literary* Criticism, p. 39. Also see: Zarrinkoob, A., *An Introduction to Literary Criticism (Ashnaee Ba Naghd-e Adabi)*, Tehran, 2004, pp. 271–388.

18 Shamisa,S., *Ma'ani (Rhetorics based on Persian literature)*, Tehran, 2004, p.13.

lifeless, inactive and unproductive level of the language to a subjective, dynamic and productive level, to make a way from ordinary and reachable meaning to an extra-ordinary network of complicated significations with numerous layers of meaning. Such function was not merely about motivating or persuading specific groups of audiences, but rather a philosophical doctrine in which the quality of sublime truth was deeply interwoven with the quality of sublime language. The linguistic journey was itself a part of the transcendental meaning. Rhetoric in Persian literature was not about a formal device, but rather about the unification of form and content in a theological and metaphysical context.

Because of theological or transcendental understanding of rhetoric, which was part of a general philosophical doctrine of Iranian medieval culture, the development of literature is affiliated with the development of intellectual and philosophical discourses. In other words, the 'decline' or 'refusal' of thought would have resulted in the decline of poetry and literature as well. With no dynamic discursive and philosophical tradition, the rhetoric devices were merely a disused form that only had one function left: naturalising and glorifying the expired or traditional idea, which eventually serves the 'despotic' political order, in other words, rhetoric would then function as ideology.

Rhetoric, when there is no dynamism and development in discursive and intellectual traditions, turns to a self-alienated device that has nothing to expose but ideology. In a despotic and arbitrary rule like that in Iran under the Qajars, ideology was no longer to do with metaphysical and ethical thoughts legitimising the despotic rule, the traditional form of 'literary self-consciousness' was ideological as well since it was part of the same metaphysical world-view. Therefore, any radical and modernist critique of literature must include the critique of rhetoric apart from criticising the philosophical or ethical statements. The 'ideology of form' is the subject of radical criticism as well as the 'ideological content' and this seems to be a good starting point for analysing Akhundzade's ideas about poetry since his most favorite term, 'Critika', deals with both of these two dimensions of Ideology.

Akhundzade's contribution to modern literary self-consciousness in Iran

Being among the pioneers of Iranian enlightenment, Mirza Fatali Akhundzade (1812–1878), as most of the scholars have concluded, had probably the most influential role on the views and works of Persian intellectuals and writers, even during his life, when he had consecutive correspondence with his Persian peers. It is true that Malkam Khan (1833–1908), the second major figure of Iranian enlightenment, developed his idea of 'new Alphabet' through his conversations with Akhundzade, who had written a monograph about the same subject before.[19] Mirza Agha Khan-e Kermani (1855–1898), another well-known modernist thinker, almost rephrased Akhundzade's views on poetry, language and literature in his works. The plays he wrote in Azari language had an enormous influence on Mirza Agha Tabrizi, the first playwright who wrote in Persian. He is also remembered as the founder of modern literary criticism in Iran, as well as the first playwright in the Middle East. He is the first Iranian thinker who introduced the novel and drama as the new forms of literary creativity to Iranian people.[20]

Akhundzade's leading position in Iranian enlightenment, in part, comes from the environment he grew up. Born into a family of Iranian origin in Shaki on the southern part of the great Caucasus, Akhundzade's intellectual development came to flourish in a cultural crossroad between Persia, Ottoman Empire, Armenia and Russia. The disastrous defeat of Persia during the Russo-Persian War of 1826–28 had a significant consequence on Akhunzade's life and evoked his patriotic emotions which later showed itself in his writings. The most important years of Akhundzade, however, were spent in Tbilisi where he joined the intellectual circles of Decembrists, Russian and Armenian writers and critics, as well as Persians. Most importantly, he acquainted himself with drama, the novel and Western materialist philosophy by attending numerous Russian theatres and reading Russian translations of European Enlightenment and literature. The literary journals, that were circulated among the intellectual circles in Tbilisi also familiarised Akhundzade with major debated on literary criticism, particularly the main currents of Russian literary criticism of the nineteenth century.

Critika, or Criticism, is seemingly the most unspecific term in Akhundzade's work. He uses it for literary assessments, journalism, socio-political criticism, and most of all, for satirical writings as opposed to didactic writings and preachment. Taking a hard position against Persian didactic literature, including Sadi's poems,

19 The project of New Alphabet was an attempt from Iranian secular modernists to use Latin alphabetical system instead of the Arabic one, as they thought modernity and new science can be understood and practice properly through the Latin alphabet and not the Arabic one. See: Algar, H., 'Malkum Khān, Ākhūndzāda and the Proposed Reform of the Arabic Alphabet', in *Middle Eastern Studies*, vol. 5, no. 2, 1969, pp. 116–130. Also for correspondence between Akhundzade and Malkam khan about the new alphabet see: Parsinejad, *Persian Enlightenment and Literary Criticism*, pp. 161–165.

20 Parsinejad, *Persian Enlightenment and Literary Criticism (Roshangaran-e Irani va Naghd-e Adabi)*, p.51. also: Adamiyat, *The Thoughts of Mirza Fatali Akhundzade*, pp.31–33.

Akhundzade alternatively emphasises notions like ridiculing, lampoon and irony as the real forms of *Critika* that has practical effects on readers. He also considers *Critika* as one of the most important achievements of European people which allowed them reaching to most developed state of intellectual wisdom and social progress:

> The European nations reached to such state of progress and knowledge because of Critika, not preaching and sermons. One must read the works of Voltaire (1694–1778), Eugen Sue (1804–1857), Alexander Dumas (1802–1870) and European philosophers such as H. Buckle (1821–1862) and Ernest Renan (1823–1892) to realize the truth of my assertion, knowing that preaching and sermons will not affect the human nature and have no use, particularly after childhood. … If preaching and sermons were to do any good, then Sa'di's *Golestan* and *Boustan*, which are full of preaches and lectures from the very beginning to the end, would have worked in Iranian minds during these six hundred years since Sa'di wrote those two books. … The reason for the significance of Critika is its being written in the forms of ridicule and mockery, discovered by European thinkers, this hidden secret is still neglected by my people [Iranians].[21]

In addition to these perceptions, it seems Akhundzade sees his philosophical arguments as a kind of *Critika* as well, particularly when he relates his philosophical analysis to his socio-political criticism.[22]

Despite having numerous meanings, a close reading of Akhundzade's thoughts can show that the basic function of *Critika* is the central concept in Akhundzade's discourse. In fact, there is logical relation between all these various conceptions and Akhundzade was probably well aware of the fact. It may seem obvious that you cannot make the most radical and effective criticism to solid and expired beliefs and traditions with the language of sermons and preaching but I believe *Critika* has one important aspect which stands above all other aspects, related to our literary discussion: that *Critika* is a specific kind of 'writing'. Almost in every instance, Akhundzade refers to *Critika* as a new art: a new form of writing. Through this term, he tries to draw the modernist writers' attention to acknowledging the form and the structure of writing even before thinking about the content. For Akhundzadeh, recognising new forms of cultural production is the precondition of

21 Cited from: Parsinejad, *Persian Enlightenment and Literary Criticism*, pp. 50–51.

22 Cited from: Parsinejad, *Persian Enlightenment and Literary Criticism*, p. 90.

understanding the modern content. Whether it is a new literary genre, the public debate in cultural media, or a form of socio-political analysis, *Critika* first and foremost is a formal and institutional acknowledgement to its independency and its individual power and effect. Therefore, according to Akhundzadeh, a modernist writer must first of all take some time to acquaint himself with the institutional nature of the genre, or the form of his writing and that is the philosophy, rules and techniques by which that particular form of writing is recognised.

The best example of this aspect of *Critika*, is Akhundzade's advice to Mirza Agha Tabrizi, the first Iranian who wrote drama in Persian and was influenced by the works of Akhundzade. There he willingly and consciously focuses on knowing the history of theatre in Europe and its social function, as well as the nature, rules and techniques of Drama and playwriting:

> Do not get worried by my instructions and recommendations about your works. They might double your hard work, but you must know that you do not need to hurry in writing. Your writings will remain after you for generations to come, so they must be written in perfection and excellence and accepted by social taste, so that your readers can rest assured that the writer knows the principles of drama, since it is essential for the playwright to be aware that his writings meet all conditions of the art of drama[23]

The most important view of Akhundzade about literature is where he tries to define 'poesy':

> poesy is a writing, about the condition and behavior of a person or a group of people as it should be illustrated, or it is a description about a specific subject as well as describing the characteristics of the existing world in verse in its most perfection and influence[24] … They do not know what Poesy has to be. They regard ignorantly any collection of verse as poesy, assuming that poesy is just about versifying the meaningless words in a specific rhythm or putting rhyme at the end of each line. Describing darlings and beloveds with unreal attributes as well as extolling spring or autumn with unrealistic and abstract similes are what they think poesy is about, like one of the poets of Tehran, *Gha'ani* (1808–1854), whose *Divan* is filled with such nonsenses. …Poesy must include a story or an objection in most perfect form and in agreement

23 Adamiat, *The Thoughts of Mirza Fatali Akhundzade*, p. 67.

24 Akhundzade, *Maktoobat*, p. 11.

> with reality and social situation either in tragic or comic manner, like the poems of Ferdowsi, may God bless his soul[25]

In *Critika*, he also argues about 'beauty of content and beauty of form' (حسن مضمون و حسن الفاظ) as two main conditions of poetry.[26] Beauty of form and content he says should create an aesthetical totality together. For Akhundzade, such a totality is what a perfect poem should be. In other words, the poem that has beauty of form is imperfect and undeveloped as much as a poem which only represents ethical and metaphysical meanings.

The philosophical aspect of Akhundzade's statement about poetry is close to the Russian criticism from the nineteenth century, of which Akhundzade learned and influenced a good deal. During his residence in Tbilisi as well as the fruitful journeys he made during 1850s and 1860s in the Caucasus region, Akhundzade studied the works of Russian critics, particularly the works of Vissarion Belinsky (1810–1848), Nikolay Chernishevsky (1828–1889) and Nikolay Dobrolyubof (1836–1861).[27] According to Rene Wellek, Russian criticism, particularly to the works of Belinsky, became 'a German speculative thought follower, first absorbed the romantic conceptions and later modified them in favor of a close approach to empirical reality, to facts, to science and to national and social needs of the time'.[28]

In Russia during that time, there was an important discursive struggle between moralistic views of literature and the view in which literature was considered a more independent and self-referential medium. The political aspect of such struggle was important as well. While moralistic views about literature were in favour of Tsarism, the oppositions usually proposed liberal and social ideas. One can observe the same political fight in Iran between those traditional poets living under a Qajar patronage system and modernist intellectuals such as Akhundzade, Mirza Agha Khan-e Kermani and Mirza Malkam Khan.

Realism is the fundamental element of Akhundzade's view of poetry. However, most of the scholars failed to see the link between Akhundzade's account of realism and Belinsky's Hegelian explanation of it. That is probably the reason for assuming that Akhundzade's realism is contradictory since he illustrates the Persian epic,

25 Akhundzade, *Maktoobat*, p. 34.

26 Adamiat, *The Thoughts of Mirza Fatali Akhundzade,* pp. 248–250.

27 Adamiyat, *The Thoughts of Mirza Fatali Akhundzade*, pp. 35–3

28 Wellek, *A History of Modern Criticism,* p. 244.

Shahname of Ferdowsi as the perfect example of poesy.[29] According to Belinsky, 'literature should be the expression of the national spirit, the symbol of the inner life of a nation, the physiognomy of a nation'; a poet has to produce 'a peculiar national spirit' as *Eugene Onegin* and *Boris Gedunov* do, since there is something 'truly national' in them.[30] Therefore, realism is the reality of the national spirit, the historical consciousness through the representation of material world. The more literary text represents the national spirit in a whole aesthetic perfection, the more realistic it may become. The 'primary task' of the artist 'is not to copy reality', but 'to create types and figures through concrete individuals, with universal significance'.[31] The concept of 'concrete individuals' in Hegel's philosophy refers to material and real manifestation of the absolute consciousness or the spirit, and the 'universal significance' expresses the function and historicity of the concrete individual as to how, through its material and historical existence, the concrete individual represents the elements of the universal spirit. Therefore, according to Hegel, the consciousness exits through the concrete manifestation necessarily, so as the concrete individual historically functions and is recognised through its signification to the universal spirit (according to Hegelian view, the 'national spirit' is part of the historical manifestation of the universal spirit). The Hegelian approach to literature considers the literary text, both in form and content, as the concrete individual which its artistic and aesthetic value can be argued based on the level of its significance to the national, and in more developed stage, the universal spirit.

I believe Akhundzade's short account about *Shahname* must be interpreted with regard to the idealist approach of Russian criticism in the nineteenth century to realism. Unfortunately, as on other occasions, Akhundzade refuses to give a thorough discussion, nonetheless, he addresses the relation between national epic and realism, explaining imaginative characters and extraordinary events in *Shahname* that have in fact real, human meanings. [32] In other words, it is not in the exotic and exaggerated characters and events we should look for realistic meanings, but in the historical and conceptual significations of those extraordinary descriptions and stories. The realist aspect of those meanings, whether they are about moralities, philosophy or politics, is in their historical contribution to the national spirit. The main criterion for realism, according to the idealist view, is not the material world

29 For instance, see: Ajoudani, M., *Ya Marg Ya Tajaddod (Either Death or Modernization)*, London, 2002, p. 96.

30 Wellek, *A History of Modern Criticism*, p. 247.

31 Wellek, *A History of Modern Criticism*, p. 247.

32 Adamiat, *The Thoughts of Mirza Fatali Akhundzade*, p. 250.

and physical appearances, but rather the national/universal identity. The mythical symbols, epical characters and epical narratives represent a moment of national consciousness in its particular stage of history, in this respect, they can be even more real than any other seemingly 'realist' text.

From this point of view, I believe the repetitive references of Akhundzade to Ferdowsi's *Shahname* do make sense and they are not the sign of contradictions in Akhundzade's thoughts any longer.

Conclusion

Akhundzade undoubtedly has a major role in initiating a modern perspective about literature in which it is not a secondary device for sublime religious meaning, but rather an independent, self-referential institution that offers progressive views through the art of critique and ridiculing the superstitions and false consciousness. For Akhundzade, the literature of enlightenment has to start from the 'existing nature', the 'true nature of humankind', but it has to signify to the national spirit and ethnical identity. Akhundzade believed one must learn the art of drama and novel since poetry is no longer capable of showing the reality of the human condition, especially the poetry that traditionally had been appropriate for explaining abstract and supernatural subjects with unrealistic rhetorical exaggerations. Moreover, he believed that acknowledging the modern forms of writing, such as drama and novel, is as important as acknowledging modern thoughts and beliefs. Searching for the reasons of social and political despotism, Akhundzade ascribes the traditional philosophy of literature as the ideology, suitable only for a subjective and unrealistic literature. For Akhundzade, the religious and ethical preaching is as ideological as the abstract and overused metaphors and useless literary exaggerations. While the first prevent reason, science and social justice to be recognised, the latter is a comic struggle to decorate such deteriorated form of discourse. However, Akhundzade as a social reformer and proto-modernist thinker refused to deliver a rich and well-articulated philosophical discourse about literature as we might see from Russian critics like Belinsky. Literature and poetry for Akhundzade was just a part of his comprehensive enlightenment project. His views are limited to poetry and mostly in the form of comments and annotations or replying to friends, without focusing more on philosophical and theoretical arguments.

His theory about the beauty of form and beauty of content, although in terms of theoretical logic, it reproduces the theory of *Lafz-o Ma'ni* (the form and the content) that had been articulated in Persian theory of rhetoric centuries ago, it is built on modern philosophical context. The content, from this new perspective, is no longer a sublime and transcendental truth, but in fact it 'starts' with the material world and the existing condition of human being. However, the idealist mind of Akhundzade somehow reproduces the problem of traditional theory and idealises the modern values and ideas to make them as the primary goal of literature. Furthermore, the lack of indigenous discourse about modern ideas, as well as having a superficial and abstract understanding of Western modern thought, caused a sort of linguistic confusion that provoked such theoretical reproduction and interrupted the process of a discursive break from traditional worldview to modernity.

Bibliography

Adamiyat, F., *The Idea of progress and the rule of law (Andishe-ye Taraghi-o Hokoomat-e Ghanoon Asr-e Sepahsalar)*, Tehran, 1972.

Adamiyat, F., *The Idea of Freedom and the Start of the Constitutional Movement (Fekr-e Azadi- o Moghaddame-ye Nehzat-e Mashroutiyat)*, Tehran, 1961.

Adamiyat, F., *The Thoughts of Mirza Fatali Akhundzade (Andishe-ha-ye Mirza Fatali Akhundzade),* Tehran, 1970.

Ajand, J., *Literary Modernism During Persian Constitutional Revolution (Tajaddod-e Adabi dar Dowreye Mashrouteh)*, Tehran, 2006.

Ajoudani, M., *Ya Marg Ya Tajaddod (Either Death or Modernization)*, London, 2002.

Akhundzade, M., *Maktoobat (The Letters)*, (ed. by Sobhdam, M.), Tehran, 1985.

Algar, H., 'Malkum Khān, Ākhūndzāda and the Proposed Reform of the Arabic Alphabet', in *Middle Eastern Studies*, vol. 5, no. 2, 1969, pp. 116–130.

Baldick, C., *The Oxford Dictionary of Literary Terms,* (3rd Edition), Oxford, 2008, available online: http://www.oxfordreference.com/view/10.1093/acref/9780199208272.001.0001/acref-9780199208272-e-586 (last accessed August 30, 2016).

Ford, A., *The Origins of Criticism*, Princeton, 2002.

Habib, M.A.R., *A History of Literary Criticism*, Oxford, 2005.

Hegel, G.W.F., *The phenomenology of Spirit,* (transl. by Miller, A. V.), Oxford, 1977.

Keddie, N., 'The Iranian Power Structure and Social Change 1800–1969: An Overview', in *International Journal of Middle East Studies*, vol. 2, no. 1, 1971, pp.3–20.

Lamarque, P., *The Philosophy of Literature*, Oxford, 2009.

Parsinejad, I., *Persian Enlightenment and Literary Criticism (Roshangaran-e Irani va Naghd-e Adabi)*, Tehran, 2001.

Pellat, Ch., 'Adab ii. Adab in Arabic Literature', in *Encyclopaedia Iranica*, vol. I, fasc. 4, pp. 439–444, available online: http://www.iranicaonline.org/articles/adab-ii-arabic-lit (last accessed: August 31, 2016).

Shamisa,S., *Ma'ani (Rhetorics based on Persian literature)*, Tehran, 2004.

Singer, P., *Hegel*, Oxford.

Tavakkoli-Targhi, M., *The indigenous modernity and rethinking of history (Tajaddod-e Boomi- o Bazandishi-ye Tarikh)*, Tehran, 2003.

Wellek, R., *A History of Modern Criticism: 1750–1950, vol. 3. The Age of Transition*, London, 1966.

Zarrinkoob, A., *An Introduction to Literary Criticism (Ashnaee Ba Naghd-e Adabi)*, Tehran, 2004

7

'To mean or not to mean?' as the underlying question of Western-inspired counter-Enlightenment discourse in Iran

Urs Goesken

Modern Western thought relevant for the constitutional movement and beyond mainly entered the Iranian scene in the form of the Enlightenment doctrine of the autonomous human subject and of various types of nineteenth-century positivism. The forms of Western thought that served as underpinnings for the official intellectual discourse in the Pahlavi era tended to be narrowed down to a kind of means-ends rationalism, mostly in the shape of technology. These ways of thought all assume a total reducibility of human being, thus essentialising human being in a reductionist fashion.

This paper tries to show that important counter currents to the official intellectual discourse starting from the early 1960s challenge the reducibilty of human being to some essence as depriving it of meaning. Many trends of the so called 'return to self' movement, in this context, draw on a combination of non-establishment religious discourse and Heideggerianism. This combination serves those intellectuals adopting it to confront the absolutist claim of positivist and Enlightenment thinking and to upgrade religion, albeit in some non-traditional form, from a mode of thinking and practice to an active force shaping the future. Beneath the surface of these particular concerns, the debate between Heidegger inspired critique of Enlightenment thought in Iran and Enlightenment thought in Iran, in the final analysis, is about whether human being has meaning or not.

Modern Western thought first entered the Iranian scene in two main forms: in the Enlightenment doctrine of the autonomy of the individual human subject grounded in ratio, and in various types of nineteenth-century positivism. In these forms, it shaped the intellectual background of many thinkers relevant to the constitutional movement.[1] As for the time following the failure of the constitutional movement, mainly those Enlightenment-inspired currents survived into political and social practice which could then be used as intellectual underpinnings for reforms from above. Thus, rationalism was officially understood and practiced as a means-ends rationalism, mostly in the form of technology.[2]

The Enlightenment-inspired doctrines relevant for the constitutional movement and, even more so, those surviving its failure can be said to essentialise the human being in a reductionist way: The Cartesian concept of the ego that grew into the accepted definition of humanity in modern Western thought defines human being as a thinking thing and, thus, as a thing.[3] Important trends of positivism and materialism adopted by Iranian thinkers, moreover, subject human being to various forms of natural-scientific, biological or historical determinism.[4] Mīrzā Āqā H̱ān Kirmānī,[5] for example, identifies human body and mind with physical and chemical processes[6] and classifies humanity according to nineteenth-century,

1 See: Atabaki, T. and Zürcher, E., J., *Men of Order: Authoritarian Modernization under Atatürk and Reza Shah*, London, 2004, pp. 1–12; Chehabi, H.E. and Martin, V. (eds.), *Iran's Constitutional Revolution: Popular Politics, Cultural Transformations and Transnational Connections*, London, 2010, pp. 165–191; Gheissari, A., *Iranian Intellectuals in the 20th Century*, Texas, 1998, pp. 13–39; Mirsepassi, A., *Intellectual Discourse and the Politics of Modernization: Negotiating Modernity in Iran*, Cambridge, 2000, pp. 55–64; Seidel, R., 'Kants Autonomiebegriff. Chance oder Gefahr für die Religion? Positionen der Kantrezeption in Iran heute.', in Hiltscher, R. and Klingner, S. (eds.), *Kant und die Religion – die Religionen und Kant*, Zürich and New York, 2012, p. 141; Seidel, R., *Kant in Teheran. Anfänge, Ansätze und Kontexte der Kantrezeption in Iran,* München, 2014, p. 31, pp. 55–58; Vahdat, F., *God and Juggernaut: Iran's Intellectual Encounter with Modernity*, Syracuse, 2002, pp. 27–74.

2 See: Atabaki and Zürcher, *Men of Order*, pp. 9–10; Gheissari, *Iranian Intellectuals in the 20th Century*, pp. 40–60; Herf, J., *Reactionary Modernism*, Cambridge, 1984, pp. 1–17; Nabavi, N., *Intellectuals and the State in Iran: Politics, Discourse, and the Dilemma of Authenticity*, Florida, 2003, p. 34; Vahdat, *God and Juggernaut*, pp. 75–90.

3 Boroujerdi, M., *Iranian Intellectuals and the West: The Tormented Triumph of Nativism*, New York, 1996, p. 1.

4 Atabaki and Zürcher, *Men of Order*, pp. 1–12; Nabavi, *Intellectuals and the State in Iran*, p. 34; Vahdat, *God and Juggernaut*, pp. 27–74.

5 Born as ʿAbd al-Ḥusayn H̱ān (1853/4–1896/7); See: Vahdat, *God and Juggernaut*, p. 36.

6 Vahdat, *God and Juggernaut*, p. 38.

racist phrenology.[7] Mīrzā Fatḥ ʿAlī Āḫūndzāda,[8] on the basis of natural-scientific determinism, rules out free will.[9] Scientism in the sense of a crossbreed of positivism and Büchnerian biological materialism as well as popularised versions of biological and social Darwinism underlay the mindset of many intellectuals in the late nineteenth and early twentieth century.[10] Religion in this mindset is often reduced to a merely social or psychological fact. Āḫūndzāda, e.g., identifies the God of monotheism with the projection of human passions.[11]

Philosophically systematic criticism of Enlightenment discourse in Iran starts in earnest in the early 1950s with the work *The Principles of Philosophy and the Method of Realism*[12] by the religious scholars Muḥammad Ḥusayn Ṭabāṭabāʾī and Murtażā Muṭahharī.[13] In it, they criticise those philosophical doctrines that they regard as intellectual roots of Western modernity in the light of the doctrine of the primordiality of existence formulated by Mullā Ṣadrā in the seventeenth century and, by their time, the leading philosophical school in the Shiʿi religious establishment.[14] Basing themselves on this doctrine that champions epistemological realism, Ṭabāṭabāʾī and Muṭahharī dismiss modern Western philosophy as idealistic and, hence, intellectually inferior to 'Islamic' philosophy.[15] Identifying Islamic philosophy with epistemological realism and Western philosophy with epistemological idealism, they proceed to construct a sort of epistemological East-West dichotomy in which 'the West' becomes essentialised as idealism and 'the East' or 'Islam', for that matter, as realism.[16] This picture is laden with religious meaning: Ṭabāṭabāʾī and Muṭahharī obviously conceive the development of Islamic philosophy, culminating, as they see it, in Mullā Ṣadrā's doctrine of the primordiality of

---

7 Vahdat, *God and Juggernaut*, p. 39.

8 (1812–1878); See: Vahdat, *God and Juggernaut*, p. 42.

9 Vahdat, *God and Juggernaut*, p. 47.

10 Atabaki and Zürcher, *Men of Order*, pp. 4–5.

11 Vahdat, *God and Juggernaut*, p. 45.

12 My translation of the original Persian *Oṣūl-e falsafe va raveš-e reʾālīsm*; cf. Bibliography.

13 Muḥammad Ḥusayn Ṭabāṭabāʾī (1903–1981), Murtażā Muṭahharī (1920–1979). For the role of these scholars in the intellectual debate of twentieth-century Iran: Gösken, U., *Kritik der westlichen Philosophie in Iran: Zum geistesgeschichtlichen Selbstverständnis von* Muḥammad Ḥusayn Ṭabāṭabāʾī und Murtażā Muṭahharī, München, 2014.

14 For Mullā Ṣadrā's philosophy and its role in intellectual history see: Kamal, M., *Mulla Sadra's Transcendent Philosophy*, Aldershot, 2006; Rizvi, S., *Mulla Sadra and Metaphysics: Modulation of Being*, London, 2009.

15 Gösken, *Kritik der westlichen Philosophie in Iran,* pp. 250–438.

16 Gösken, *Kritik der westlichen Philosophie in Iran,* p. 438.

existence, as the gradual fulfilment of salvation history, whereas the West, characterised by idealism, is on the path to perdition.[17] Thus, the philosophical East-West dichotomy in terms of realism versus idealism becomes intertwined with a religious one in terms of salvation history versus perdition history. While, in the eyes of Ṭabāṭabā'ī and Muṭahharī, Islamic philosophy attains perfection in the doctrine of the primordiality of existence formulated by Mullā Ṣadrā, 'Western' idealism culminates in dialectic materialism, championed in Iran in their day by the Iranian left.[18] Claiming opinion leadership in dealing with Western philosophical teachings, especially dialectic materialism, in order to prevent the younger generation from intellectual and spiritual confusion has in fact been Ṭabāṭabā'ī's and Muṭahharī's main motive behind the project of *The Principles of Philosophy and the Method of Realism*.[19] In order, of course, to assume opinion leadership with regard to Western philosophy, the two thinkers had to provide themselves with what they considered sufficient knowledge of the topic. They did this by reading the, at the time, most authoritative Persian source about Western philosophy, the *History of Philosophy in Europe*[20] by the scholar and elder statesman Muḥammad 'Alī Furūġī. Furūġī, whose overall educational background including knowledge of several European languages allowed him to access many philosophical sources in the original, in fact had authored this book in order to enlighten the educated Iranian public about what he felt was a constituent part of Western culture.[21] What he deals with as European philosophy ranges from the pre-Socratics to Bergson, however dialectic materialism is conspicuously absent.[22] Ṭabāṭabā'ī and Muṭahharī fill in this gap by relying on the Iranian Marxist Taqī Arānī.[23] On the other hand, they do not discuss Nietzsche, a thinker, to note, that Furūġī deals with. Another philosopher whose absence in their account raises questions is Martin Heidegger[24] whom we shall discuss more deeply later in this paper. While, in the case of Ṭabāṭabā'ī, this lack may be explained by the fact that, when he had completed the main text of *The Principles of Philosophy and the Method of Realism* in the early 1950s,

17 Gösken, *Kritik der westlichen Philosophie in Iran,* p. 443.

18 Gösken, *Kritik der westlichen Philosophie in Iran,* p. 443; Muṭahharī, M., *Ṭabāṭabā'ī, Muḥammad-Ḥusayn,*1381 HŠ, I:32f

19 Gösken, *Kritik der westlichen Philosophie in Iran,* p. 170.

20 Gösken, *Kritik der westlichen Philosophie in Iran,* pp. 173–175.

21 Boroujerdi, *Iranian Intellectuals and the West*, p. 59; Naṣrī, 'A., *Rūyārūyī bā taǧaddod. 2 Bde,* Tehrān, 1386 HŠ, II:21.

22 Gösken, *Kritik der westlichen Philosophie in Iran,* p. 174.

23 Gösken, *Kritik der westlichen Philosophie in Iran,* p. 184.

24 Gösken, *Kritik der westlichen Philosophie in Iran,* pp. 436–437.

Heidegger was barely making his first appearance on the Iranian intellectual stage, this assumption cannot hold true with regard to Muṭahharī. For Muṭahharī, one of Ṭabāṭabāʾī's students, had been asked by his teacher to comment on the main text in order to make it understandable to a wider audience,[25] and he worked on this task over a period of nearly three decades during which time he can be proved to have kept himself constantly up to date on new trends in Western philosophy.[26] But this silence on such a key thinker like Heidegger was only one more reason why Ṭabāṭabāʾī's and Muṭahharī's challenge to modern Western philosophy soon proven outdated. First, given that both authors, besides their native Persian, were only fluent in Arabic, they had only limited access to original sources.[27] Second, their criticism opposes realism against idealism, whereas Western philosophy from the nineteenth century had evolved into overcoming this divide, Heidegger's philosophy playing a main part in this development.[28] Third, taken at face value, their summary dismissal of Western philosophy as intellectually inferior to Islamic philosophy, if not utterly worthless, would make any further dealing with it pointless.[29] The story, clearly, couldn't end there and, in fact, didn't.

Starting from the early 1960s, Enlightenment discourse as reflected in the rationalism promoted by the Pahlavīs is challenged by counter-Enlightenment movements conventionally subsumed under the heading 'return to self'.[30] Recent scholarship accounts for this trend by feelings of cultural and intellectual alienation as a result of modernisation with its concomitant phenomena like urbanisation, industrialisation, social and economic individualisation, the rise of a new bourgeois middle class and secularisation, all coupled with a lack of freedom in the political, cultural and intellectual sphere.[31] Since these phenomena reflected the

25 Gösken, *Kritik der westlichen Philosophie in Iran,* pp. 181–182.

26 Gösken, *Kritik der westlichen Philosophie in Iran,* pp. 186–187.

27 Gösken, *Kritik der westlichen Philosophie in Iran,* pp. 173–175.

28 Rentsch, T., *Philosophie des 20. Jahrhunderts: Von Husserl bis Derrida*, München, 2014, pp. 7–20.

29 Gösken, *Kritik der westlichen Philosophie in Iran,* p. 474.

30 Boroujerdi, *Iranian Intellectuals and the West*, p. 106, pp. 112–113, p. 217; Mirsepassi, *Intellectual Discourse and the Politics of Modernization,* pp. 96–127; Nabavi, N., *Intellectuals and the State in Iran:* pp. 57–58; Vahdat, *God and Juggernaut*, pp. 113–127; Vahdat, F., 'Return to which Self? Jalal Al-e Ahmad and the Discourse of Modernity', in *Journal of Iranian Research and Analysis,* vol. 16, no. 2, 2000.

31 Herf, J., *Reactionary Modernism*, Cambridge, 1984, pp. 1–17; Mirsepassi, A., *Intellectual Discourse and the Politics of Modernization,* pp. 129–158; Mirsepassi, A., *Political Islam, Iran, and the Enlightenment: Philosophies of Hope and Despair*, Cambridge , 2011, pp. 85–128; Nabavi,

state sponsored understanding of rationalism, they came to be identified both with the state and with rationalism itself. The latter point is borne out by the fact that those same counter movements to rationalism likewise rejected the dialectic materialism advocated by the Iranian left.

It may be claimed that movements fitting the definition of 'return to self' had cropped up before in the nineteenth- and twentieth-century history of Iran, often in the context of developments going on in the Middle East as a whole. One of them can be considered what is known as salafism, understood by its adherents as the return to the idealised teaching and practice of Islam at the time of the Prophet and the pious ancestors – Arabic: *salaf*, hence salafism – the early Muslims.[32] This version of 'return to self' defines the self in religious terms, relating it to 'true Islam', a truth that it identifies with an historic reality in the past. Accordingly, the present situation of Muslims is perceived as the result of an alienation from their true essence caused by the developments having taken place between the idealised situation in the past and the far-from-ideal present. Realising the true self, according to this view, goes hand in hand with re-enacting that past ideal situation in the present. Another 'return to self' movement may be seen in the doctrine of modern Iranian nationalism as championed, among others, by the nineteenth-century thinker Mīrzā Āqā Ḫān Kirmānī.[33] Applying nineteenth-century racist phrenology to distinguish the Arabs and Jews as Semites from the Iranians as Aryans, he declares the domination of Iran by the Arabs and 'their' religion, Islam, as lying at the root of the degeneration of Iranians and of their alienation from their 'ethos of superiority, magnanimity and nobility'.[34] Consistently, he advocates the return of Iranians to the pre-Islamic religion of Iran, Zoroastrianism, and the glories of Iran's pre-Islamic dynasties as the solution to this form of national 'alienation'.[35] The latter part of this suggested solution was to become integrated into the nationalism of the Pahlavīs, whereas return to Zoroastrianism was dropped as a requirement.[36]

As for the counter-Enlightenment movements subsumed under the heading 'return to self', they combine non-establishment religious discourse[37] and Iranian

N., *Intellectuals and the State in Iran,* pp. 92–96.

32 Seidensticker, T., *Islamismus: Geschichte, Vordenker, Organisationen*, München, 2014, pp. 24–28.

33 Vahdat, *God and Juggernaut*, pp. 36–39.

34 Vahdat, *God and Juggernaut*, p. 39.

35 Vahdat, *God and Juggernaut*, p. 39.

36 Vahdat, *God and Juggernaut*, pp. 80–81.

37 Nabavi, N., *Intellectuals and the State in Iran,* pp. 100–106, pp. 128–134.

Heideggerianism.[38] As the common denominator in this combination appears the French philosopher and orientalist Henry Corbin, who first introduced Heidegger's philosophy to the Iranian intellectual scene in the late 1940s and early 1950s – the time when he started to work and live in Iran as a researcher into Islamic mysticism and philosophy.[39] Corbin, on the one hand, accepted Heidegger's phenomenology as a hermeneutic key for his understanding of what he termed the Iranian-Islamic philosophical tradition, an intellectual and spiritual tradition that, in his view, has been substantially constituted by the two thinkers Šihāb al-Dīn Suhrawardī (executed 1191) and Ṣadr al-Dīn Šīrāzī, commonly referred to by the honorific title Mullā Ṣadrā (d. 1640). On the other hand, Corbin replaced Heidegger's delimitation of the horizon of human being in terms of 'being-towards-death' by 'being-towards-beyond-death'.[40] What brings Corbin to this extension of human being's horizon is his understanding of what he calls the 'religious fact' as a non-reducible dimension of human existence.[41] Historic religion, for Corbin, is but an appearance of the religious fact and the Iranian-Islamic tradition the most authentic manifestation of it.[42]

The first Iranian thinker who, inspired by Corbin, became fascinated by Heidegger's thought was the philosophy teacher Aḥmad Fardīd.[43] He had studied

---

38 About this combination see: ʿAbd al-Karīmī, B., *Hāydiggir dar Īrān. Nigāhī bi zindigī, āsār va andīša- hā-yi Sayyid Aḥmad Fardīd,* Tihrān, 392HŠ, pp. 127–153; Boroujerdi, *Iranian Intellectuals and the West*, pp. 65–76; Mirsepassi, A., *Intellectual Discourse and the Politics of Modernization,* pp. 96–128; Mirsepassi, *Political Islam, Iran, and the Enlightenment*, pp. 85–128; Mirsepassi, A., 'Religious Intellectuals and Western Critiques of Secular Modernity', in *Comparative Studies of South Asia, Africa and the Middle East*, vol. 26, no.3, 2006; Vahdat, *God and Juggernaut*, pp. 113–127.

39 Henry Corbin (1903–1978): See: ʿAbd al-Karīmī, *Hāydiggir dar Īrān.*, pp. 69–71, pp. 86–87; Landolt, H., 'Henry Corbin, 1903–1978: Between Philosophy and Orientalism', in *Journal of the American Oriental Society*, vol. 119, no. 3, 1999; van den Bos, M., 'Transnational Orientalism. Henry Corbin in Iran', in *Anthropos,* bd. 100, h. 1, 2005, pp. 113–125.

40 ʿAbd al-Karīmī, *Hāydiggir dar Īrān.*, pp. 101–106; Corbin, H., 'De Heidegger à Sohravardî: Entretien avec Philippe Nemo', in Jambet, C. (ed.), *Cahiers de l'Herne: Henry Corbin*, Paris, 1981, p. 31; Landolt, 'Henry Corbin, 1903–1978: Between Philosophy and Orientalism', p. 488; Seidel, *Kant in Teheran*, pp. 62–63; van den Bos, M., 'Transnational Orientalism. Henry Corbin in Iran', p. 115, p. 118.

41 'fait religieux': See: Corbin, H., *Itinéraire d'un enseignement*, Téhéran, 1993, pp. 23–26.

42 ʿAbd al-Karīmī, *Hāydiggir dar Īrān.*, pp. 107–126; Corbin, 'De Heidegger à Sohravardî: Entretien avec Philippe Nemo', pp. 28–30; Landolt, 'Henry Corbin, 1903–1978: Between Philosophy and Orientalism', pp. 484–485; Seidel, R., *Kant in Teheran*, pp. 62–63; van den Bos, 'Transnational Orientalism. Henry Corbin in Iran', p. 114.

43 Aḥmad Fardīd (1909[according to other sources: 1912]-1994): see. ʿAbd al-Karīmī, *Hāydiggir*

philosophy in France where he seems to have become very much attracted to Bergson's doctrine.[44] Considering that Bergson, like Heidegger, whose thought shall be discussed shortly, develops a philosophy that aims at overcoming positivistic reductionism, this affinity to Bergson may have predisposed him to be susceptible to Heidegger's thinking. Fardīd became acquainted with Corbin in the early 1950s.[45] In turn Corbin had become interested in Heidegger's thought as early as the 1930s. He had personally met the philosopher and translated some of his writings into French on Heidegger's behalf, thus introducing this thinker to the French intellectual scene.[46] Fardīd obviously read Heidegger first in French, but he is reported to have proceeded to study German very soon in order to access Heidegger's texts in the original language.[47] He soon gathered a circle of Iranian Heideggerians, featuring some prominent figures of Iranian pre- and post-revolutionary intellectual life like Riżā Dāvarī Ardakānī and Dāryūš Šāyigān.[48] Fardīd's adaptation of Heidegger's critique of technology, moreover, influenced the writer Ǧalāl Āl-i Aḥmad in his book *Westoxication*[49], a term coined by Fardīd. The Persian original *ġarb-zadagī* derives from *ġarb-zada*, which can be translated by 'West-struck' or 'West-infected'. At the merely formal level, *ġarb-zada* looks like an imitation by the devices of Persian word formation of the pseudo-Arabic term

dar Īrān., pp. 155–170; Boroujerdi, *Iranian Intellectuals and the West*, pp. 63–65; Mirsepassi, *Political Islam, Iran, and the Enlightenment*, pp. 30–43; van den Bos, 'Transnational Orientalism. Henry Corbin in Iran', p. 122.

44 ʿAbd al-Karīmī, *Hāydiggir dar Īrān.*, pp. 56–57.

45 ʿAbd al-Karīmī, *Hāydiggir dar Īrān.*, pp. 69–71, pp. 156–157.

46 Landolt, 'Henry Corbin, 1903–1978: Between Philosophy and Orientalism', p. 485.

47 ʿAbd al-Karīmī, *Hāydiggir dar Īrān.*, p. 33.

48 Riżā Dāvarī Ardakānī (1933-), Dāryūš Šāyigān (1935-): See: ʿAbd al-Karīmī, *Hāydiggir dar Īrān.*, pp. 265–275; Boroujerdi, *Iranian Intellectuals and the West*, p. 63, pp. 156–175; Mirsepassi, *Political Islam, Iran, and the Enlightenment*, pp. 28–43; van den Bos, 'Transnational Orientalism. Henry Corbin in Iran', pp. 119–122.

49 Just one of many translations of the original Persian 'ġarbzadagī': See: ʿAbd al-Karīmī, *Hāydiggir dar Īrān.*, pp. 144–147; Boroujerdi, *Iranian Intellectuals and the West*, pp. 65–76; Lenze, F., *Der Nativist Ǧalāl-e Āl-e Aḥmad und die Verwestlichung Irans im 20. Jahrhundert: eine Analyse der ethnographischen Monographien Awrāzān, Tāt-nešīnhā-ye bolūk-e Zahrā und Ǧazire-ye Ḫārg, dorr-e yatīm-e ḫalīǧ unter besonderer Berücksichtigung seiner Programmschrift Ġarbzadegī, Berlin*, 2008, pp. 38–39; Mirsepassi, *Intellectual Discourse and the Politics of Modernization*, pp. 97–114; Mirsepassi, *Political Islam, Iran, and the Enlightenment*, pp.119–124; Nabavi, N., *Intellectuals and the State in Iran*, pp. 57–64; Seidel, *Kant in Teheran*, pp. 60–61; Vahdat, *God and Juggernaut*, pp. 114–117, pp. 186–191.

mufarang that we come across in ʿAbd al-Raḥīm Ṭalibūf's[50] writings.[51] Ṭalibūf uses this term in his criticism of those Iranians who, as he sees it, have betrayed their cultural identity by adopting the trappings of Western civilisation without understanding its essence.[52] Such criticism is grounded in the assumption on the part of Ṭalibūf of an essential opposition between East and West in terms of a cultural dichotomy. As we shall see later in this paper, the East-West dichotomy that Ṭalibūf constructs at the cultural level assumes an ontological dimension in Fardīd and other Iranian Heideggerians.

Now, Fardīd's attraction to Heidegger's thought was largely due to his conviction that Heidegger's analysis of human being's situation in the world contained the potential of a paradigm shift in understanding Iran's cultural and intellectual situation.[53]

First of all, given Heidegger's de(con)struction of Western intellectual tradition, including Enlightenment thought, Fardīd and like-minded Iranian thinkers could find in this particular philosopher an invaluable key witness in their own criticism of the intellectual foundations of Western culture. Moreover, the link between Heidegger and religion established by Corbin in his application of Heideggerian hermeneutics and phenomenology to the analysis of the Iranian-Islamic tradition allowed Iranian intellectuals to re-contextualise religion as a meaningful manifestation of a metahistorical dimension of human being, thereby absolving it from the objection of backwardness on the part of positivist thinkers.[54] In short, Heideggerianism allows Iranians to deal with 'the West' without feelings of inferiority. From this perspective, 'the West' is no longer understood as a necessary frame of reference for human thought and practice, but rather as no more than itself one of many merely contingent human ways of thought and practice. 'The West', thus, is no longer the necessary point of view from which to perceive any possible 'other', but can just as well itself be subjected to perception from some 'other' point of view.

50 (1832–1910); See: Vahdat, *God and Juggernaut*, pp. 48–54.

51 Vahdat, *God and Juggernaut*, p. 52.

52 Vahdat, *God and Juggernaut*, pp. 52–53.

53 ʿAbd al-Karīmī, *Hāydiggir dar Īrān.*, pp. 156–158, pp. 266–268; Boroujerdi, *Iranian Intellectuals and the West*, pp. 63–65; Gheissari, *Iranian Intellectuals in the 20th Century*, p. 89; Mirsepassi, *Political Islam, Iran, and the Enlightenment*, pp. 30–43; Seidel, *Kant in Teheran*, pp. 60–61; van den Bos, 'Transnational Orientalism. Henry Corbin in Iran', p. 122.

54 ʿAbd al-Karīmī, *Hāydiggir dar Īrān.*, pp. 156–158, pp. 266–268, pp. 282–291; Corbin, 'De Heidegger à Sohravardî: Entretien avec Philippe Nemo', pp. 30–31; Landolt, 'Henry Corbin, 1903–1978: Between Philosophy and Orientalism', pp. 484–485; van den Bos, 'Transnational Orientalism. Henry Corbin in Iran', pp. 114–115.

Beyond and above these considerations, however, Heidegger's thinking can be used to challenge not only individual tenets of the Western intellectual trends introduced to the Iranian scene, but also to take issue with their absolutist claim to validity as a theoretical or practical approach to the world. This debate touches upon some core issues of Heidegger's philosophy such as the concept of 'world'[55] and the question of meaning or meaningfulness.[56] 'World' according to Heidegger does not mean the totality of objectifiable entities whose being is defined as their being constituted by an objective essence.[57] Instead, Heidegger conceives of world as a referential context of significance[58] in which the being of entities is defined as their being understood, interpreted, given meaning or made sense of as this or that. So, e.g., if I drop the item that in London we conventionally understand and refer to as a 'can opener' on an undiscovered tribe in the heart of the Brazilian jungle, I cannot predict as what the tribespeople will understand, and refer to, that item. But I can predict that they will not understand it and refer to it as 'can opener'. For, on the one hand, in their living context, or in their 'world', if you will, there are no cans and, therefore, no cans to be opened. On the other hand, and more crucially, however, the item dropped on them would not communicate with them in whatever metaphorical way we may take the term 'communicate' – 'telling' them, as it were: 'Call me "can opener" because this is what I *am* because this is my *objective essence*.' There is no point in supposing that entities on their part do anything in terms of making themselves understood to us and, thus, enter our communication on their own. It is we, as human beings, who communicate them by understanding them and referring to them as this or that. If the term 'being' with reference to entities serves any purpose at all, then 'being' cannot be understood as going on by virtue of any essence of the entity in question, but as a being understood as this

55 Heidegger, M., *Sein und Zeit*, Tübingen, 2001, pp. 63–66; Lafont, C., 'Hermeneutics', in Dreyfus, H., L. and Wrathall M., A. (eds.), *A Companion to Heidegger*, Oxford, 2005, pp. 270–274; Sheehan, T., 'Dasein', in Dreyfus, H., L. and Wrathall M., A. (eds.), *A Companion to Heidegger*, Oxford, 2005, pp. 200–202.

56 Couzens Hoy, D., 'Heidegger and the hermeneutic turn', in Guignon, C., B. (ed.), *The Cambridge Companion to Heidegger*, Cambridge, 2006, pp. 188–194; Heidegger, *Sein und Zeit*, pp. 142–160; Lafont, 'Hermeneutics', pp. 265–266, p. 270, p. 275; Sheehan, 'Dasein', p. 193, pp. 196–207.

57 Lafont, 'Hermeneutics', p. 270.

58 German original: 'Verweisungszusammenhang der Bedeutsamkeit'; See: Guignon, C., B., 'Introduction', in *The Cambridge Companion to Heidegger*, Cambridge, 2006, pp. 10–11; Lafont, 'Hermeneutics', p. 270; Sheehan, 'Dasein', p. 199.

or that on the part of meaning-givers or sense-makers.[59] In 'world' according to Heidegger, there can be no question of an objective essence of entities that could serve as an absolute point of reference for naming them and speaking about them.

Now, if what constitutes 'world' is meaning and not being in the sense of essence-constitutedness, human being in the world is constituted by its role in the giving of meaning and not by getting to the essence in some act of object-cognition. Thus, human being's involvement with the world cannot be described as that of a detachable subject posed over against an object like in the subject-object model of traditional philosophy.[60] Human being's role in the bestowal of meaning cannot be identified with object cognition, but must be regarded as interpretation, making sense of or, in short, as understanding. This concept grounds philosophy in hermeneutics.[61] As for the concepts of perception, object cognition, intuition or thinking of traditional philosophy, Heidegger goes to some lengths to demonstrate that they can in their turn be explained within the framework of understanding, but not vice versa.[62] On the basis of grounding philosophy in hermeneutics, then, the ontological and epistemological concepts underlying Western Enlightenment thought can all be embedded in Heidegger's concept of understanding, thus losing their claim of absolute validity. If human being's relation to the world, as we have seen, is not constituted by perception according to the subject-object model, but by understanding and interpretation – we need to consider that interpretation requires a standpoint, and therefore human being's stance towards the world is always already presupposition-dependent.[63]

The fact that the approach of human being *in* the world *to* the world is presupposition-dependent, in turn, means that human being's knowledge is necessarily mediate and partial and, hence, imperfect.[64] Human being's knowledge, then, falls short of perfect knowledge as in the case of God, where it is defined as the being one of the knower with the knowable, which constitutes immediate knowledge.[65] Rather, human being's knowledge does not mean an exhaustive grasp of the know-

59 Guignon, C., B., 'Introduction', p. 9; Sheehan, 'Dasein', p. 200.

60 Lafont, 'Hermeneutics', pp. 265–266, p. 270.

61 Couzens Hoy, 'Heidegger and the hermeneutic turn', pp. 177–201; Heidegger, *Sein und Zeit*, pp. 142–148; Lafont, 'Hermeneutics', pp. 265–266, pp. 270–274.

62 Heidegger, *Sein und Zeit*, pp. 154–160; Lafont, 'Hermeneutics', p. 265, pp. 274–276, pp. 279–282.

63 Lafont, 'Hermeneutics', pp. 276–278.

64 Lafont, 'Hermeneutics', pp. 276–278; Sheehan, 'Dasein', p. 200, pp. 205–206.

65 Sheehan, 'Dasein', pp. 204–205.

able. Human being 'knows' this or that in the sense of knowing it 'as' this or that. So, for example, I can express knowledge of Heidegger by saying 'Heidegger is a philosopher'. But in so doing, I neither exhaust the class 'philosopher' nor do I achieve a full grasp concerning 'Heidegger'.[66] My knowledge proves partial. By the same token, it proves contingent because the knowledge expressed in 'Heidegger is a philosopher' is only one merely possible way beside other merely possible ways of knowing Heidegger. Moreover, returning to the item I dropped on the Brasilian jungle earlier in this paper, I can only understandingly refer to it as 'can opener' if I understand it in a relationship – in a relationship, that is, to cans and the opening of them. The very possibility of the meaningfulness of 'can opener' lies in the possibility of relating it to, and mediating it by, cans and opening. The necessary mediatedness of human being's knowledge, then, spells meaningfulness.[67] And both mediatedness and being only partial define human being's knowledge as necessarily imperfect knowledge and, therefore, human being itself as a necessarily imperfectly knowing being.[68]

In an adaptation of Heidegger's definition of human being's necessary imperfection constituted by the necessary presupposition-dependence of human being's approach to the world, we can likewise define meaning as constituted by the necessarily imperfect identifiability between signifying and signified in the act of reference. If there were perfect identifiability between signifying, say 'cup' as a word, and signified, say 'cup' as a thing, the very act of referring-to would prove pointless, since it would make no difference whether I deal with the thing 'cup' or the word 'cup'. On the other hand, if there were no identifiability at all between signifying and signified, the very act of referring-to, which I could visualise as an arrow, would prove pointless, too, since the reference arrow would point to nowhere. Perfect identifiability as well as zero identifiability, then, spell meaninglessness.

Now, the forms of Enlightenment thought relevant for Iranian intellectual life, as we have said, essentialise human being in a reductionist fashion in one way or another. The very fact that they do so implies that they presuppose an essence for human being on the one hand and a total reducibility of human being on the other. Total reducibility in its turn implies perfect identifiability. Perfect identifiability, however, as we have seen, spells meaninglessness. Thus, the presupposition of an essence for human being to which human being can be reduced and in whose realisation human being attains fulfilment and perfection according to whatever

66 Sheehan, 'Dasein', pp. 200–201.

67 Sheehan, 'Dasein', pp. 205–207.

68 Sheehan, 'Dasein', p. 205.

ideal definition of it comes at a price, namely that of depriving human being of meaning. If human being has essence,[69] it has no meaning. If, then, e.g., we essentialise human being as a subject-thing standing in front of object-things after the Cartesian model, human being, reduced to object-cognition and unable to make sense of the world in terms of meaning-giving, cannot in its turn be given meaning. Viewed from this angle, criticism of Enlightenment in Iran is not just about pointing out intellectual shortcomings of this or that particular theory or the difficulty or undesirability of this or that resulting practice, but what is implicitly at issue is the question of whether human being is meaningful or meaningless.

This question acquires another momentum if we bring God into play, as, indeed, many Iranian Heideggerian Enlightenment critics have done, first and maybe most prominently Aḥmad Fardīd himself.[70] Of course, the example of Corbin may have played its part in giving Heidegger reception in Iran a religious dimension in the first place.[71] But we may be justified in assuming other factors that account for the lasting attraction of understanding Heidegger in a religious way.

On the one hand, Enlightenment thought, by positing the absolutely autonomous human subject, makes the assumption of a divine subject that we, then, would have to conceive of as even more absolutely autonomous problematic, to say the least. Indeed, this problem brought many Enlightenment thinkers the world over into conflict with religion. Heidegger's thought, however, since it does not posit human being as a subject according to the subject-object model in the first place, at least on this count does not rule out some concept of God whatsoever, provided we do not again conceive of God as a subject or an object according to the subject-object model.[72] Thus, adopting Heidegger's philosophy need not conjure up a conflict with religion.

On the other hand, while there need not be any contradiction between Heideggerian thought and religious discourse, Heidegger's thinking allows or even forces

69 If we take 'essence' as a translation of German 'Wesen', we have to bear in mind that Heidegger uses this word in a meaning different from classical philosophical terminology. At any rate, 'essence' in Heidegger's terminology, when applied to human being, cannot be taken to mean a final point at which human being in its movement arrives. In fact, there is no final arriving for human being in his movement: See: Sheehan, T., 'Dasein', p. 205.

70 ʿAbd al-Karīmī, *Hāydiggir dar Īrān.*, pp. 127–147, 155–170, 284–291, 297–308; Boroujerdi, *Iranian Intellectuals and the West*, pp. 63–65, 156–165; Mirsepassi, *Political Islam, Iran, and the Enlightenment*, pp. 116–119.

71 ʿAbd al-Karīmī, *Hāydiggir dar Īrān.*, pp. 155–170; van den Bos, 'Transnational Orientalism. Henry Corbin in Iran', pp 115–116.

72 ʿAbd al-Karīmī, *Hāydiggir dar Īrān.*, pp. 297–319.

the intellectual adopting it to understand religion in a way different from traditional religious discourse considered backward by Enlightenment thinkers. Placing Heidegger's philosophy in a religious dimension, a dimension, by the way, that in its turn may be influenced by Heidegger's thought, upgrades religion from an either cherished or despised thing of the past to a productive force shaping the future.[73] This is why many religious Enlightenment critics in Iran can be defined as what Jeffrey Herf, referring to the case of Germany, calls 'reactionary modernists'[74]: They are reactionary in that they fall back behind the French Revolution, and they are modernists in that they try to leave behind what they perceive as bourgeois stagnation in intellectual and cultural life.[75] Taking this thought a step further, we can build upon Mirsepassi's understanding of the 1979 revolution as an attempt at reconfiguring the course of modernity in a local context rather than as a manifestation of antimodernism[76] and call it a movement driven by thinkers and activists who fit the definition of reactionary modernists.

Aside from the level of more recent events, however, the combination of Heidegger's philosophy and religious thought can be seen as a joining forces of two modes of thinking that affirm the meaningfulness of human being as against Enlightenment thought that is seen to deny human being meaningfulness by reducing it in terms of perfect identification. In Heidegger's philosophy, human being is defined as playing a role in giving meaning to entities. In fact, this definition of human being in its turn constitutes human being's own meaningfulness. Hence, meaningfulness as constituting human being and human being's situation in the world is definitely ensured. Arguing from this angle, we could say that likewise in Islam meaningfulness for human being and his situation in the world is ensured in the sense that it is God who gives meaning to entities by creating them as meaningful. The meaningfulness of entities in this religious understanding could in fact be interpreted in several, mutually non-exclusive ways: Entities can be referred to as meaningful insofar as they must have meaning for God, who cannot be thought to

73 ʿAbd al-Karīmī, *Hāydiggir dar Īrān.*, pp. 284–295, pp. 359–375; Boroujerdi, *Iranian Intellectuals and the West*, pp. 65–76, pp. 105–115; Mirsepassi, *Intellectual Discourse and the Politics of Modernization,* pp. 96–128; Mirsepassi, *Political Islam, Iran, and the Enlightenment,* pp. 116–128; Vahdat, 'Return to which Self? Jalal Al-e Ahmad and the Discourse of Modernity', pp. 60–63.

74 Herf, J., *Reactionary Modernism*, Cambridge, 1984, pp. 1–17; Mirsepassi, *Political Islam, Iran, and the Enlightenment,* p. 121.

75 Herf, *Reactionary Modernism*, pp. 11–13; Mirsepassi, *Intellectual Discourse and the Politics of Modernization,* p. 97, pp. 131–135.

76 Mirsepassi, *Political Islam, Iran, and the Enlightenment,* p. 116.

have created them if he did not care in the first place.[77] They can further be considered meaningful in the sense that their very meaning is to have been created by God. In addition, they can be regarded as meaningful in the way that God in the Qur'ān, besides stating that he has created all entities and what the entities are that he has all created, often also indicates as what or for what he has created them[78] and in what relationship to them he placed other entities and human being. As for human being in particular, God is also said to have taught Adam all the names,[79] human being alone, moreover, accepting the responsibility – *amāna* – that God offered it.[80] God, then, is the original and ultimate meaning-giver, and human being in his situation in the world imitates – 'responds to' –, however imperfectly, God's original and final meaning-giving in the act of understanding.

Without attempting a comparative study between Heidegger's thought and whatever interpretation of Islam, we may nevertheless hint at some consequences resulting from a religious understanding of Heidegger's philosophy. In this philosophy, human being is constituted by understanding which, as we have said, is in itself a necessarily imperfect act. And since the act of understanding that constitutes human being is necessarily imperfect, human being himself can be said to be necessarily imperfect.[81] Human being's understanding is imperfect in the sense that it never brings human being into perfect oneness with the knowable and that in sense-making it can only refer to this or that entity by way of relating it to other entities.[82] Now, if we bring God into play, we posit a non-relative, absolute point of reference in relation to which and in the light of which this and that entity and, indeed, all entities can be made *perfect* sense of. Since God as the absolute point of reference is the original meaning-giver to all entities, if only human being became God, his understanding would be perfect. Of course, how far human being can become God and thus ever reach that absolute point of reference in meaning-giving is a debated issue in religious discourse. However, the very positing of God as the absolute point of reference for all of human being's referencing and meaning-giving gives human being's meaning-giving itself another meaning.

77 From a believer's point of view, this thought could be confirmed by reference to Qur'ān 23/115 and 75/36 where God explicitly rules out the possibility of any act on his part without purpose and meaning (عَبَثاً، سُدًى).

78 E.g. Qur'ān 45/3–5 where the function of God's creatures as signs for man is emphasised.

79 Qur'ān 2/31.

80 Qur'ān 33/72.

81 Sheehan, 'Dasein', p. 193, p. 205.

82 Sheehan, 'Dasein', p. 193, pp. 205–206.

Whatever meaning human being may give any entity, he now believes in that there is a perfect meaning-giving performed by God, and he does not regard this belief itself as yet another instance of his necessarily imperfect understanding. The frame within which human being's meaning-giving takes place is then not defined itself by human being's meaning-giving. On the one hand, this positing of a frame can be taken as a limitation of the range of human being's action in the act of meaning-giving. On the other hand, considering that this frame is God's meaning-giving, human being's finite meaning-giving is ultimately related to God the Infinite Meaning-Giver.[83] Of course, the meaning-giving on the part of God, the perfect meaning-giver, is itself perfect, constituting perfect identification between signifying and signified. In human being's terms, such perfect identification ineluctably spells meaninglessness. In God's perspective, however, this seeming meaninglessness in human being's terms in fact is absolute meaningfulness. This identifying of meaninglessness with absolute meaningfulness in the case of God, the ultimate origin of meaning, is but a translation into the hermeneutic-philosophical paradigm of the identification of not-being with absolute being in the case of God, the ultimate origin of being, in traditional metaphysical ontology.

In addition, however, the observation that important currents of Heidegger reception in Iran are characterised by a religious dimension gives rise to questions about the fundamental understanding of Heidegger's thought by Iranian Heideggerians. As we have seen, Corbin, who had introduced Heidegger's thought to Iran, adopted Heidegger's phenomenology as a hermeneutic key to understanding the contents of the Iranian-Islamic tradition, rejecting, on the other hand, Heidegger's concept of human being as being-towards-death. Moreover, Corbin valued the Iranian-Islamic intellectual and spiritual tradition as offering the prospect of constructing an alternative metaphysics, grounded in knowledge by presence, to modern Western philosophy so that de(con)struction of Western metaphysics, crucial to Heidegger's philosophical project, would become redundant.[84] As for the Iranian Heideggerians, one of their motives in adopting Heidegger's thought was precisely that it allowed them to re-evaluate 'their' Iranian-Islamic tradition. On the other hand, it could be argued that this might result in some internal ambivalence of their Heidegger reception. For on the one hand, interpreting the Iranian-Islamic tradition in the light of their understanding of Heidegger's thought allows them to upgrade that tradition to the level of global intellectual discourse. On the other

83 About the ineluctable finitude of human being's understanding see: Sheehan, 'Dasein', p. 193, p. 198, p. 200.

84 Landolt, 'Henry Corbin, 1903–1978: Between Philosophy and Orientalism', p. 486, p. 488.

hand, the doctrines of the Iranian-Islamic tradition all qualify as metaphysical and, as such, would not escape Heidegger's de(con)struction of metaphysics. The question how far Iranian Heideggerians are aware of this possible ambivalence and, if so, how they react to it invites further research.[85] The question is all the more pressing since the way Iranian-Islamic tradition deals with what Heidegger calls the 'question about being' can be shown to be fundamentally different from Heidegger's. The main schools of the Iranian-Islamic tradition are the philosophy of illumination developed by Suhrawardī and the doctrine of the primordiality of being founded by Mullā Ṣadrā. The ontology contained in Suhrawardī's illuminationist philosophy was posthumously called 'doctrine of the primordiality of essence'.[86] This is because Suhrawardī's remarks on the relationship between essence and existence were mainly understood in the sense that, for him, essence is real, thus constituting reality, whereas existence is a mere mental concept.[87] Mullā Ṣadrā, while owing much to illuminationist philosophy, reversed this relationship between essence and existence, claiming that it is existence that is real and constituting reality, essence being a mere mental concept.[88] For all the material differences between these two doctrines, the question underlying both of them is a question about being, one that could be formulated as 'What *is* being?'. The question underlying Heidegger's thinking, however, although constituting a question about being, refers to the meaning of being and could be formulated as 'What does being *mean*?'.[89] In the final analyis, then, every philosophy of the Iranian-Islamic tradition is a philosophy of being, whereas Heidegger's thought is a philosophy of meaning.[90] This point can further be borne out by the fact that the validity of Heidegger's philosophy heavily depends on the trivial truth of the assumption that meaning determines reference, which assumption is a meaning issue, not a being issue.[91] Iranian Heidegger reception, hence, as it seems, is beset with yet another internal ambivalence lying behind the one mentioned above, an ambivalence that

85 This question is the topic of an upcoming project by the author of this article.

86 'Aṣālat al-māhiyyah; See: Kamal, M., *Mulla Sadra's Transcendent Philosophy*, Aldershot, 2006, pp. 12–23; Muvaḥḥid, Ṣ., *Nigāhī bi sarčišma-hā-yi ḥikmat-i išrāq va mafhūm-hā-yi bunyādī-i ān*, Tihrān, 1383HŠ.

87 Kamal, M., *Mulla Sadra's Transcendent Philosophy*, pp. 12–23.

88 Gösken, *Kritik der westlichen Philosophie in Iran*, pp. 139–140; Kamal, *Mulla Sadra's Transcendent Philosophy*; Rizvi, S., *Mulla Sadra and the Later Islamic Philosophical Tradition*, Edinburgh, 2013.

89 'der Sinn von Sein'; See: Sheehan, 'Dasein', p. 193.

90 Sheehan, 'Dasein', p. 193.

91 Lafont, 'Hermeneutics', p. 269, p. 282.

could be cast in the following questions, questions that require further research, too: If Iranian Heideggerians understand Heidegger's thinking as a philosophy of meaning, how do they link this philosophy of meaning to the philosophies of being of the Iranian-Islamic tradition? And if they understand it as a philosophy of being, how much may this understanding have suggested itself to them by the attempt to link it to the Iranian-Islamic tradition?

To take a step further, these considerations may be placed in the wider context of the construction of West-East dichotomies in Iranian intellectual history since the nineteenth century. The East-West dichotomy that Ṭālibūf supposes, as we have seen, is a cultural dichotomy.[92] Ṭabāṭabā'ī and Muṭahharī in *The Principles of Philosophy and the Method of Realism* construct an East-West dichotomy that we could call epistemological or religious at the same time: epistemological in that it identifies the East with realism and the West with idealism; religious in that it narrates the development of Islamic philosophy as the gradual fulfilment of salvation history, whereas it sees the West on a road to perdition. Iranian Heideggerians, following Heidegger's de(con)struction of metaphysical thought since antiquity, identify the West with metaphysics.[93] Given that Heidegger criticises the metaphysical tradition of Western thought on the ground that it leaves the crucial question about being unposed, which has resulted in what he calls the forgetfulness of being, they also identify the West with forgetfulness of being.[94] What Iranian Heideggerians identify the East with may vary from one thinker to another. Some, basing themselves on Corbin's construction of an Iranian-Islamic tradition as the manifestation of a metahistoric fact, identify the West with representational cognition and the East with cognition in terms of knowledge by presence, which, again, results in some form of epistemological dichotomy.[95] Along similar lines, some thinkers identify the East with truth and the West with reality.[96] At a more detached level, however, since both the representatives of the Iranian-Islamic tradition and Heidegger adopt different approaches to being on the basis of explicit or implicit questions about being, the East-West dichotomies constructed by thinkers dealing with the Iranian-Islamic tradition as well as with Heidegger may also be said to be ontological dichotomies. On the other hand, considering that the question about

92 Vahdat, *God and Juggernaut,* p. 53.

93 ʿAbd al-Karīmī, *Hāydiggir dar Īrān.,* pp. 274–275.

94 Vahdat, *God and Juggernaut,* p. 125; pp. 190–191.

95 Mirsepassi, *Political Islam, Iran, and the Enlightenment,* pp. 30–31, p. 34.

96 Mirsepassi, *Political Islam, Iran, and the Enlightenment,* pp. 112–113; Vahdat, *God and Juggernaut,* pp. 190–191

being underlying the Iranian-Islamic tradition results in philosophy of being, whereas the question about being that Heidegger asks results in a philosophy of meaning, the resulting construction of East-West dichotomy would be a dichotomy between ontology and hermeneutics.

Leaving aside the construction of East-West dichotomies, the appeal of Heidegger's philosophy to Iranian intellectuals can also be assessed if we examine its connection with the 'return to self' movement of the early 1960s. Whereas the salafist 'return to the self' is religious, thus not holding any attraction for Iranian nationalists, and the nationalist vision of 'return to the self' in terms of reviving the glories of the pre-Islamic past alienates religious minds, a 'return to the self'in terms of the Iranian-Islamic tradition, a tradition that in its turn can be connected to Heidegger's philosophy and to his criticism of Western thought, in some way bridges the gap: The formula 'Iranian-Islamic' can appeal to nationalists and religious thinkers alike, depending on which part of the formula they choose to stress. At the same time, adopting the Iranian-Islamic tradition and Heideggerianism alike allows Iranians, religious minded and others, to get involved with Western thought and practice without being forced to attribute it any superiority.

Thus, Iranian Heideggerianism, by recontextualising the concept of God and religion, played its role in reconciling hitherto opposed strands of Iranian intellectual life into one potent counter culture to official discourse and practice.[97] And insofar as the Iranian Heideggerians adopted and adapted Heidegger's thought in opposition to Enlightenment discourse that posits the final reducibility of human being, positing God in this scenario can be seen as an additional measure to ensure the final non-reducibility of human being. God itself could indeed be understood as the non-reducibility of human being. Anyway, while the issue between Iranian Heideggerianism and religious discourse is only about whether there is an absolute point of reference for meaningfulness in general and for the meaningfulness of human being in particular, the issue between Heideggerian thought in Iran and Enlightenment discourse in Iran is about whether human being has meaning at all or not.

97 Mirsepassi, *Political Islam, Iran, and the Enlightenment*, pp. 28–43, pp. 85–128.

Bibliography

ʿAbd al-Karīmī, B., *Hāydiggir dar Īrān. Nigāhī bi zindigī, āṯār va andīša- hā-yi Sayyid Aḥmad Fardīd,* Tihrān, 392HŠ.

Atabaki, T. and Zürcher, E., J., *Men of Order: Authoritarian Modernization under Atatürk and Reza Shah*, London, 2004.

Boroujerdi, M., *Iranian Intellectuals and the West: The Tormented Triumph of Nativism*, New York, 1996.

van den Bos, M., 'Transnational Orientalism. Henry Corbin in Iran', in *Anthropos,* bd. 100, h. 1, 2005, pp. 113–125.

Chehabi, H.E. and Martin, V. (eds.), *Iran's Constitutional Revolution: Popular Politics, Cultural Transformations and Transnational Connections*, London, 2010.

Corbin, H., 'De Heidegger à Sohravardî: Entretien avec Philippe Nemo', in Jambet, C. (ed.), *Cahiers de l'Herne: Henry Corbin*, Paris, 1981, pp. 23–37.

Corbin, H., *Itinéraire d'un enseignement*, Téhéran, 1993.

Couzens Hoy, D., 'Heidegger and the hermeneutic turn', in Guignon, C., B. (ed.), *The Cambridge Companion to Heidegger*, Cambridge, 2006, pp. 177–201.

Dabashi, H., *Theology of Discontent: The Ideological Foundation of the Islamic Revolution in Iran*, New York, 1993.

Gheissari, A., *Iranian Intellectuals in the 20th Century*, Texas, 1998.

Gösken, U., *Kritik der westlichen Philosophie in Iran: Zum geistesgeschichtlichen Selbstverständnis von Muḥammad Ḥusayn Ṭabāṭabāʾī and Murtażā Muṭahharī*, München, 2014.

Guignon, C., B., 'Introduction', in *The Cambridge Companion to Heidegger*, Cambridge, 2006, pp. 1–41.

Heidegger, M., *Sein und Zeit*, Tübingen, 2001

Herf, J., *Reactionary Modernism*, Cambridge, 1984.

Kamal, M., *Mulla Sadra's Transcendent Philosophy*, Aldershot, 2006.

Kandil, F., *Nativismus in der Dritten Welt*, St. Michael, 1983.

Lafont, C., 'Hermeneutics', in Dreyfus, H., L. and Wrathall M., A. (eds.), *A Companion to Heidegger,* Oxford, 2005, pp. 265–284.

Landolt, H., 'Henry Corbin, 1903–1978: Between Philosophy and Orientalism', in *Journal of the American Oriental Society*, vol. 119, no. 3, 1999, pp. 484–490.

Lenze, F., *Der Nativist Ǧalāl-e Āl-e Aḥmad und die Verwestlichung Irans im 20. Jahrhundert: eine Analyse der ethnographischen Monographien Awrāzān, Tāt-nešīnhā-ye bolūk-e Zahrā und Ǧazire-ye Ḫārg, dorr-e yatīm-e ḫalīǧ unter*

besonderer Berücksichtigung seiner Programmschrift Ġarbzadegī, Berlin, 2008.
Mirsepassi, A., *Intellectual Discourse and the Politics of Modernization: Negotiating Modernity in Iran*, Cambridge, 2000.
Mirsepassi, A., 'Religious Intellectuals and Western Critiques of Secular Modernity', in *Comparative Studies of South Asia, Africa and the Middle East*, vol. 26, no.3, 2006, pp. 416–433.
Mirsepassi, A., *Political Islam, Iran, and the Enlightenment: Philosophies of Hope and Despair*, Cambridge , 2011
Muṭahharī, M., cf. *Ṭabāṭabāʾī, Muḥammad-Ḥusayn,*1381 HŠ
Muvaḥḥid, Ṣ., *Nigāhī bi sarčišma-hā-yi ḥikmat-i išrāq va mafhūm-hā-yi bunyādī-i ān*, Tihrān, 1383HŠ.
Nabavi, N., *Intellectuals and the State in Iran: Politics, Discourse, and the Dilemma of Authenticity*, Florida, 2003.
Naṣrī, ʿA., *Rūyārūyī bā taǧaddod. 2 Bde*, Tehrān, 1386 HŠ.
Rentsch, T., *Philosophie des 20. Jahrhunderts: Von Husserl bis Derrida*, München, 2014.
Rizvi, S., *Mulla Sadra and Metaphysics: Modulation of Being*, London, 2009.
Rizvi, S., *Mulla Sadra and the Later Islamic Philosophical Tradition*, Edinburgh, 2013.
Seidel, R., 'Kants Autonomiebegriff. Chance oder Gefahr für die Religion? Positionen der Kantrezeption in Iran heute', in Hiltscher, R. and Klingner, S. (eds.), *Kant und die Religion – die Religionen und Kant*, Zürich and New York, 2012, pp. 137–158.
Seidel, R., *Kant in Teheran. Anfänge, Ansätze und Kontexte der Kantrezeption in Iran,* München, 2014.
Seidensticker, T., *Islamismus: Geschichte, Vordenker, Organisationen*, München, 2014
Sheehan, T., 'Dasein', in Dreyfus, H., L. and Wrathall M., A. (eds.), *A Companion to Heidegger,* Oxford, 2005, pp. 193–213.
Ṭabāṭabāʾī, M., *Uṣūl-i falsafa va raviš-i riʾālīsm*, 5 vols., Tihrān,1381/2 HŠ.
Vahdat, F., 'Return to which Self? Jalal Al-e Ahmad and the Discourse of Modernity', in *Journal of Iranian Research and Analysis,* vol.16, no. 2, 2000, pp. 55–71.
Vahdat, F., *God and Juggernaut: Iran's Intellectual Encounter with Modernity*, Syracuse, 2002.

8

In Search of the Secret Center in Constitutional Tabriz

Evan Siegel

The role of secret societies in the Iranian Constitutional Revolution has been recognised by all scholars of this event. This essay reviews the available evidence about the role and nature of one such society, the Tabriz Secret Center.

Secret Societies in the Iranian Constitutional Revolution

In her pioneering work on secret societies in the Constitutional Revolution, Ann Lambton writes. '[T]he way for the adoption of a modern Western system of government [was] prepared by secret or semi-secret societies in the direct line of Islamic tradition.'[1] Although she doesn't go into any detail about the Islamic tradition of secret societies and how they compare to the secret societies in the Constitutional Revolution, her broader point seems valid.

Indeed, the record which comes down to us indicates that, rather than esoteric Masonic practices which would bring Iran under the baleful control of Western Enlightenment values,[2] awaken it with them,[3] or using ancient practices perfected by religious schismatics, the Iranian constitutionalist secret societies were rather mundane and familiar operations. The most detailed record we have of such an operation, *Tarīkh-i Bīdārīyi Īrānīyān*,[4] written by a follower of perhaps the leading religious authority in the constitutional movement, Sayyid Muḥammad Ṭabaṭabā'ī, reveals a secret society lacking occult doctrines, rituals, and uniforms (aprons, etc.). Hamid Algar, in his masterful essay on Freemasonry in Iran, marshals considerable evidence to show that Freemasonry had not recovered from its suppression under Nāṣir al-Dīn Shah, although individual Masons actively participated in the Constitutional Revolution and Masonry might have contributed to the tools of modern political organisation.[5]

On the other hand, there is considerable interest in the role of Caucasian social-democracy and its presence in the secret societies which sprang up during the Constitutional Revolution, particularly in Tabriz.[6] This article studies the most significant of these societies, the Secret Center.

---

1 Lambton, Ann K. S., 'Secret Societies and the Persian Revolution of 1905–6', in *St. Antony's Papers*, vol. 4, 1958, p. 60.

2 Rā'īn, I., *Farāmūshkhāna va Farāmūsānarī dar Īrān*, London, 1978, pp. 148–218. Particularly charming is his page-long congratulations to Adolf Hitler for alerting the world to the dangers of Judeo-Masonry. *Ibid.*, p. 153.

3 Bayat, M., 'Freemasonry and the Constitutional Revolution in Iran: 1905–1911', in Önnerfors, A. and Sommer, D. (eds.), *Freemasonry and Fraternalism in the Middle East*, Sheffield, 2008, pp. 109–150.

4 And whose Masonic character Bayat argues for so vigorously. Bayat, 'Freemasonry and the Constitutional Revolution in Iran: 1905–1911', pp. 140–142.

5 Algar, H., 'An Introduction to the History of Freemasonry in Iran,' *Middle Eastern Studies*, vol. 6, no. 3, 1970, p. 292.

6 The literature on this left by left-nationalist writers deserves a separate treatment. As examples, see Sardārīnīyā, Ṣ., *Naqsh-i Markaz-i Ghaybīyi Tabrīz dar Inqilāb-i Mashrūṭiyyat*, Tehran, 1984,

The Beginning of Secret Societies in Tabriz

It is well known that Azerbaijan was a centre of progressive ideas in early modern Iran. Aḥmad Kasravī, the great historian of the Constitutional Revolution, underlines the role of the Iranian merchants in their diffusion into Iran.[7] Members of this class wrote about the promise of rationalism and modernity and the weaknesses of Iranian society. Prominent among them were 'Abd al-Raḥīm Tālibuf and Ḥājī Zayn al-'Ābidīn Marāgha'ī. Their books had to be read in secret. Indeed, even after the constitution was established, an Iranian bookseller was arrested, tortured, and held for a massive fine by the reactionaries for dealing in them.[8]

Kasravī wrote of Zayn al-'Ābidīn's *Sīyāhatnāmayi Ebrāhīm Bey* that 'many people were awakened by reading this book, became ready to struggle for their country's improvement, and joined with other activists.'[9] Indeed, it is credited with having inspired Sayyid Muḥammad Ṭabaṭabā'ī to launch a constitutionalist secret society which, in turn, set the Constitutional Revolution in motion, according to the memoirs of one of his followers.[10]

In the meantime, members of the budding Tabrizī intelligentsia were exploring new ideas under the inspiration of Caucasian Muslim intellectuals, Turkish Ottoman journals, Arabic newspapers published in British-ruled Egypt, and the Persian émigré press. The budding apostle of modernism in constitutional and post-constitutional Iran, Sayyid Ḥasan Taqīzāda, born into a clerical-landlord family, records the awakening this produced in him.[11] He gathered a small circle which went on to put out a short-lived journal, *Ganjīnayi Funūn*, starting in January 1903.[12] We will soon see that it played a vital role in the formation of the Secret Center.

Origins of Tabriz Social Democracy and the Secret Center, and Its Leader

Rizā Hamrāz, an avid student of the role of Iranian Azerbaijan in the Iranian Constitutional Revolution, commented in an introduction to his recent collection

---

and Riżāzāda-Malak, R., *Chakīdayi Inqilāb: Ḥaydar Khān 'Amūoghlū*, Tehran, 1972. Probably the best source of this material is posted on the website run by Riżā Hamrāz (http://www.salarsolmaz.blogfa.com/)

7 Kasravī, A., *Tārīkh-i Mashrūṭayi Īrān*, Tehran, 1975, p. 126.

8 Kasravī, *Tārīkh-i Mashrūṭayi Īrān*, p. 820.

9 Kasravī, *Tārīkh-i Mashrūṭayi Īrān*, p. 45.

10 Nāżim al-Islām, see: Kirmānī, *Tārīkh-i Bīdārīyi Īrānīyān*, Tehran, 1982, p. 245.

11 Taqīzāda, Ḥ., *Zindigīyi Tūfānī: Khāṭirāt-i Sayyid Ḥasan Taqīzāda* (ed. Afshār, Ī.), Tehran, 1989, p. 25 ff.

12 Taqīzāda, *Zindigīyi Tūfānī: Khāṭirāt-i Sayyid Ḥasan Taqīzāda*, pp. 35–36.

of essays on the Secret Center, 'Unfortunately, … the Secret Center was an underground organization and information about it is very limited for precisely this reason, since almost all the documents about it have regrettably been lost…' He continues that its leader, ʿAlī Monsieur, has also 'so far remained unknown.'[13]

The Secret Centre and its leader have found a status in left-nationalist historiography as the power behind the constitutional movement in Tabriz. Kasravī, who had access to a leader of the Centre, Ḥājī Rasūl Sidqīyānī, writes that soon after the Constitutional Revolution broke out, ''Alī Monsieur, Ḥājī ʿAlī Davāfurūsh , Ḥājī Rasūl Sidqīyānī and others translated the platform [of a Baku-based Iranian social democratic party] into Persian and formed the mujahid party. They themselves formed a secret society called the Secret Center which ran it.'[14] Here, the Secret Center works as the underground core or central committee of a mujahid party. Again, he writes, a dozen people 'formed a secret society called the Secret Center… [T]he movement was secretly controlled by the Secret Center.'[15] Again, 'The Secret Center, which was mostly convened in the home of … ʿAlī Monsieur, followed what Muḥammad ʿAlī Mīrzā [the Crown Prince, domiciled in Tabriz] and his circle were doing, both eyes wide open, and led the mujahids, which had just been formed.'[16] Note that in Kasravī's rendering, neither the mujahids nor the Secret Center are explicitly socialist.

The version of his history of the Iranian Constitutional Revolution Kasravī published in his journal *Paymān* in the 1930s gives a more spontaneous and less pre-planned depiction of the Secret Center: 'Before long, people united these squads [of mujahids, which were carrying out military drill] and ties with the Social Democratic Party of the Caucasus emerged. Eventually, a secret society called the Secret Center took control of these squads.'[17] This Center was not often mentioned in the history of the period, but its members were competent, firm, and courageous. '[M]ost of them were merchants who in the meantime refrained from work and took their losses. They never accepted jobs or posts.' He continued, 'During this

13 Hamrāz, R., ''Alī Monsieur', in *Mahd-i Tamaddun*, vol. 1, no. 16, 2014, p. 49 and 'Markaz-i Ghaybīyi Tabrīz', in *Mahd-i Tamaddun*, vol. 1, no. 16, 2014, p. 53. After the Soviet invasion of Azerbaijan, his surviving son was so terrified that he destroyed his memoirs and other documents, written in Persian and French, plus many photographs. (Sardārīnīyā, *Naqsh-i Markaz-i Ghaybīyi Tabrīz dar Inqilāb-i Mashrūṭiyat*, p. 296)

14 Kasravī, *Tārīkh-i Mashrūṭayi Īrān*, p. 391.

15 Kasravī, *Tārīkh-i Mashrūṭayi Īrān*, pp. 175–176.

16 Kasravī, *Tārīkh-i Mashrūṭayi Īrān*, p. 183.

17 Kasravī, A., *Tārīkh-i Hijda Sālayi Āzarbāyjān*, no date, no publisher, vol. 2, p. 45.

zealous outcry, too, it was the Secret Center which was the most active.'[18] Here, the Center and the Party are described as separate entities. This impression is reinforced by one of the descriptions of the founding of the Center Kasravī gave in the final version of his *History*. Here, he has the Center mentioned as having been set up by a group of intellectuals with no mention of any Social Democratic Party.[19]

According to Chosroe Chaqueri, social democracy got its start in Tabriz with the Social Democratic Party [*Firqayi Ijtimāʿīyūn ʿĀmmīyūn*]. According to secondary Soviet-era material which he himself considered of indifferent reliability, it was founded some time in 1905.[20] The first date he gives of its being active on any level is the autumn of 1907.[21]

Chaqueri then devotes a few paragraphs to the Secret Center (or, as he calls it, the Occult Center). He tells us that while the prominent Soviet Iranist M. S. Ivanov believes it to have been 'a small social-democratic group', he himself agrees with the Soviet academic N. K. Belova who said that 'no historical evidence has ever confirmed its existence.'[22] Indeed, he writes: 'Almost all the recurrent treatment of this curious centre is based on the as yet unverified discussion in Kasravī's two volumes of historiography of the Persian Revolution.'[23]

Karīm Ṭāhirzāda-Bihzād, in his memoirs as a member of the Center, begins with the Center's combat with the *farrāsh* (the constabulary) in order to maintain order; there is no mention of its defending the constitutional order in its early months,[24] although he recognises that it had been founded *after* the constitutional order had been proclaimed.[25] He describes the Center as a sort of underground leadership of the local Social Democratic Party, the latter being 'politically connected' to the party of the same name in the Caucasus, and that it was founded by ʿAlī Monsieur, who would become the Center's leader.[26] In a footnote to nothing in particular, he writes that the Social Democratic Party was actually founded towards

18 Kasravī, *Tārīkh-i Hijda Sālayi Āzarbāyjān*, p. 48.

19 Kasravī, *Tārīkh-i Mashrūṭayi Īrān*, p. 167, p. 175.

20 Chaqueri, C., *Origins of Social Democracy in Modern Iran*, Seattle, 2001, p. 120.

21 Chaqueri, *Origins of Social Democracy in Modern Iran*, p. 122.

22 Chaqueri, *Origins of Social Democracy in Modern Iran*, p. 137. But see footnote 139 where he shows how she apparently reverses herself.

23 Chaqueri, *Origins of Social Democracy in Modern Iran*, pp. 137–138.

24 Ṭāhirzāda-Bihzād, K., *Qīyām-i Āzarbāyjān dar Inqilāb-i Mashrūṭīyyat-i Īrān*, Tehran, 1984, p. 134. See also p. 453.

25 Ṭāhirzāda-Bihzād, *Qīyām-i Āzarbāyjān dar Inqilāb-i Mashrūṭīyyat-i Īrān*, p. 453.

26 Ṭāhirzāda-Bihzād, *Qīyām-i Āzarbāyjān dar Inqilāb-i Mashrūṭīyyat-i Īrān*, p. 45. See also p. 453.

the end of November 1904 under cover of mourning services for the universally-recognised Shiʿite authority ʿAlāma Fāżil Sharbīyānī.[27]

Nusrat Allāh Fatḥī's portrayal of the rise of the Secret Center is similar to Kasravī's original depiction (from his 1930's serialisation of his history). He has it that it was the result of a spontaneous accretion of households which armed themselves realising what was in store for them as the crown prince, with whose despotic ways the Tabrizīs had become acquainted as he lived among them, advanced to the throne.[28]

The aforementioned, Rižā Hamrāz, simply considers the Secret Center to be 'the Social-Democrats' underground apparatus.'[29]

E. G. Browne's *Letters from Tabriz*, consisting of his translations of letters from the great scholar's friends during the 1911 Russian occupation of Tabriz, is one of the earliest sources on the Secret Center and its leader ʿAlī Monsieur. In one of these letters, written by Taqīzāda[30] soon after the former's death, we read:

> The late Karbalāʾī ʿAlī, known as 'Monsieur', was one of the old Liberals and leaders of the earlier Constitutionalists. He lived for some time at Constantinople, and afterwards came to Tabriz and started a china-manufactory, for his eldest son Ḥājī had learned this craft…. His factory flourished for a long time at Tabriz, but after the establishment of the Constitution Karbalāʾī ʿAlī 'Monsieur' because [he was] one of the heroes of the Constitution, and during the days of the Revolution he was Chief and Elder of the National Volunteers of Tabriz, whose Director and Guide he became in spite of the fact that he never bore arms and was not a fighting man [h]e enjoyed a great influence amongst them, and ostensibly headed the third place after Sattār Khān and Bāqir Khān in authority. He was especially obnoxious to the Russians. He was very brave and devoted, and a most capable administrator and organizer, and is to be reckoned one of the chief organizers of the Revolution in Azerbaijan.[31]

27 Ṭāhirzāda-Bihzād, *Qīyām-i Āzarbāyjān dar Inqilāb-i Mashrūṭīyyat-i Īrān*, pp. 48–49.

28 Fatḥī, N., *Didār bā Hamrazm-i Sattār Khān*, Tehran, 1972, p. 7. Its author never makes it clear whether this book is a work of fiction or not. But given his wealth of knowledge, it is a valuable source of constitutional lore. He put these words in the mouth of the unnamed constitutionalist khan's illiterate servant, whose memory is somehow failing.

29 Hamrāz, 'Markaz-i Ghaybīyi Tabrīz', p. 53.

30 Browne, E. G., *Letters from Tabriz* (ed. by Javadi, H.), Washington, DC, 2008, p. xxix.

31 Browne, *Letters from Tabriz*, p. 193.

Indeed, he later adds, he and his comrade Ḥājī ʿAlī Davāfurūsh held 'the very soul of the Tabriz Revolution' in their hands.[32] In agreement with Kasravi, we can see pivotal roles being ascribed to ʿAlī Monsieur, though there is no mention yet of a Secret Center. The social democratic presence is only rarely alluded to.[33]

The Secret Center's Membership

The names of the Center's founders overlap greatly with the aforementioned *Ganjīnayi Funūn* group of Europeanising intellectuals and given this, we may conclude, in agreement with Suhrāb Yazdānī and K. Belova,[34] that the Center had more the character of a group of modernising intellectuals than socialists. Comparing the list of members of the *Ganjīnayi Funūn* group presented by Kasravī:

> Mīrzā Ḥadād Ḥakkākbāshī, Mīrzā Maḥmūd, Sayyid Ḥasan Taqīzāda, Mīrzā Sayyid Ḥusayn Khān 'ʿAdālat', Sayyid Muḥammad Shabastārī 'Abūz-Zīyā', Sayyid Ḥasan Sharīfzāda, Mīrzā Muḥammad ʿAlī Khān Tarbīyyat, Ḥājī ʿAlī Davāfurūsh, Mīrzā Maḥmūd Ghanīzāda, Ḥājī Mīrzā Āqā Farshfurūsh, Karbalāʾī ʿAlī Monsieur, Ḥājī Rasūl Sidqīyānī, Mīrzā ʿAliqulū Khān Safaruf, Āqā Muḥammad Salmāsī, Jaʿfar Āqā Ganjaʾī, Mīrzā ʿAli Asghar Khuiʾī, Mīrzā Maḥmūd Uskūʾī, and Mashhadī Ḥabīb[35]

with the members of the Secret Center provided by Kasravī (where we italicise the names of the Secret Center members who were members of the *Ganjīnayi Funūn* group):

> *Karbalāʾī ʿAlī Monsieur, Ḥājī Rasūl Sidqīyāni , Ḥājī ʿAlī Davāfurūsh , Sayyid Ḥasan Sharīfzāda, Mīrzā Muḥammad ʿAlī Khān Tarbīyyat, Jaʿfar Āqā Ganjaʾī,* Āqā Mīr Bāqir, *Mīrzā ʿAlī Asghar Khuiʾī,* Āqā Taqī Shujāʿī, Āqā Muḥammad Sādiq Khāmina, and Sayyid Riżā.[36]

---

32 Browne, *Letters from Tabriz*, p. 217.

33 Browne, *Letters from Tabriz*, p. 191–192, 238. It is worth mentioning that Taqīzāda would never mention ʿAlī Monsieur, whom he here depicts as the pivot of constitutional Tabrīz, in his future writings, not to mention the Secret Center.

34 Yazdānī, S., '*Dar bārayi Firqayi Ijtimāʿīyyūn ʿĀmīyyūn-i Īran*', *Faslnāmayi ʿIlmi-Takhassusīyi Tārīkh*', vol. 1, no. 3, 2006, p. 151.

35 Kasravī, *Tārīkh-i Mashrūṭayi Īrān*, pp. 150–151.

36 Kasravī, A., *Tārīkh-i Mashrūṭayi Īrān*, pp. 166.

shows that at least two thirds of the Secret Center came from the *Ganjīnayī Funūn* circle. In an autobiography provided in his memoirs, Ṭāhirzāda-Bihzād mentions that ʿAlī Monsieur, the future leader of the Secret Center, and Taqīzāda, Tarbīyyat, and other prominent reformists were members of a discussion group founded in the year preceding the constitution's being granted, a clear reference to the abovementioned circle.[37]

Unsurprisingly, the list of members of the Secret Center varies from author to author. Ṭāhirzāda-Bihzād gives a partial list of names, of which two people (Ḥadād Ḥakkākbāshī and Mīr ʿAlī Akbar Sarrāj) are not present in Kasravī's list.[38] In the aforementioned odd footnote to his memoirs, he gives a very different list and claims, *inter alia*, that the military hero of the Tabriz constitutionalist, Sattār Khān, had joined the Social-Democratic Party.[39]

The aforementioned memoirs by Nusrat Allāh Fatḥī has a servant of a constitutionalist Khān he was visiting give a detailed but almost definitely apocryphal story of Sattār Khān's induction into the Secret Center.[40]

According to Riżā Hamrāz, Salam Allāh Jāvīd, a Tudeh Party leader and scholar of constitutional Azerbaijan, includes Taqīzāda in 'a liberal cell based in Baku and [later] organized in Tabriz,' a clear reference to the Secret Center.[41]

Lengthy passages of the (possibly apocryphal) unpublished memoirs of Mīrzā Javād Khān Nātiq, one of the three great Tabriz constitutionalist preachers, are quoted in Nusrat Allāh Fatḥī's biography of these constitutionalist orators.[42] In them, Mīrzā Javād claims to have been a member of a group of Tabriz intellectuals which included Taqīzāda on the one hand and another which included ʿAlī

37 Ṭāhirzāda-Bihzād, *Qīyām-i Āzarbāyjān dar Inqilāb-i Mashrūṭīyyat-i Īrān*, pp. 468 ff.

38 Ṭāhirzāda-Bihzād, *Qīyām-i Āzarbāyjān dar Inqilāb-i Mashrūṭīyyat-i Īrān*, pp. 45. He is commonly mentioned in other lists. See for instance, Jāvīd, S., http://www.tabrizinfo.com/tabriz/shahrdaran/tarbiat.htm (last accessed August 8, 2016) where he is referred to as a member of 'that group of liberals which was founded in Baku and then organized in Tabrīz,' a clear reference to the Social-Democratic party.

39 Ṭāhirzāda-Bihzād, *Qīyām-i Āzarbāyjān dar Inqilāb-i Mashrūṭīyyat-i Īrān*, pp. 48–49.

40 Fatḥī, *Dīdār-i Hamrazm-i Sattār Khān*, pp. 8–9.

41 Hamrāz, 'Markaz-i Ghaybī' *Mahd-i Tamaddun*, pp. 58–59. This is particularly odd given the Tudeh Party's deep and long-standing enmity with Taqīzāda.

42 Fatḥī, N., *Sokhangūyān-i Sigānayi Āzārbāyjān dar Inqilāb-i Mashrūṭīyyat-i Īrān*, Tehran, 1977, pp. 98 ff. His daughter, Homa Nateq, was editing these memoirs when she passed away. (http://www.mirasmaktoob.ir/fa/news/5743, last accessed August 8, 2016)

Monsieur, paralleling the usual description of the *Ganjīnayi Funūn* group and the Secret Center, but writing himself into them.[43]

It is not necessary to choose among the membership lists of the Secret Center to recognise that all of these intellectuals were members of the same reformist milieu in Tabriz. Despite its reputation for strict secrecy, it is hard to imagine that a group whose meeting place was well known to the public (ʿAlī Monsieur's home) could actually function clandestinely. Rather, the Secret Center was less a tightly disciplined underground organisation than a relatively loose association of radical intellectuals with long-standing links to each other who blended into a social periphery which shared its values. On this latter point, when ʿAlī S̱iqat al-Islām, a valuable moderate observer of the constitutional movement in Tabriz, remarks on the Secret Center, he includes among its ranks people best described as its periphery. Moreover, his diary also shows that the leadership and possibly the membership of the Secret Center was actually rather well known. He includes in it ʿAli Monsieur and continues:

> A certain Ḥājī Ṣamad Khayyāt and Qalʿavānbāshī the Customs employee, who are both extremists, jumped in among the people and devoted themselves to insulting the aristocrats and the grandees. Among them was a group of toughs and thugs – Yūsuf Khazdūz, Ḥājī Aḥmad Naqqāsh, Mīr Taqī Chāychī, etc. – who kept the pot boiling and incited disturbances.[44]

---

43 Fatḥī, *Sokhangūyān-i Sigānayi Āzārbāyjān dar Inqilāb-i Mashrūṭīyyat-i Īrān*, pp. 131–144.

44 S̱iqat al-Islām-i Tabrīzī, ʿA., *Majmūʿayi Ās̱ār-i Qalmīyi S̱iqat al-Islām-i Tabrīzī*, (ed. Fatḥī, N.), Isfahan, no date, p. 52.

Jaʿfar Āqā was a member of Taqīzāda's circle. Ṣamad Khayyāt was a mujahid leader (Browne, *Letters from Tabriz*, p. 189. He is listed simply as a mojahed in Ṭāhirzāda-Bihzād, as opposed to by his political affiliation (Social Democrat, etc.); Ṭāhirzāda-Bihzād, *Qīyām-i Āzarbāyjān dar Inqilāb-i Mashrūṭīyyat-i Īrān*, p. 351). Qalʿavānbāshī led a disastrous expedition to Marāgha, in which he treated the city like an occupying army and acted like a degenerate dictator, leading to a disastrous reversal for the Constitutionalists. (Kasravī, *Tārīkh-i Mashrūṭayi Īrān*, pp. 816–821 and S̱iqat al-Islām-i Tabrīzī, *Majmūʿayi Ās̱ār-i Qalmīyi S̱iqat al-Islām-i Tabrīzī*, p. 130.) Ṭāhirzāda-Bihzād calls Aḥmad Naqqāsh a commander of the socialists' mojaheds (Ṭāhirzāda-Bihzād, *Qīyām-i Āzarbāyjān dar Inqilāb-i Mashrūṭīyyat-i Īrān*, p. 351). Kasravī mentions him in his *Tārīkh-a Hijda Sālayi Āzarbāyjān*, saying, 'Some call him bloodthirsty and blame the killings of many on him. But it seems it is not as simple as that. He was involved in the Tabriz constitutional movement from the start and was among the militia leaders and was always there when the fighting was tough… It was in 1908 that he captured some of the constitution's enemies and executed them in the Citadel, but fled to the Caucasus and from there to Gilan, where he was among the founders

Of these, Ḥājī Ṣamad Khayyāt, Qalʿavānbāshī, Ḥājī Aḥmad Naqqāsh, and Mīr Taqī Chāychī – half of those mentioned – are rarely or never mentioned as members of the Secret Center.

The Secret Center's Social Basis

In order to understand this Center better, let us look at some biographical information about some of its members.

- ʿAlī Monsieur. Karīm Ṭāhirzāda-Bihzād writes in his memoirs that he was an enlightened merchant of Nawbar. He had set up a porcelain factory in Tabriz with a considerable investment. He won his sobriquet because of his knowledge of French. He was deeply impressed with the French Revolution.[45] The only reference to him in the Tabriz constitutionalist periodical of record, *Anjuman*, is his presiding over a fundraising effort in his borough of Nawbar for a public school, which shows that he had amiable relations with the local merchants and moneylenders.[46]
- Ḥājī ʿAlī Davāfurush. He made his fortune in using dyes in the fireworks he sold; this brought him business with the local government. This business also put him in contact with other countries, from which he learned about Western political institutions.[47] *Anjuman* regularly referred to him as a leading constitutionalist and he had a significant public presence, unlike ʿAlī Monsieur.

---

of the Sattār Committee in Rasht.' He played a leading role in the constitutionalist march on Qazvin, after which he returned to Tabriz. When the Russians occupied Tabriz, he was a leader of the resistance to the Russian army. But he soon realised that it was impossible to take on its many millions of troops. He then drew up a list of enemies of the nation and said, 'After us, they will stop at nothing in persecuting those who survive us. So it is better to kill them all while we live and rid the country of them. (Kasravī, *Tārīkh-a Hijda Sālayi Āzarbāyjān*, pp. 347–8) Ṭāhirzāda-Bihzād labels him as a Social-Democratic commander. (Ṭāhirzāda-Bihzād, *Qīyām-i Āzarbāyjān dar Inqilāb-i Mashrūṭīyyat-i Īrān*, p. 351) Elsewhere, he is reported as being exiled to Rasht by the party for an unspecified breach of discipline. (Ṭāhirzāda-Bihzād, *Qīyām-i Āzarbāyjān dar Inqilāb-i Mashrūṭīyyat-i Īrān*, p. 38, note 1.) We will meet Mīr Taqī Chāychī later in this essay.

45 Ṭāhirzāda-Bihzād, *Qīyām-i Āzarbāyjān dar Inqilāb-i Mashrūṭīyyat-i Īrān*, pp. 452–455.

46 '*Bishārat va Iʿlān*' in *Anjuman*, vol. 2, no. 41, 25 Zi'l-Hijja, 1324, p. 4. It should be pointed out that in the period leading up to the Constitutional Revolution, schools were very political. See Kasravī, A., *Tārīkh-i Mashrūṭayi Irān*, pp. 25–26.

47 Ṭāhirzāda-Bihzād, *Qīyām-i Āzarbāyjān dar Inqilāb-i Mashrūṭīyyat-i Īrān*, pp. 449–450.

- Ḥājī Rasūl Sidqīyānī. The owner of a powerful and respected merchant firm in Istanbul.[48] He was from a religious family in the conservative borough of Shuturbān. His career as a merchant brought him to the Caucasus and Austria as well as the Ottoman Empire. Having returned to Tabriz, he plunged into reformist activity. A year before the Constitution was granted, he helped form the Social Democratic Party along with ʿAlī Monsieur.[49]
- Sayyid Ḥasan Sharīfzāda. He was in his mid-twenties during the constitutional period. He was from a respected and wealthy clerical family.[50] From his youth, he was fascinated by Western learning, which he studied methodically. He learned 'some French' and later studied in the American missionary school in Tabriz. He taught in the American school, where the students idolised him.[51] When fighting broke out in Tabriz, he took refuge in the French embassy, only emerging after the fighting was over.[52] He was assassinated by a pair of drunken mujahids after he'd upbraided a crowd of their comrades for including adventurist elements in their ranks.[53]
- Muḥammad ʿAlī Tarbīyyat. Along with Taqīzāda, whose brother-in-law he was, he lead the *Ganjīnayī Funūn* circle. He spent most of his adult life in the libraries and bookstores of the Ottoman Empire and Europe. There is no record in the literature of the period of his being a constitutionalist activist. Perhaps his biggest contribution to the constitutionalist cause was his book which Browne translated and published under his own name, *The Press and Poetry in Persia*. His brother, ʿAlī Muḥammad Tarbīyyat, was 'a volcano' politically and an active mujahid.[54]
- Karīm Ṭāhirzāda-Bihzād. Although he does not appear on any of the list of Secret Center members, he states in his memoirs that he was a

48 Ṭāhirzāda-Bihzād, *Qīyām-i Āzarbāyjān dar Inqilāb-i Mashrūṭīyyat-i Īrān*, p. 359.

49 Ṣanīʿzada, Ṣ., 'Farazhāyi az Zindigīyi Shādravān Ḥaj Rasūl Sidqīyanī', *Mahd-i Tamaddun*, vol. 1, no. 16, 2014, p. 59.

50 Amīrkhīzī, I., *Qīyām-i Āzarbāyjān va Sattār Khān*, Tehran, 1960, p. 60.

51 Mahdī Mujtahidī, *Rijāl-i Āzarbāyjān dar ʿAṣr-i Mashrūṭīyyat*, Tehran, 1949, p. 208.

52 Amīrkhīzī, *Qīyam-i Āzarbāyjān va Sattār Khān*, p. 92.

53 Taqīzāda, Ḥ., *Tārīkh-i Avāyil-i Inqilāb va Mashrūṭīyyat-i Īrān*, in Afshār, Ī. (ed.), *Maqalāt-i Taqizāda*, Tehran, vol. 5, 1970, p. 320.

54 Mujtahidī, M., *Rijal-i Āzarbāyjān dar ʿAṣr-i Mashrūṭīyyat*, pp. 50–52. See also: http://zamaaneh.com/morenews/2006/12/_6_1.html, last accessed August 8, 2016.

member. Mahdī Mujtahidī, in his indispensable *Rijāl-i Āzārbāyjān dar 'Aṣr-i Mashrutīyyat*, says that his father, Mīrzā Ḥusein Khān Mozīn al-Soltān, was an outstanding artist and professor of fine arts in Istanbul. He continues that he authored a scholarly book on the fine arts in Iran and made a career as an architect in Berlin, but gives no reference to any political activity.[55]

The upper class quality of the social democratic Secret Center is underlined in Ṭāhirzāda-Bihzād's memoirs. The Secret Center inductee, he is told, will be given a membership card 'after a thorough investigation into … his family's good repute.'[56] This memoirist chastises Kasravī for overemphasising the mujahids' role in the struggle, saying that it was the political activists (all of whom were upper class), above all Taqīzāda, who gave it direction. The mujahids, he wrote, were not reliable sources, since they tried to exaggerate their services to the cause.[57] Indeed, the real leaders were the intellectuals[58] and not the mujahids, whom the author deprecates.

Fatḥī, in his story of a visit to a constitutionalist khān, has the servant character talk about Sattār Khān's induction into the Secret Center. However improbable it is, it reveals the way the members of the Center saw themselves. He has the servant say, 'Sattār Khān joined them, although he supports himself by horse trading.'[59] Such a common trade was beneath the status of the run of the Secret Center cadre. Only a few pages later, this same source is made to say that of the few Center members he met, 'most of them were bazaar craftsmen, sugar dealers, shoemakers, and weavers' and that he himself was a carpet weaver[60] and elsewhere, the comrade in arms of Sattār Khān featured in Fatḥī's book says, 'the social position of the first founders of the Secret Center [were] from the third and fourth classes,' giving an example Sattār Khān.[61] But the (admittedly fanciful) list of Secret Center founders he presents when he resumes discussing it contradicts this claim.[62] The author asserts that the Secret Center was composed of *sans-culottes* when he's

55 Mujtahidī, M., *Rijāl-i Āzarbāyjān dar 'Aṣr-i Mashrūṭīyyat*, p. 201.

56 Ṭāhirzāda-Bihzād, *Qīyām-i Āzarbāyjān dar Inqilāb-i Mashrūṭīyyat-i Īrān*, p. 63.

57 Ṭāhirzāda-Bihzād, *Qīyām-i Āzarbāyjān dar Inqilāb-i Mashrūṭīyyat-i Īrān*, p. 17.

58 Ṭāhirzāda-Bihzād, *Qīyām-i Āzarbāyjān dar Inqilāb-i Mashrūṭīyyat-i Īrān*, p. 21, note 1.

59 Fatḥī, *Dīdār-i Hamrazm-i Sattār Khān*, p. 9.

60 Fatḥī, *Dīdār-i Hamrazm-i Sattār Khān*, p. 12.

61 Fatḥī, *Dīdār-i Hamrazm-i Sattār Khān*, p. 70.

62 Fatḥī, *Dīdār-i Hamrazm-i Sattār Khān*, p. 133.

consciously addressing its class composition, but otherwise he recognises the very upper-class names of its founding fathers.

The Secret Center's Ideology

For all Ṭāhirzāda-Bihzād's emphasis on the role of the men of ideas in the Constitutional Revolution, the level of political indoctrination in the Secret Center as he portrays it was low. He recalls a speech by ʿAlī Monsieur in which he called on members to be fearless and prepared to sacrifice life and property in the cause, referring to the martyrs at Kerbala. It closed with an exposition on the French Revolution. The talk is designed to fire up the ranks but gives no political analysis except the general view that Iran had to be freed.[63] Rather, loyalty and unquestioning obedience were stressed. In addition, they were to treat the people kindly and have no contact with the absolutists.[64] As for enforcing discipline, there is only one (extreme) example of its enforcement, as we will see below.

A rather more substantial essay by ʿAlī Monsieur has recently been found by the veteran scholar of Constitutionalist Tabriz, ʿAbd al-Ḥusayn Nāhīd-Āzar. It uses as reference the 1603 liberation of Tabriz by Shah ʿAbbās' armies after it had been occupied by the Ottomans for almost a century. He uses the self-sacrifice of the people in that battle to illustrate how Iran belongs to all its people equally. The duty of rulers (elected or otherwise) is to protect the country. If they fail in this obligation, they are to be deposed. Unfortunately, Iranians, in their ignorance, have allowed unworthy absolutists to stay in power. He cites Imām ʿAlī's celebrated injunction that since the oppressed are so much more numerous than their oppressors, it is the latter's duty to rise up against them. He illustrates this with the execution of King Louis XVI. The essay closes by declaring that it is the task of the people of Azerbaijan to win over the rest of Iran to the struggle for freedom and that the unity of the Iranian people will be irresistible.[65]

---

63 Ṭāhirzāda-Bihzād, *Qīyām-i Āzarbāyjān dar Inqilāb-i Mashrūṭīyyat-i Īrān*, pp. 74–76.

64 Ṭāhirzāda-Bihzād, *Qīyām-i Āzarbāyjān dar Inqilāb-i Mashrūṭīyyat-i Īrān*, p. 64. According to Fatḥī's servant character, the four conditions were, '1) being Iranian, 2) being a Muslim, 3) preserving the group's secrets, and 4) unconditional obedience.' Fatḥī, *Dīdār-i Hamrazm-i Sattār Khān*, p. 7.

65 Hamrāz, 'Markaz-i Ghaybīyī Tabrīz', pp. 55–56.

The Secret Center in Action

On the power of the Secret Center, Kasravī states:

> [T]he movement was secretly controlled by the Secret Center. The expulsion of Mīr Hāshim and the Friday Imam and keeping the Anjuman from being closed was all their doing.[66] They knew well that autocracy had not disappeared, that nothing would come of the name 'constitution' alone, and that forces must be assembled and prepared for combat. They knew well that if the people were left to themselves, they would gradually weaken and lose enthusiasm. So [the Center] would keep finding occasions to get them to go into action and not abandon the struggle against autocracy.[67]

And yet, Secret Center member Ṭāhirzāda-Bihzād scarcely mentioned these events that Kasravī claims the Center had played such a pivotal role in. He said that he[68] and ʿAlī Monsieur had participated in taking refuge in the British consulate, but there is certainly no indication of them playing any leadership role in it.[69]

Taqīzāda, for his part, never refers to the Center in his recollections of the period even though, as pointed out above, a number of close friends of his were founding members.[70]

Even Kasravī, in his own narrative of the events, makes it clear that the idea for taking refuge in the British consulate was decided on by the leaders of the borough of Shuturbān and the constitutionalist preachers and that it was Mīrzā Ḥusayn Vāʿiz, one of the three great constitutionalist preachers in Tabriz, who confronted Mīr Hāshim in the Anjuman and led the movement that ended in his exile from Tabriz. As for Kasravī's report on the threat to the Anjuman, he only

66 Mīr Hāshim was a leading cleric from the borough of Shuturbān in Tabriz. He led the constitutional movement there, but when it became clear that he could not monopolise it, it was said, he went over to the anti-constitutional camp. People claimed to have seen him visiting the autocratic Crown Prince. 'It was said, "The Crown Prince was told that whoever got a camel on the roof could get it down."' (Kasravī, *Tārīkh-i Mashrūṭayi Īrān*, p. 171.) The Anjuman was elected originally to supervise the Majlis elections in Tabriz, the Anjuman survived pressure by the central government to close after the elections and became a local government.

67 Kasravī, *Tārīkh-i Mashrūṭayi Īrān*, pp. 175–176.

68 Ṭāhirzāda-Bihzād, *Qīyām-i Āzarbāyjān dar Inqilāb-i Mashrūṭīyyat-i Īrān*, p. 453.

69 The constitutional movement in Tabriz as such began with the city's leading citizens taking refuge in the British embassy.

70 See especially his *Tārīkh-i Inqilāb-i Īrān*, republished in *Maqalāt-i Taqīzāda*, vol. 5, pp. 340–341.

said that it was the 'mujahids' who blocked it, much too vague a statement to count for much.[71] The best contemporary source on these events, S̲iqat al-Islām's diary of these events, reported on them pretty much the way Kasravī did.[72]

Kasravī also claimed that the Secret Center was secretly directing the arming of the people:

> Distributing weapons among the people could have meant any variety of dreadful things. Wise leaders who knew what they were doing were needed to prevent chaos and bloodshed and make progress. This Secret Center showed that it was up to the task.
>
> This Center struggled to form a group of fighters called the Mujahids. Indeed, they were arming a militia drawn from among the people. It was to advance this aim of theirs that, with the help of orators and others, this business of buying rifles and target practice started and the Center did not cease from supporting it.[73]

Ṭāhirzāda-Bihzād in his memoirs doesn't give a very impressive picture of these Secret Center mujahids as a fighting force. He writes that in their inexperience, they one night mistook some trees for Raḥīm Khān, the tribal marauder the central government had sent against the Tabriz constitutionalists, and ignited a massive volley on the constitutionalist side, and in another 'engagement' mistook the approach of a milkman for that of Raḥīm Khān's cavalry.[74] He does give examples of real heroism by his comrades as the fighting wore on, but it is clear that by this time that the Secret Center played no role in setting up these latter constitutionalist fighting forces.

The claim that the Secret Center played a significant role in setting these armed squads in motion is also belied by the contemporary record.

The first reference to military drill appears in *Anjuman*. In November 1906, it wrote:

> The shops and the bazaars shall be closed on Friday and the people shall gather in the mosques… The three preachers will preach the benefits of

71 Kasravī, *Tārīkh-i Mashrūṭayi Īrān*, pp. 153–157, pp. 171–177.

72 Fatḥī, *Majmū'aya Ās̲ār-i Qalmīyi S̲iqat al-Islām-i Shahīd Tabrīzī*, pp. 13–17, pp. 28–31, pp. 35–36, pp. 48–50.

73 Kasravī, *Tārīkh-i Mashrūṭayi Īrān*, p. 237.

74 Ṭāhirzāda-Bihzād, *Qīyām-i Āzarbāyjān dar Inqilāb-i Mashrūṭīyyat-i Īrān*, pp. 71–73.

> constitutionalism and the merits of unity and the advantage of the union of government and people, to make the people aware.[75]

It made the source of inspiration for this movement to have been the three leading constitutionalist preachers in Tabriz, Shaikh Salīm, Mīrzā Javād Nātiq, and Mīrzā Ḥusayn.

It is worth nothing that Kasravī cites this after having claimed that the Secret Center was behind this agitation.[76] He writes that the Secret Center was actually behind the agitation and had just formed its armed wing, the Mujahids. He then cites (without attribution) the above-mentioned article but replaces 'mujahids' for '*jam*ʿ*ī az ahālī*', a group of the people, in a clear attempt to prove his assertion about the pivotal role of the Secret Center in these events.

Five months later, *Anjuman* writes:

> In several boroughs of Tabriz, zealous youths and men from among the people have been gathering on Fridays in the afternoon and on other days two hours before dusk outside of town, with specialized and sound training, busy with military drill for a jihad, which is one of Islam's obligations.[77]

The next month, *Anjuman* reported that a band of mujahids from the conservative Tabriz borough of Shuturbān held a military parade at the home of one Muḥammad Bāqir, a sponsor of this military activity. This parade inspired excitement among the spectators and caused the author of the article to ask the Shah to be kind to his people, who have repaid his guidance so handsomely, and said that the treacherous ministers will feel miserable when they see that Iran will no longer tolerate their absolutism and oppression. The article continued:

> These zealous youths and mujahids, who are prepared to lose their all, even their very lives, have undertaken this arduous task for the sake of the country and to spread the shariat of the Prophet (upon whom be blessings and peace!), and have therefore busied themselves with learning the science of jihad, which is an obligation of Islam, lest it occur to the traitors and absolutists that this movement is a joke or a whim or that they have dressed in military

---

75 'Al-Jumʿa Sayyid al-Ayyām wa Man Shuʿāʿ al-Islām', in *Anjuman*, vol. 1, no. 11 (9 Shawwal, 1324).

76 Kasravī, *Tārīkh-i Mashrūṭayi Īrān*, p. 183.

77 'Hayajān-i Ghayūrāna va Moʾadabāna', in *Anjuman*, vol. 1, no. 67, p. 3 (6 Rabīʿ I, 1325).

> uniforms and learned the science of jihad in order to (God forbid!) rebel against the dynasty and the people (We take refuge with God!). Rather, we are all guildsmen and craftsmen of the bazaar and of our noble people who are striving for the sake of the country and to raise the banner of His Imperial Majesty, the King of Islam, and for the progress of the realm and the advancement of the Constitution. O God, protect the Crowned Father of we the Iranians, His Imperial Majesty Muḥammad ʿAlī Shah (May God immortalize his reign!) from calamity, and may he be kind and generous to his subjects, who are as his children, and grant him success in strengthening and advancing the sacred great National Consultative Assembly [the *Majlis*] and disseminating the just commandments [of Islam].[78]

It should be noted here in connection with Kasravī's claim about a role of the Secret Centere in these events that the center had no connection with the mujahids in Shuturbān, and, in fact, soon went to war with them.

The next month, *Anjuman* carried an article by the same author reporting that military drill in three other boroughs of Tabriz had commenced a month before. The twice-weekly drill was kept orderly, with people who practiced target shooting at unauthorised places to be severely punished.[79]

In the earlier version of his history of the Iranian constitutional revolution serialised in his monthly magazine, *Paymān*, Kasravī himself recalls:

> I will never forget that one day, I saw the young son of a merchant stop His Eminence Mīr Javād and ask him, 'Your Eminence, did you deliver a fatwa that we should buy rifles and drill?' The prayer leader replied, 'Yes! Today it is obligatory upon all Muslims to buy rifles and drill. We must deliver the Caucasus from the hands of the infidel!' It was as if the youth had discovered a treasure trove, the way he walked on happily and with a prayer on his lips. He probably bought a rifle that very day and drilled and exercised. As for me, it was as if my every wish had been granted; I was so happy I thought I'd burst, and went on, thanking [God].[80]

In the final version of his *History*, Kasravī recalls:

78 No title, *Anjuman*, vol. 1, no. 75 (23 Rabīʿ I, 1325), pp. 1–2.

79 'Ikhtār,' *Anjuman*, vol. 1, no. 79, (29 Rabīʿ I, 1325), pp. 3–4.

80 Kasravī, A., *Tārīkh-i Hizhda Sālayi Āzarbāyjān* (*Paymān*) vol. 1, pp. 99–100.

In Tabriz, a very valuable thing began that spring: military drill and shooting practice. This had begun during the winter, but progress was actually made during the spring.

… [F]or several months, upon of the Anjuman's instructions, the bazaars would be shut down on Fridays and the people would gather in three mosques. Three preachers – Shaykh Salīm, Mīrzā Javād, and Mīrzā Ḥusayn – would each mount a mosque's pulpit and preach to the people. This was very successful, particularly with Mīrzā Ḥusayn, who became an institution unto himself. This man, with his expressive and gripping voice, would recite inspiring poems in Persian and Turkish, make powerful speeches, and stir the people's hearts. The people turned to him and the Mīrzā Mahdī Mosque, for all its vastness, would be completely filled, and people would have to stand in the hallway up to the door…

[T]hey would be very stirring in speaking of the country's weakness and recounting Fatḥ ʿAlī Shah's defeat and the loss of the Caucasus and similar events and inspired the people to get guns and learn how to use them and to drill…

And so, a barracks sprung up in every borough and they assembled musical instruments and other things. Squads also sewed and wore their own uniforms. They were so inspired that Fridays were not enough, and they decided to do this every day. The bazaars would close every evening and chintz dealers, rock sugar dealers, coppersmiths, used goods vendors and merchants … would rush off to their houses, change their clothes, pick up a rifle, head for the local barracks, and drill there with the rest. Every evening the sound of drum and bugle and the chanting of the cadence rose from every borough. The grandeur and splendor of that effort increased day by day.

The city completely changed character. Everyone talked about buying a rifle, drilling, military preparations, and self-sacrifice.

Kasravī then adds, as an afterthought, his comment about the importance of the Secret Center's wisdom mentioned above.[81] But he makes no mention of what the Center was supposed to have done.

Social Unrest and the Social Democrats

One of the turning points of the Constitutional Revolution in Tabriz was the Qara Chaman affair, in which a local notable village's peasants disobeyed the bailiff

81 Kasravī, *Tārīkh-i Mashrūṭayi Īrān*, pp. 235–237.

and a punitive expedition was sent there, spreading murder and mayhem. As it happened, this atrocity was committed with the blessing of Mujtahid Mīrzā Ḥasan, Tabriz's most prestigious religious authority.[82] This in turn led to a major confrontation between the constitutionalists, led by Shaykh Salīm and his two clerical comrades, and the Mujtahid and the local establishment. Kasravī's account leaves unclear the issues involved, but the gap is filled by S̱iqat al-Islām, a staunch member of the landowning class. According to him, the peasants beat the landlord, threw him out of the village, imprisoned his relatives, and looted whatever they found.[83] He continued:

> Some say that the cause of the sedition from the start was some *talaba*s who got together and went to the Anjuman. These, in turn, were stirred up by two or three *talaba*s who had been talking about Qara Chaman all along. Servants and laborers and people from Qazalcha [the village owned by Tabriz's Friday Imam, an absolutist and an infamous grain hoarder] and a bunch of others and some socialists were also mixed in…[84]

This passing reference to socialists being involved is the only such reference in his recollections of this crisis. When he gets specific about the instigators, he blames the constitutionalist preacher Shaykh Salīm.[85] It is worth noting that the context of this quotation shows that the 'sedition' referred to the *results* of the Qara Chaman disturbance, and not its cause, which he saw in a Russian conspiracy to destabilise Iran which would only lead to the ruin of Iranian agriculture and the rise of foreign domination.[86] He sees the situation in Tabriz as different from what was unfolding in Rasht, in which trouble-makers were being prepared by Russia-based social democrats.[87] Later, he says that the villages are in an upheaval, and that the polite, law-abiding peasants have entered the Parisian schools, emerging as anarchists and refusing to pay their taxes. 'They loot the granaries and talk back

---

82 Kasravī, *Tārīkh-i Mashrūṭayi Īrān*, pp. 239–40; S̱iqat al-Islām, *Majmū'ayi Ās̱ār-i Qalmīyi S̱iqat al-Islām-i Tabrīzī*, p. 48.

83 Letter dated 17 Ṣafar, 1325, in S̱iqat al-Islām, A., *Nāmahāyi Tabrīz* (ed. by Afshār, Ī.), Tehran, 2000, p. 36.

84 1 Rabī' I 1325, in S̱iqat al-Islām, A., *Nāmahāyi Tabrīz*, p. 40.

85 S̱iqat al-Islām-i Tabrīzī, *Majmū'ayi Ās̱ār-i Qalmīyi S̱iqat al-Islām-i Tabrīzī*, p. 48.

86 Letter dated 1 Ṣafar, 1325, in S̱iqat al-Islām, *Nāmahāyi Tabrīz*, p. 41.

87 Letter dated 15 Rabī' I, 1325, in S̱iqat al-Islām, *Nāmahāyi Tabrīz*, p. 56.

to the bailiff.' They refuse to sow the grain they are given and the cities starve.[88] Again, for the most part there is only mention of agitation and not of agitators. He reports these events as if they are spontaneous.[89] Indeed, there is an increasing public indifference or hostility towards the landed class.[90]

Thus, there is no evidence that the social democrats or the Secret Center participated in this peasant agitation; the name associated with it was Shaykh Salīm, followed by other, anonymous, turbulent preachers.

In another instance, bread rioters lynched a hoarder (who happened to have been a constitutionalist).[91] S̱iqat al-Islām noted in passing that the hoarder had been under the protection of the Secret Center.[92]

The social democrats, however, had no scruples about extorting guns and funds from the people. This became an issue particularly with the conservative clergy which would go over to fight the constitutionalists. 'By day they go to the people asking for money and guns. The Caucasians and Mīrzā Āqā Esfahānī and Ḥājī ʿAlī Davāfurūsh and ʿAlī Monsieur must not remain in our province,' said a group of clerics who followed Mīr Hāshim, one of the first Tabriz constitutionalists who would soon betray the cause.[93]

---

88 Letter dated 29 Rabīʿ I, (1325), in S̱iqat al-Islām, *Nāmahāyi Tabrīz*, p. 72. See also S̱iqat al-Islām-i Tabrīzī, *Majmūʿayi Ās̱ār-i Qalmīyi S̱iqat al-Islām-i Tabrīzī*, p. 34.

89 Letter dated 8 Jumadā II, 1325, in S̱iqat al-Islām, *Nāmahāyi Tabrīz*, p. 170; Letter dated 21 Jumadā II, 1325, in S̱iqat al-Islām, *Nāmahāyi Tabrīz*, p. 180.

90 Letter dated 21 Jumadā II, 1325, in S̱iqat al-Islām, *Nāmahāyi Tabrīz*, p. 180.

91 Kasravī, *Tārīkh-i Mashrūṭayi Īrān*, pp. 354–355.

92 Letter dated 24 Jumadā II, 1325 in S̱iqat al-Islām, *Nāmahāyi Tabrīz*, p. 98. S̱iqat al-Islām identified him as a Caucasian Social Democrat, but he throughout confused the Caucasian and the Tabrīz Social Democrats/Secret Center. Thus, at one point, he identifies ʿAlī Monsieur, the leader of the Secret Center, as a supporter of the Caucasian faction. Again, he identified Nawbar and Charandāb as boroughs of Tabrīz supporting the Caucasians, but Nawbar was the base of the Secret Center and ʿAlī Monsieur's home borough! (S̱iqat al-Islām, *Nāmahāyi Tabrīz*, p. 118, p. 125, p. 126), although Laylabad seems to have been pro-Caucasian (Ṭāhirzāda-Bihzād, *Qīyām-i Āzarbāyjān dar Inqilāb-i Mashrūṭīyyat-i Īrān*, p. 290) Since this lynching was near the telegraph post and the Secret Center had dispatched agents there (Ṭāhirzāda-Bihzād, *Qīyām-i Āzarbāyjān dar Inqilāb-i Mashrūṭīyyat-i Īrān*, p. 471), it seems clear that this mujahid was a member of the Secret Center.

93 Letter dated 8 Jumadā II, 1325, in S̱iqat al-Islām, *Nāmahāyi Tabrīz*, p. 168. See also Letter 21 dated Jumadā II, 1325, in S̱iqat al-Islām, *Nāmahāyi Tabrīz*, p. 186.

War with Shuturbān

A forgotten event which served as a prelude to the civil war in Tabriz was an attack by the Secret Center's mujahids on Shuturbān, which occurred in mid-June 1907. S̱iqat al-Islām writes that there were four fedayi factions in Tabriz:

> The Caucasian faction run by ʿAlī Monsieur, the Shuturbān faction, another led by one Mashhadi Ḥasan, and one led by Mīr Hāshim, each with its own seal and membership cards. (The Shuturbān faction is likely identical with Mīr Hāshim's.) 'Ḥājī Ṣamad, Qalʿavānbāshī, Yūsuf Khazdūz, Mīr Taqī Chāyfurūsh [Chāychī], etc. are members of the Caucasian fedayis, at whose helm ʿAlī Monsieur has established himself, and went and gave a group of Shuturbānīs what for. There were not more than a handful of Caucasian mujahid .... They went under the command and banner of this few, which called itself the [Secret] Center. Mīrzā Ghaffār Zunūzī[94], who had come here in Muharram and makes speeches and sermons and causes disturbances, is a member of this Center.'

He continued:

> In early Jumadā I [mid June, 1907], there was an outbreak of violence between two members of the ... Shuturbān mujahids and the [Secret] Center mujahids. A [Secret Center] detail went to the former's home and threw their wives and children into the street and a commotion ensued. A deputation was sent from the Ottoman Embassy but [the Secret Center mujahids] didn't accept it, saying, 'We follow the [Secret] Center....' That night, the Shuturbān mujahids summoned Ḥājī Ṣamad and Qalʿavānbāshī to their borough and threatened them and they promised to leave them alone....

Then a Caucasian went missing and so its mojaheds tried but failed to shut the Shuturbān bazaar down. A Caucasian mojahed was captured in the process. The Caucasians came back and attacked a coffee shop, killing an employee in the process. The Caucasians[95] asked S̱iqat al-Islām to intercede with the Shuturbānīs and recover one of their men whom they'd captured and got him released.

---

94 Identified by Kasravī as a Caucasian mujahid of surpassing eloquence in *Tārīkh-i Mashrūṭayi Irān*, p. 355, p. 455, and p. 473.

95 And accusing him of being a member of the Caucasian mujahid. Letter dated 12 Jumadā I, 1325, in S̱iqat al-Islām, *Nāmahāyi Tabrīz*, p. 118.

The next episode in this conflict had the qualities of a comic opera. That night, a group of Shuturbānīs were standing guard when a group of people from the Tabrizī borough of Ahrāb (which was a rival of Shuturbān) surrounded the house of the Russian consul as sentries. When the consul returned, he saw the sentries and asked them to leave. Not having succeeded,[96] the consul summoned his Cossacks and ordered them to shoot the sentries, who fled or surrendered, many abandoning their weapons.[97]

In the meantime, a victim of the Secret Center attack died of his wounds and a *taʿzīyya*, or Shiite passion play, was held in his memory, inflaming popular emotions. Ultimately, the Caucasians, including ʿAlī Monsieur, left town on their own and Mīr Hāshim was ordered out of town for staging the *taʿzīyya*, which was considered a provocation.

The Anjuman held a meeting a few days later at which it was decided that no more party membership cards were to be issued. Ḥājī Mahdī Kūzikanānī, a leader of the Anjuman and future secretary to Sattār Khān, rose up and demanded the expulsion of the Caucasians. The people of Nawbar, ʿAlī Monsieur's home borough, escorted the Caucasians back, but the government sent cavalry to drive them out.

This expulsion of the Caucasians was taken as an opportunity to settle scores. ʿAlīqulū Khān, the editor of *Āzarbāyjān*,[98] for instance, was also exiled, along with thirty others. The municipality arrested ʿAlī Monsieur, who seems to have managed to return to Tabriz, but he was freed by force by Mīr Taqī Chāychī with a band of Caucasians. The repressive measures sparked an outburst of anger among the more militant constitutionalists. 'Shaykh Salīm went to the pulpit and screamed that in the two hours we've been inattentive, the autocracy has returned.'

The Anjuman decided to organise an exchange of visits between delegations from each borough.[99] S̱iqat al-Islām explained that forging bonds between the

96 They left to call Mr. Zakarīya, who told them to return to their positions. S̱iqat al-Islam found this baffling, but said that this story was given by all the people from Laylabād he questioned. Letter dated 12 Jumadā I, 1325, in S̱iqat al-Islām, *Nāmahāyi Tabrīz*, pp. 117–118.

97 The Shuturbānīs said that the sentries were sent there on allegations that the people of Shuturbān were going to attack the consul's home. They added that this was a provocation by the neighboring borough of Laylabād, which supported the Caucasians, led by ʿAlī Monsieur, to bring them under suspicion. Letter dated 12 Jumadā I, 1325, in S̱iqat al-Islām, *Nāmahāyi Tabrīz*, pp. 117–118.

98 A strongly Iranian nationalistic journal, written in a mixture of Azerbaijani Turkish and Persian. See Motika, Raoul, *Die politische Öffentlichkeit Iranisch-Aserbaidschans während der Konstitutionellen Revolution in Spiegel der Täbriser Zeitung Āzarbāyǧān*, Frankfurt am Main, 2001.

99 Kasravī, *Tārīkh-i Mashrūṭayi Īrān*, pp. 393 ff. provides a detailed report on this based on *Anjuman*.

boroughs would help undo the mischief done by the social democrats because the boroughs were divided along pro-Caucasian and anti-Caucasian lines.[100]

Even after this, however, the social democrats and their fellow travelers made trouble. Thus, Mīr Taqī Chāychī established himself as 'the General of Nawbar', seizing the arsenal and arresting and imprisoning people at will.[101]

This conflict led to a flurry of angry flyers being published by the conservatives in Shuturbān as well as articles in the conservative *Mullā ʿAmū*.[102] One of these is translated into Persian and published in Aḥmad Kasravī's *History*.[103] It called on the pious Muslim Iranians who 'for long ages ... did not bow [their] heads in obedience to despotic kings' not to 'become prisoners of five or six vagrants from the Caucasus.' It called on the boroughs of Tabriz targeted by the Secret Center and its allies to resist the death sentence they imposed on them. When Mīr Taqī Chāychī and Īt Khalīl[104] brazenly told them to stick to their religious studies, not a single zealous Muslim answered that the principle aim of the constitution is learning the shariat and applying it and not peddling bitter tea.[105] A constitutionalist cleric went to Shuturbān and came to see the justice of their side and tried to reason with their enemies, asking them, 'Why do you consider yourself obliged to murder and loot the people in the boroughs of Sorkhāb and Shuturbān?' The article continues that ʿAlī Monsieur replied, 'You yourself came as a pauper and have accumulated wealth in our borough. Now you have learned absurdities from the boroughs of Sorkhāb and Shuturbān.' He eventually left the constitutionalist militants in disgust.[106]

Nāhīd-Āzar unearthed a number of these documents. This excerpt must suffice here:

---

100 Kasravī, *Tārīkh-i Mashrūṭayi Īrān*, pp. 121–122. He later lists Laylabād, Nawbar, and Charandāb as being pro-Caucasian. Khīyaban he considers to be acting according to it expedience. Kasravī, *Tārīkh-i Mashrūṭayi Iran*, p. 125.

101 S̱iqat al-Islām, *Majmuʿayi Ās̱ār-i Qalmīyi S̱iqat al-Islām-i Tabrīzī*, p. 65. In a letter dated 15 Jumadā I, 1325, in S̱iqat al-Islām, *Nāmahāyi Tabrīz*, p. 135, he calls him a dragon who has fallen upon the people.

102 The only other discussion of this broadsheet I've seen in the literature is Motika, *Die politische Öffentlichkeit Iranisch-Aserbaidschans während der Konstitutionellen Revolution in Spiegel der Täbriser Zeitung Āzarbāyǧān*, pp. 187 ff.

103 Kasravī, *Tārīkh-i Mashrūṭayi Irān*, pp. 536–538.

104 Literally 'Dog Khalīl', a killer deployed by ʿAlī Monsieur, discusses elsewhere in this article.

105 Chāychī means 'tea merchant' in Turkish.

106 Kasravī, *Tārīkh-i Mashrūṭayi Īrān*, pp. 536–538. See also ʿAbd al-Husayn Nāhīd-Āzar, in Hamrāz, R., 'Markaz-i Ghaybīyi Tabrīz', p. 57.

> Didn't you see how some atheists ... for no reason but because of the orders of a foolish madman and under the instigation of seductive heretics for two days descended on all the neighborhoods of the Muslims, who are mostly descendants of His Holiness the Prophet, and the blessed shrines of Sayyid Ḥamza, Sayyid Raḥīm, and Sāḥib al-ʿAmr, which are in the boroughs of Sorkhāb and Shuturbān, like wolves with their guns.... These gentlemen the hooligans who call themselves Caucasian, have allied themselves with degenerates and troublemakers and invaded Sorkhāb and Shuturbān upon orders of the atheist ʿAlī Monsieur and Mīrzā Muḥammad ʿAlī Khān the Uneducated [*bītarbīyyat* for *tarbīyyat*, education]. You sons of bitches, do you imagine that they won't settle their score with you?

The Caucasian Mujahids and the Tabriz Mujahids

While this was going on, fighting broke out, this time between social democratic factions. Even before the fighting between the Secret Center and the Shuturbān mojaheds had broken out, there was 'a violent falling out between the Caucasian Social Democrats and the Tabriz Social Democrats.'[107]

The Caucasian social-democrats (so-called because they dressed like Caucasians, although they were from Tabriz) were more cosmopolitan and less respectful of the clergy, and this troubled the population. What set off the conflict, though, was their obedience to the social democratic center in Baku and not the Secret Center in Tabriz, and they intrigued against ʿAlī Monsieur and his comrades. As the tension mounted, the bazaar closed on 8–10 Jumada I (June 19–21). Kasravī writes, 'But since most of the leaders of both sides were wise and experienced, they prevented bloodshed and made peace with each other without any publicity. Starting Sunday, the bazaars opened, and the people went about their business. Nothing had happened in public and nothing was written about it in the newspapers. ʿAlī Monsieur and his comrades showed here their competence.'[108]

As we shall see, things were not so simple.

A primary source on this struggle was Ṭāhirzāda-Bihzād, who is surprisingly frank about ʿAlī Monsieur's aims and methods. With Kasravī, he writes that the Caucasian party took its orders directly from the Caucasus (which he refers to as

107 Letter dated 25 Rabīʿ II, 1325 in S̱iqat al-Islām, *Nāmahāyi Tabrīz*, p. 106. Note that the Tabrīz Social Democrats, who followed ʿAlī Monsieur, had heretofore been referred to as 'Caucasian.' This term is now reserved for their factional rivals.

108 Kasravī, *Tārīkh-i Mashrūṭayi Īrān*, p. 391.

Tiflis rather than Baku) rather than the Secret Center. However, he mentions the killing of several Caucasian mujahids in the struggle.[109]

S̱iqat al-Islām wrote in rather more detail that, 'the Caucasian social democrats became more powerful after they occupied the [Tabriz] telegraph post. Sedition and disturbances exceeded all bounds.' 'The Tabriz social democrats dislike the Caucasian social democrats, whom they see as a source of trouble.[110] A day doesn't go by without murder and mayhem.'[111] He blamed the smuggling of guns into town on the Caucasian social democrats.[112]

In the end, he reports, fighting did not break out on Friday as expected.[113] But all was not over. The forces under Ḥājī Ṣamad Khayyāt 'the Caucasian faction's sword-bearer' (whom we've mentioned before) went to the house of a baker who was a member of the other faction and trouble arose which was exacerbated by the Caucasian faction and the women fled from the house. But this, too, was patched up.[114]

The Assassination of opponents

Two months after ʿAlī Monsieur crushed this threat to his leadership, another arose.

Little enough of Mashhadī Yūsuf Khazdūz's role in the Constitutional Revolution is known. I have not found his name mentioned in contemporary sources such as the newspaper *Anjuman*, until his execution at the hands of his comrades.

Our chief source about him in the memoir literature is Ṭāhirzāda-Bihzād's. He reports Khazdūz was a member of the leadership body of the Secret Center.[115] He lists him among Tabriz's twenty 'orators and principle writers,'[116] singling him out for his ability to transport his audience and fire it up to charge into battle.'[117] He was called 'the Mirabeau of Tabriz.'[118]

Unfortunately, the thing that he is best known for is his execution, on 2 Shaʿbān

---

109 Kasravī, *Tārīkh-i Mashrūṭayi Īrān*, pp. 455–456.

110 Letter dated 1 Jumadā I, 1325, in S̱iqat al-Islām, *Nāmahāyi Tabrīz*, p. 109.

111 Letter dated 1 Jumadā I, 1325, in S̱iqat al-Islām, *Nāmahāyi Tabrīz*, p. 107.

112 Letter dated 1 Jumadā I, 1325, in S̱iqat al-Islām, *Nāmahāyi Tabrīz*, p. 108.

113 Letter dated 5 Jumadā I, 1325, in S̱iqat al-Islām, *Nāmahāyi Tabrīz*, p. 115.

114 Letter dated 5 Jumadā I, 1325, in S̱iqat al-Islām, *Nāmahāyi Tabrīz*, p. 115.

115 Ṭāhirzāda-Bihzād, *Qīyām-i Āzarbāyjān dar Inqilāb-i Mashrūṭīyyat-i Īrān*, p. 62.

116 Ṭāhirzāda-Bihzād, *Qīyām-i Āzarbāyjān dar Inqilāb-i Mashrūṭīyyat-i Īrān*, p. 21.

117 Ṭāhirzāda-Bihzād, *Qīyām-i Āzarbāyjān dar Inqilāb-i Mashrūṭīyyat-i Īrān*, p. 386.

118 Ṭāhirzāda-Bihzād, *Qīyām-i Āzarbāyjān dar Inqilāb-i Mashrūṭīyyat-i Īrān*, p. 425.

1325 (September 10, 1907), by his comrades.[119] A rather terrifyingly exultant report of this is given in the pages of *Anjuman*,[120] where he was accused of posing as a fedaii to advance unnamed personal interests. As a result, he was spied on by his comrades who uncovered unspecified malfeasance on his part which called for execution. He was then repeatedly warned that the job of a mujahid was strictly limited to protecting Islam and Iran and freeing the people from oppression, and that he must comport himself accordingly, but in some unstipulated way he did not do so.

Ṭāhirzāda-Bihzād believed that it was the result of a sense of arrogance and conceitedness which led him to see himself as superior to leaders more senior than himself. 'He was repeatedly warned orally and in writing by the Secret Center's elders, but when he persisted with his wayward speech, he was killed…'[121] Later in his memoirs, he is a bit more skeptical of the assassination. Of Khazdūz, he wrote:

> A member of the Central Committee who had an astonishing influence over the party members and the people had overshadowed ʿAlī Monsieur, who ordered him assassinated in broad daylight… The next day, the assassins had lunch in a chelo kabab shop and no one troubled them.

Having cowed his enemies, ʿAlī Monsieur could rest secure.[122] But in a footnote, the author added, 'He was overshadowing ʿAlī Monsieur. Perhaps he had also been guilty of some crime, although I don't know.'[123]

Kasravī himself saw this as part of a policy of purging the mujahids in the aftermath of violent or potentially violent conflicts in their own ranks.[124]

ʿAlī Monsieur had already faced down one challenge to his authority, and he showed he was ready to resort to arms if necessary to do so again. That rivalry between mujahid factions almost led to civil war made the Secret Center's absolute leader anxious about a challenge from within.

Another instrument in intimidating the population was the aforementioned Īt Khalīl, whose ability to reach and destroy his enemies was used to great effect. When Tabriz's popular new governor, Mahdiqulū Khan Mukhbir al-Salṭana,

119 Kasravī, *Tārīkh-i Mashrūṭayi Īrān*, p. 467.

120 'Vaqʿāyi Shāhri-Mokāfāt-i Mujahid-i Muharibi' in, *Anjuman*, vol. 1, no. 133 (6 Shaʿban, 1325), p. 3.

121 Ṭāhirzāda-Bihzād, *Qīyām-i Āzarbāyjān dar Inqilāb-i Mashrūṭīyyat-i Īrān*, pp. 385–387.

122 Ṭāhirzāda-Bihzād, *Qīyām-i Āzarbāyjān dar Inqilāb-i Mashrūṭīyyat-i Īrān*, p. 454.

123 Ṭāhirzāda-Bihzād, *Qīyām-i Āzarbāyjān dar Inqilāb-i Mashrūṭīyyat-i Īrān*, p. 453.

124 Kasravī, *Tārīkh-i Mashrūṭayi Īrān*, p. 391.

confronted ʿAlī Monsieur with his alliance with Īt Khalīl, he was told that he needed him to protect him against assassination, referring to a recent attempt on his life. Īt Khalīl finally went too far and murdered someone in broad daylight. Upon his arrest, he brazenly confessed to all his murders, believing that ʿAlī Monsieur's power would save him, not realising that the social democrats had abandoned him because his wanton acts of brutality had turned the people against them, and he paid for this with his life.[125] In any case, it was generally believed in Tabriz that ʿAlī Monsieur's killers could take the life of anyone who challenge him.[126]

The End of the Social Democrats

Ultimately, Ṭāhirzāda-Bihzād took his group out of the rest of the social democrats because the latter were including undisciplined elements of dubious character, including old *farrāsh*es. This group called itself the National Guard and was composed of 'literate and educated youth'. The run of the mujahids thought these well-heeled fighters were unfit for the rigors of battle. On the other hand, put off by their perceived snobbery, the mujahid leaders sent them to the most dangerous fields of combat. For all one might imagine that the snappily-dressed National Guardsmen were softies, they contributed many martyrs in some of the most dangerous and decisive battles for the defense of Tabriz.[127] The Democratic Party, recently founded by Taqīzāda, also looked down on the mujahids, for the same reason.

It appears that ʿAlī Monsieur met his fate before the Russians arrived in Tabriz.[128] One story is that he was poisoned at the Russian consulate; no reason for his visit is given.[129] Another is that he died of natural causes.[130]

---

125 Ṭāhirzāda-Bihzād, *Qīyām-i Āzarbāyjān dar Inqilāb-i Mashrūṭīyyat-i Īrān*, pp. 136–137, which gives a portrait of the rise and fall of him as a popular hero.

126 Ṭāhirzāda-Bihzād, *Qīyām-i Āzarbāyjān dar Inqilāb-i Mashrūṭīyyat-i Īrān*, pp. 454–455.

127 Ṭāhirzāda-Bihzād, *Qīyām-i Āzarbāyjān dar Inqilāb-i Mashrūṭīyyat-i Īrān*, pp. 263–65, pp. 301–312.

128 Neither Kasravī nor Ṭāhirzāda-Bihzād mention the circumstances of his death. They both have him as having certainly died before the rising. Indeed, there is no mention of his participating in rising itself. Kasravī, *Tārīkh-i Hijda Sālayi Āzarbāyjāni*, p. 321; Ṭāhirzāda-Bihzād, *Qīyam-i Āzarbāyjān dar Inqilāb-i Mashrūṭīyyat-i Īrān*, p. 456.

129 The source for this is given as Browne, E. G., *Nāmahā'i az Tabrīz*, p. 206, referred to in Sardārīnīyā, *Naqsh-i Markaz-i Ghaybīyi Tabrīz dar Inqilāb-i Mashrūṭiyyat*, p. 30. But there is no reference to ʿAlī Monsieur having been poisoned in the English original.

130 Jāvīd, S. takes this position in his *Fidākāran-i Farāmūsh Shuda*, p. 23 (cited in Sardārīnīyā, Ṣ., *ʿAlī Monsieur*, Tehran, 1980, p. 84).

With the entrance of Russian troops into constitutionalist Tabriz to relieve the city of its eleven-month siege by royalist forces, the central government prevailed upon the mujahids to disband.[131] The Russians imposed a reign of terror on the beleaguered city, leading to a spontaneous and, for a short time, very successful uprising against the Russian occupiers.[132] But the Anjuman saw that there was nothing to do ultimately but to negotiate a settlement with the Russians, and this settlement called for the exile of the anti-Russian mujahids.[133] The dispersal of the mujahids followed by the brutal Russian occupation of Azerbaijan effectively ended a political era. A new era of mass party party politics began. A hybrid creation like the Secret Center, part political party, part old-fashioned street fighters, saw its day come and go. It was replaced by the democrats and the moderates of the second *Majlis* period.

131 Ṭāhirzāda-Bihzād, *Qīyām-i Āzarbāyjān dar Inqilāb-i Mashrūṭīyyat-i Īrān*, pp. 260–62.

132 Kasravī, *Tārīkh-i Hijde Sālayi Āzarbāyjāni*, pp. 262 ff.

133 Kasravī, *Tārīkh-i Hijde Sālayi Āzarbāyjāni*, pp. 287, 297.

Bibliography

Newspapers

Anjuman

Āzarbāyjān

Books and Articles

Algar, H., 'An Introduction to the History of Freemasonry in Iran,' *Middle Eastern Studies*, vol. 6, no. 3, 1970.

Amīrkhīzī, I., *Qīyām-i Āzarbāyjān va Sattār Khān*, Tehran, 1960.

Bayat, M., 'Freemasonry and the Constitutional Revolution in Iran: 1905–1911', in Önnerfors, A. and Sommer, D. (eds.), *Freemasonry and Fraternalism in the Middle East*, Sheffield, 2008, pp. 109–150.

Browne, E. G., *Letters from Tabriz* (transl. by Javadi, H.), Washington, DC, 2008.

Chaqueri, C., *Origins of Social Democracy in Modern Iran*, Seattle, 2001.

Fatḥī, N., *Didār bā Hamrazm-i Sattār Khān*, Tehran, 1972.

Fatḥī, N., *Sokhangūyān-i Sigānayi Āzārbāyjān dar Inqilāb-i Mashrūṭīyyat-i Īrān*, Tehran, 1977.

Hamrāz, R., '‘Alī Monsieur', in *Mahd-i Tamaddun*, vol. 1, no. 16, 2014.

Hamrāz, R., 'Markaz-i Ghaybīyi Tabriz', in *Mahd-i Tamaddun*, vol. 1, no. 16, 2014

Kasravī, A., *Tārīkh-i Hizhda Sālayi Āzarbāyjān* (*Paymān*) vol. 1, no date

Kasravī, A., *Tārīkh-i Hejda Sālayi Āzarbāyjān*, vol. 2 no date.

Kasravī, A., *Tārīkh-i Mashrūṭayi Īrān*, Tehran, 1975.

Lambton, Ann K. S., 'Secret Societies and the Persian Revolution of 1905–6', in *St. Antony's Papers*, vol. 4, 1958.

Mahdī M., *Rijāl-i Āzarbāyjān dar ‘Aṣr-i Mashrūṭīyyat*, Tehran, 1949.

Motika, Raoul, *Die politische Öffentlichkeit Iranisch-Aserbaidschans während der Konstitutionellen Revolution in Spiegel der Täbriser Zeitung Āẕarbāyǧān*, Frankfurt am Main, 2001

Rā’īn, I., *Farāmūshkhāna va Farāmūsānarī dar Īrān*, London, 1978.

Riżāzāda-Malak, R, *Chakīdayi Inqilāb: Ḥeydar Khān ‘Amūoghlū*, Tehran, 1972.

Ṣanī‘zada, Ṣ., 'Farāzhāyi az Zindigīyi Shādravān Ḥaj Rasūl Sidqīyānī', *Mahd-i Tamaddun*, vol. 1, no. 16, 2014.

Sardārīnīyā, Ṣ., *Naqsh-i Markaz-i Ghaybīyi Tabriz dar Inqilāb-i Mashrūṭiyyat*, Tehran, 1984.

S̱iqat al-Islām, A., *Nāmahāyi Tabriz* (ed. by Afshār, Ī.), Tehran, 2000.

S̲iqat al-Islām-i Tabrizī, ʿA., *Majmūʿayi Ās̲ār-i Qalmīyi S̲iqat al-Islām-i Tabrizī*, (ed. by Fatḥī, N.), Isfahan, no date.
Ṭāhirzāda-Bihzād, K., *Qīyām-i Āzarbāyjān dar Inqilāb-i Mashrūṭīyyat-i Īrān*, Tehran, 1984.
Taqīzāda, Ḥ., *Tārīkh-i Avāyel-i Enqelāb va Mashrūṭīyyat-i Īrān*, in Afshār, Ī. (ed.), *Maqalāt-i Taqizāda*, Tehran, vol. 5, 1970.
Taqīzāda, Ḥ., *Zindigīyi Tūfānī: Khātirāt-i Sayyid Ḥasan Taqīzada* (ed. by Afshār, Ī.) , Tehran, 1989.
Yazdānī, S., 'Dar bārayi Firqayi Ijtimāʿīyyūn ʿ Āmīyyūn-i Īran', *Faslnāmayi ʿIlmi-Takhassusīyi Tārīkh*, vol. 1, no. 3, 2006.

9

Early Translations of Modern European Philosophy. On the Significance of an Under-Researched Phenomenon for the Study of Modern Iranian Intellectual History

Roman Seidel

One distinct feature of Iranian intellectual history in the Qajar era was the beginning of the reception of European philosophical trends which took place in the larger context of various processes of knowledge-transmission between Europe and the Middle East. Although the contribution of many outstanding intellectuals who played a major role in the appropriation of Enlightenment thought and other European intellectual trends are known to us, we still now very little about which European writings were explicitly discussed in their intellectual networks, which of these were actually accessible to them and in which rendition or edition. Throughout the scholarly literature on the reception of Enlightenment thought by Iranian thinkers we find statements and some evidence that they have adopted various doctrines of eminent European thinkers such as Voltaire, Rousseau, John Stuart Mill and the like. However, accurate references to the sources the Iranian intellectuals might have used are still usually very rare in most of these studies. An important case in point in this context is the phenomenon of the translation of philosophical works in that period, that in many respects deserves more attention. For one thing we are far from having an even approximate picture of which European philosophical works were translated into Persian, for another some of theses translations were carried out in a mediated way. Either because they did not rely on the original but were conducted by proxy of an already translated version (Ottoman Turkish, Russian, Arabic) or they were shortened, extended, commented upon and merged with other text and thereby not immediately recognisable as translations. The paper discusses some examples of this phenomenon (for instance Descartes' Discours de la Méthode or the question of textbook translations) and argues for the urgent need for an increased and focussed scholarly commitment in this field of study.

One of the most important topics in modern Iranian intellectual history is often discussed under the heading 'Iran's encounter with the West'.[1] The reception of ideas from Enlightenment thought as the foundation of modern European philosophy is, undoubtedly, a highly significant facet of this 'encounter'. What we call 'the Enlightenment' and 'modern European philosophy', however, are multifaceted entities and the image of an encounter between seemingly two parties or 'cultures' is perhaps not an accurate one. What is meant by this encounter is better characterised by manifold mediated and reciprocal processes of knowledge transmission between Europe and the Middle East: an entangled intellectual history. With regard to the Iranian intellectuals in the Qajar era right before the Constitutional Revolution these processes narrate the story of the adaptation of ideas, of experimentation with different literary genres and of writing as a means for political activism. Translations of modern European philosophical texts constitute an important aspect of this story and a sophisticated evaluation of this aspect could contribute significantly to our understanding of the narratives of the Enlightenment in Iran.

Prior to an extensive analysis of relevant source material, it may be helpful to start with some preliminary reflections on the issue of Enlightenment and European philosophy on the one hand, and the question of what counts as 'translation of philosophy' on the other. The notion of Enlightenment is an ambiguous term as it is for one thing related to certain ideas and doctrines and for another to an intellectual movement which, heterogeneous with regard to its different protagonist, had a tremendous impact on the social reality of European societies. Moreover, it is, for that reason, often misleadingly regarded as an exclusive cultural heritage of Europe.

With regard to the aforementioned ideas and doctrines one would identify a number of general tendencies of thought characteristic of the phenomenon of Enlightenment thinking. Among them is the critique of religious dogmatism (not necessarily of religion in itself) – a departure from classical metaphysics and an orientation towards empiricism. All of this culminates in a confidence in the power of human reason to achieve true knowledge of the world (nature) and the right guidelines of morality. To be sure all of these general ideas were not unprecedented in the history of philosophy, what *was* new, however, is that they turned into a broader social discourse which had enormous political consequences, most significantly the

1 See for instance: Boroujerdi, Mehrzad, *Iranian Intellectuals and the West. The Tormented Triumph of Nativism*, Syracuse, NY, 1996; Gheissari, A., *Iranian Intellectuals in the 20th Century*, Austin, TX, 1998; Vahdat, F., *God and Juggernaut: Iran's Intellectual Encounter with Modernity*, Syracuse, NY, 2002.

French Revolution and its aftermath. The intellectual paradigm shifts of enlightenment that laid the foundations of modern philosophy did not happen all of a sudden rather it was the result of a long process of interpretation, refutation and modification that was carried by various thinkers, intellectuals and representatives of state and church. From a certain point in history – the second half of the nineteenth century – Middle Eastern thinkers were also part of this discourse, not merely in the role of passive emulators but as creative political activists and writers.

The significance of expatriate intellectuals is very well known and can hardly be exaggerated.[2] These thinkers began to organise themselves in various circles and intellectual networks in Europe, the Ottoman Empire (especially Istanbul and Egypt), and the Caucasus region under Russian control. Within these networks the public, yet always precarious, debate about ideas of truth and reality became visible as the very character of the Enlightenment as such and resulted in a variety of intellectual writings. A comprehensive (intellectual) history of these expatriate communities, their inner circles and their translocal interconnectedness in general as well as their significance for Iranian history in particular has yet to be written. One specific aspect of the intellectual activities of these networks is the engagement with the ideas of eminent European philosophers. Throughout the scholarly literature on the reception of Enlightenment thought by Iranian thinkers we find statements and some evidence that they adopted various doctrines of eminent European thinkers such as Voltaire, Rousseau, John Stuart Mill, David Hume and the like. However, accurate references to the actual sources these Iranian intellectuals might have used are usually still very rare in most of these studies.[3]

The circulation of writings by expatriate Iranian thinkers played a decisive role in the dissemination of modern European philosophy. Although it was not

2 A reasonable vantage point for such an endeavour would be a systematic examination of expatriate journals, their themes and contributors. For an exemplary case study in this field, see Pistor-Hatam, A., *Nachrichtenblatt, Informationsbörse und Diskussionsforum: Aḫtar-e Estānbūl (1876–1896): Anstöße zur frühen persischen Moderne*, Münster, 1999. This study, however, does not specifically deal with the reception of European philosophy.

3 See: Bayat-Philipp, M., 'Mīrzā Āqā Khān Kirmānī: A Nineteenth-Century Persian Nationalist', in *Middle Eastern Studies*, vol. 10, no. 1, 1974, pp. 36–59; Bayat-Philipp, M., 'The Concepts of Religion and Government in the Thought of Mirza Aqa Khan Kirmani, a Nineteenth-Century Persian Revolutionary', in *International Journal of Middle East Studies*, vol. 5, no. 4, 1974, pp. 381–400; Masroori, C., 'European Thought in Nineteenth-Century Iran: David Hume and Others', in *Journal of the History of Ideas,* vol. 61, no. 4, 2000, pp. 657–674, Sanjabi, M. B., 'Rereading the Enlightenment: Akhundzada and His Voltaire', in *Iranian Studies* vol. 28, no. 1–2, 1995, pp. 39–60.

introduced into the Iranian intellectual realm in a scholarly fashion it encouraged subsequent thinkers to engage with it either exclusively or in comparison with Islamic thought.[4] The most prominent protagonists popularising Enlightenment thought in Iran are perhaps eminent intellectuals, such as Mirzā Malkum Khān (d.1909), Mirzā Āqā Khān Kermanī (d.1896), Mirzā Fatḥʿalī Akhundzāda (d. 1878), Abd al-Raḥīm Tālibuf (d. 1910) and Sayyid Jamāl ad-Dīn Asadābādī, known as Afghānī, (d. 1897).[5] They closely followed the intellectual discourses in their host countries and related them to the Islamic intellectual tradition as well as to recent political developments in the Muslim world in general, or Iran in particular. Although the writings of these thinkers appear to be the most influential ones, it is important to bear in mind that an enormous number of intellectual writings by scholars of the Qajar period have yet to be examined with respect to the early reception of European philosophy. Important sources that have to be considered for such an endeavour are, for example, correspondences, memoirs, travelogues, textbooks and fiction.

Broadly speaking, the intellectual commitment of theses Iranian reformers materialised in two sorts of writings which sometimes are not easily separated from each other: on the one hand, there were politically engaged essays, which primarily appeared in exile journals,[6] and monographs, also mainly published abroad but likewise circulated in Iran – some of these writings were not even published but circulated as handwritten copies.[7] On the other hand, we find various adaptations

4 Literature, particularly that focusing on the reception of European philosophy, is rather limited. Mention should be made to Mujtahidī, K., *Āšināʾī-yi īrānīyān bā falsafahā-yi ğadīd-i gharb* [The acquaintance of the Iranians with Modern Western Philosophy], Teheran, 1384/2005–6, and Heydari, A. A., *Rezeption der westlichen Philosophie durch iranische Denker in der Kadscharenzeit*, unpublished Dissertation, Rheinische Friedrich-Wilhelms-Universität, Bonn, 2003.

5 The most influential scholarly evaluation of the reception of Europe thought by Iranian intellectual is a series of monographs by Firidūn Ādamiyyat: *Amīr Kabīr va Īrān* (1969); *Andīšihā-yi Mīrzā Fatḥʿalī Ākhundzāda* (1970); *Andīšihā-yi Mīrzā Āqā Khān Kirmānī* (1978); *Andīšihā-yi Ṭālibuf Tabrīzī* (1984).

6 For an overview of the relevant journals and their significance, see various entries on the respective journals in *Encyclopaedia Iranica*; see also Āriyanpūr, Y., *Az Ṣabā tā Mīnā*, vol. 1, [5th edition], Teheran, 1372/1993–4, pp. 249–252; for *Akhtar* see Pistor-Hatam, *Nachrichtenblatt, Informationsbörse und Diskussionsforum*.

7 The question as to which of these writings were circulated in Iran, by whom, and to what extent they were read still remains to be studied in more detail. What is known, however, is that there were various circles in Iran who organised the distribution of the exile journals. An important case

of specific doctrines from modern European philosophical works rendered into Persian in different forms, length and accuracy. These texts were either integrated into the mentioned essayistic writings or written as independent translations of articles and sometimes even of entire books translated from European languages into Persian. They therefore not only influenced the intellectual discourse in Iran but also had an impact on Persian as a philosophical language.[8]

Translation and Appropriation

The appropriation of Enlightenment thought is therefore closely related to the phenomenon of translation, especially of philosophical writings. The early translation of modern European philosophy is, as I shall argue, a phenomenon that deserves more scholarly attention, both with regard to the European reference texts and their transmission until they were received by the Iranian intellectuals, as well as with regard to the translations themselves and their subsequent reception by Iranian thinkers.

As for the issue of the European source texts, we still know very little about exactly which European philosophical writings were explicitly discussed in intellectual networks of expatriate Iranian thinkers and which of these were actually accessible to them, and if accessible, in which rendition or edition. In other words, what do we make of the fact that, for instance, Akhundzada made reference to Voltaire, Rousseau, David Hume and John Stuart Mill? Did he have copies of their writings at his disposal? If so, which writings had he read and in which form? Since we know he didn't read either French or English it could only have been in Turkish or Russian or perhaps already in a Persian translation. Or perhaps it was rather paraphrases and summaries of certain doctrines he picked up from introductory writings, essays of, for instance, Russian intellectuals who commented on the ideas of European thinkers. He may have also been inspired by discussions with fellow reformist thinkers in Tbilisi, which in the late nineteenth century was a vibrant intellectual melting pot much like Istanbul, where thinkers, merchants, dissidents and diplomats from Europe and the Middle East would meet. That is to say that the ideas of eminent Enlightenment thinkers from Europe such as the

---

in point is the journal *Qānūn* edited by Malkum Khān. See: Algar, H., *Mirza Malkum Khan: A Study in the History of Iranian Modernism*, Oakland, 1973, pp. 193.

8 The issue of how and to what extent the philosophical language of modern Persian was influenced by these writings, for instance via the introduction of European loan words or the creation of new technical terms, is again a question that has yet to be researched in detail.

ones previously mentioned already had a history of reception within and outside Europe before they were received by Iranian intellectuals. It would perhaps be a methodological short circuit to immediately link these receptions back to the major philosophical works of these European thinkers. Then again, in a mediated way, they are of course instances of appropriations of these works.

The other issue is related to the nature and number of the relevant Persian translations themselves. As it seems we are far from having an even approximate picture of which European philosophical texts were translated into Persian in the Qajar period. More than that there are a number of further questions that still need to be addressed more thoroughly: for instance, which texts translated in that period can actually be considered as philosophical text? Is it only major philosophical treatises or also intellectual fiction, novels or travelogues? Then again which of these texts are to be categorised as translations at all? What different types of translations do we encounter? Besides attempts for literal translations we find mediated and hybrid forms of translations as well: for instance, translations, conducted by proxy of an *already* translated version (Ottoman Turkish, Russian, Arabic) or Persian versions which are either short paraphrases of the original or modifications of the source text, sometimes even longer than the original. One may also find translations merged with commentary sequences not contained in the original. As a result these writings may not immediately be recognisable as translations. What is needed though is both a sort of typology of philosophical texts translated into Persian as well as an inventory of Persian texts that can be regarded as translations of European philosophy. All of this remains to be explored in more detail in future research.

In what follows I present some preliminary observations and reflections on the issue of early translation of modern European Philosophical Texts into Persian that may be helpful as a heuristic device for a more extensive evaluation of the primary sources. For that purpose I roughly differentiate between three types of translations of philosophical texts: First, translations of major works from European philosophy; second, translations of minor philosophical texts; and third, hybrid forms of intellectual writings, which merge translation and creative adaptation of modern European philosophy.

The Translation of Major Works from European Philosophy

a) The first translation of Descartes' 'Discours de la méthode'

Let me begin with the first phenomenon, namely comprehensive translations of complete philosophical works written by eminent European thinkers. As far as we are aware, their number is very few. This may be one reason why the question of translation with regard to the appropriation of modern European philosophy has so far not been the focus of research.

Interestingly, the first complete translation of a major modern European philosophical text, René Descartes' *Discours de la méthode,* which undoubtedly counts as a foundational treatise for modern European philosophy, was not conducted by one of the expatriate thinkers. This translation emerged from a different intellectual milieu as it was initiated by the French diplomat and scholar Arthur Comte de Gobineau who resided in Tehran in the years 1855–8 and again as ambassador of France from 1861 to 1864.[9] Gobineau showed a specific interest in the philosophical tradition of Iran and obviously interacted with some of the leading philosophers of the time. Amongst them was Āqā ʿAlī Mudarris Ṭihrānī az-Zunūzī (1819–1890) a scholar who played a leading role in establishing the philosophical tradition of Mullā Ṣadā in the new Qajar capital Tehran. It was he from whom Gobineau gathered knowledge on the philosophical discourse in Iran.[10] Based on that information Gobineau gave a valuable genealogical account of Iranian post-Sadrian philosophers in his work *Les Religiones et les philosophies dans l'Asie centrale.*[11] Yet he was not only interested in observing and describing the philosophical discourse in Iran, he also intended to contribute to it by way of personal engagement. For instance, he gave introductory private lessons on European philosophy in order to enhance, in his own understanding, the development of philosophy in Iran.[12]

In his aforementioned work Gobineau tells us that he had discussed some

9 For Gobineau and his significance for Iranian Intellectual History see, Calmard, J. 'GOBINEAU, Joseph Arthur de', in *Encyclopeadia Iranica*, vol. XI, fasc. 1, 2001, pp. 20–24. See also: Seidel, R., *Kant in Teheran. Anfänge, Ansätze und Kontexte der Kantrezeption in Iran*, Berlin, 2014, pp. 43–48.

10 Āqā ʿAlī wrote a short account of the history of Iranian philosophers (starting from Mīr Sayyid Sharīf Jurjānī and ending with himself) on the request of Gobineau. The *Risāla tārīkh al-ḥukamāʾ* (History of the Philosophers) consists of two chapters the first ending with Mollā Ṣadrā the second dealing with post-Ṣadrian philosophers: The autograph, split into two parts, is kept at the library of the University of Strasburg (University of Strasburg Gobineau-Collection MSS 66 and 68). The first part has been published in the collected writings of Āqā ʿAlī, see: Mudarris Ṭihrānī, Ā., 'Risāla-yi Tārīkh al-ḥukamāʾ', in Kadīvar, M. (ed.), *Majmūʿa-yi muṣannafāt*, vol. 3, 1999, pp. 125–142 The second part is unedited. Beyond that there are also reports that Gobineau had – unsuccessfully – tried to convince Āqā 'Alī to teach Islamic Philosophy at the Sorbonne in Paris, see Kadīvar, M. (ed.), 'Muqaddama-yi Majmūʿa' [Introduction to the edited works], in *Majmūʿa-yi muṣannafāt*, p. 49.

11 De Goubineau, J. A. C., *Les religions et les philosophies dans l'Asie centrale*, Paris, 1865.

12 See note 13 below.

chapters of Descartes' work in some of his private lessons and that he is convinced that the notion of the 'Cogito, ergo sum' is a new idea for the Asian intellectual context and could hence have a positive impact on the minds of Iranian thinkers. He also states that some Iranians had been particularly curious about the doctrines of Spinoza and Hegel, yet Gobineau considered their way of reasoning too close to the 'Asian mindset' so that it would not be an innovative input for the Iranian discourse.[13] Descartes' doctrines, in contrast, he regarded as inherently European and therefore more suitable for making a complementary contribution the philosophical discourse in Iran.[14] Moreover, in a private letter he also mentions that he was explicitly asked by some fellow Iranians to translate the *Discours* into Persian.[15]

Consequently, Gobineau decided to introduce that particular work into the Iranian context and commissioned a Jewish scholar called Lālazār Hamadānī to

---

13 See: de Goubineau, *Les religions et les philosophies dans l'Asie centrale*, pp. 113–114. 'J'ai donc procuré aux Persan le Discours sur la Méthode. Il m'a paru que, dans toute notre philosophie, rien ne pouvait avoir chance de produire des résultats plus singuliers parmi eux. Ils ne sont pas des gens à tomber dans les excès de la méthode expérimentale, et il n'y a pas d'apparence qu'on supprime jamais chez eux l'abus de l'induction. On n'en voit pas davantage qu'ils arrivent à tirer du *cogito, ergo sum* le partie modéré auquel les Européens ont la prétention de s'arrêter. En réalité, ils en feront probablement quelques chose, et, pour moi, je ne saurais oublier les séance dans lesquelles les cinq chapitres du chef d'œuvre de Descartes ont été communiqués à quelques hommes d'une vraie intelligence et d'une science hors linge. Ils en ont éprouvé une impression remarquable, et il n'est pas probable que cette impression s'efface sans résultats.' For a Persian version of this passage see : Mujtahidī, *Āšinā'ī-yi īrānīyān bā falsafahā-yi jadīd-i gharb*, p. 135.

14 See: de Goubineau, *Les religions et les philosophies dans l'Asie centrale*, p. 114 'Mais, toutefois, les deux hommes que les philosophes de ma connaissance ont la plus grande soif de connaître, c'est Spinosa [sic!] et Hegel; on le comprend sans peine. Ces deux esprits sont des esprits asiatiques et leurs théories touchent par tous les points aux doctrines connues et goûtées dans le pays du soleil. Il est vrai que, pour cette raison même, elles ne sauraient introduire là des éléments vraiment nouveaux.'; see also: Seidel, *Kant in Teheran*, p. 45. On Gobineau's intentions behind this translation project, see also Manāf Zāda, ʿA. R., 'Nakhustīn matn-i falsafa-yi jadīd-i gharbī bi zabān-i fārsī', in *Īrānnāma*, no. 33, 1369 (1991), pp. 98–108, who, despite the fact that he makes no reference to it, more or less follows Mujtahidī's account, which originally appeared in 1354 (1975) in *Rahnamā-yi kitāb*. Manāf Zāda adds some more quotations from Gobineau's *Trois ans en Asie* and *Religions et philosophies dans l'Asie centrale* concerning his intentions to initiate this translation (pp. 98–105) and some quotations from the translator's introduction (pp. 105–7).

15 This is mentioned in a letter to Anton Graf Prokesch von Osten (1795–1876), an Austrian diplomat who served in Cairo and Istanbul and with whom Gobineau corresponded over many years. In the letter he does not mention, though, who these Iranians were. See Seidel, *Kant in Teheran*, p. 46 and Mujtahidī, *Āšinā'ī-yi īrānīyān bā falsafahā-yi jadīd-i gharb*, p. 133.

carry out the translation with the support of the French diplomat Emile Berney. A lithographed version of this translation was published in Tehran in 1862 under the title *Ḥikmat-i Nāṣiriyya* which indicates that it was dedicated to Nāṣir ad-Dīn Shāh.[16] The text is about 164 pages long and contains a preface of about fifteen pages, in which the translator highlights the benefits of translations of modern European philosophical works into Persian.[17] And yet Lālazār's translation did not meet the expectations Gobineau had expressed. This was largely due to the fact that the translator seems to have had only some rudimentary philosophical knowledge and he obviously was not very much acquainted with philosophical terminology in either French or Arabic and Persian, so that in the end his Persian equivalents, especially of Descartes' technical terms, were rather incomprehensible, even to a philosophically trained readership, and the translation as a whole failed to convey a consistent philosophical argument.[18] This is one reason why this translation doesn't seem to have had any impact on the philosophical discourse in Iran or, at least, we don't have any exact knowledge about its reception by Iranian scholars of the time. Another reason may also be found in the fact that materially this translation was not destined to last long, since only very few copies of it have survived. There is even some evidence that most of the copies of the translation were burned. Although not unlikely this incident is, as far as we know, not clearly documented and we have no clear evidence about the circumstances of

---

16 According to Danishpazhūh, it was published by Āqā Moḥammad Ḥosayn as a lithograph in a *nastaʿlīq ductus*. See Danishpazhūh, M. T., 'Nakhustīn kitābhā-yi falsafah wa ʿulūm-i jadīd dar Īrān', in *Nashr-i dānish,* no. 8, 1360 (1982), p. 89. A copy of the lithographed version printed in 1862 is kept in the national library in Tehran. This text has just recently been edited by Farāmarz Muʿtamid Dizfūlī, see: Descates/Hamadānī(transl.)/Berney(transl.), Ḥikmat-i Nāṣiriyya (Kitāb-i Diyākart). Nakhustīn tarjuma-yi 'Guftār dar ravish'-i Dikārt dar ʿaṣr-i Qajar, (ed. by Muʿtamid Dizfūlī), Tehran 1393/2014. The edition, however, is not a critical one, it only contains a short introduction by the editor (pp. 9–18) which merely gives some very general information about the original text by Descartes, its significance and the circumstances of its translation into Persian. The edited text itself contains ony very few editorial remarks, no references are given. Yet the editor is to be credited for making the text available in print.

17 For this introduction see: Descates/Hamadānī(transl.)/Berney(transl.), *Ḥikmat-i Nāṣiriyya*, pp. 21–28; see also: Mujtahidī, *Āšināʾī-yi īrānīyān bā falsafahā-yi ǧadīd-e ġarb*, pp. 131–41.

18 Thus the evaluation in Mujtahidī, *Āšināʾī-yi īrānīyān bā falsafahā-yi ǧadīd-e ġarb*, pp. 139–41 and Danishpazhūh, 'Nakhustīn kitābhā-yi falsafah wa ʿulūm-i jadīd dar Īrān', p. 89. Muʿtamid Dizfūlī doesn't share this opinion, in his view the synonyms for technical terms used by the translator are by and large well chosen and justified. Unfortunately he doesn't elaborate his argument in the preface or elsewhere in the edition, see Descates/Hamadānī(transl.)/Berney(transl.), Ḥikmat-i Nāṣiriyya, p. 16.

this incident.[19] However, this translation, apart from the fact that is one of the first examples of a major philosophical work recorded, is an important source for the adaptation process of modern European philosophy precisely because it is a rather unusual example. The fact that it was initiated by a European diplomat may further explain why it didn't have a significant impact, as it was not produced by Iranian thinkers deeply engaged with modern European thought. It was hence situated in a different context as it was addressed to traditional Iranian philosophers who had their own thematic (metaphysical) concerns and were, apart from some basic curiosity, not intrinsically interested in modern philosophy.[20]

b) The 2nd translation of the 'Discours' and the phenomenon of proxy-translation

The case of the second translation to be discussed here was different with respect to the one who produced it as well as with regard to the targeted audience. It was again Descartes' treatise that was rendered into Persian. This time however by one of the expatriate Iranian intellectuals. In the first decade of the twentieth century Afżal al-Mulk Kirmānī, like Gobineau, came to the conclusion that this particular text would be an appropriate way to introduce modern European

19 Mujtahidī also refers to rumours that the 1279/1862 edition was indeed the second edition and that it was actually a first edition of 1270 which was entirely burned by a group of unspecified radicals (*ʿidiʾī mutaʿaṣib*). But, as Mujtahidī argues, there is no evidence of an earlier edition; indeed, the 1862 dating fits better with the period of Gobineau's stay in Iran. See: Mujtahidī, *Āšināʾī-yi īrānīyān bā falsafahā-yi jadīd-i gharb*, pp. 137. Danishpazhūh states that on the back of a folio version he has consulted on microfilm there is a note saying that copies of it were burned during the reign of Nāṣir ad-Dīn Shāh. See: Danishpazhūh, 'Nakhustīn kitābhā-yi falsafah wa ʿulūm-i jadīd dar Īrān', p. 89.

20 One might, as a working hypothesis, compare Gobineau's attempts for 'philosophical development aid' with the activity of Christian missionaries who produced Persian translations of the Bible, see for instance: Amanat, A., 'Mutahids and Missionaries: Shiʿi Responses to Christian Polemics in the Early Qajar Period', in Gleave, R. (ed.), *Religion and Society in Qajar Iran,* London, 2004. In both examples the translations were not conducted by Iranians out of their own curiosity but commissioned by Europeans for educational purposes. Although it appears that traditional Mullā Ṣadrian philosophers were not much interested in European philosophy, there were also exceptions. Most importantly one should mention Badīʿ al-Mulk Mīrzā, for his attempts to draw the attention of his classical philosophy teachers, among them Āqā 'Alī Tehrānī. On European Philosophy, see Mujtahidī, *Āšināʾī-yi īrānīyān bā falsafahā-yi jadīd-i gharb*, pp. 238–44. For his interest in anti-positivist post-Kantian philosophy see Mujtahidī, *Āšināʾī-yi īrānīyān bā falsafahā-yi jadīd-i gharb*, pp. 245–252; Seidel, R., *Kant in Teheran*, pp. 86–88.

philosophy and with it new perspectives into the Iranian discourse. The circumstances under which this translation came about once again shed light on the relationship between the reception of ideas and political and intellectual contexts from which they emerge. Afżal al-Mulk was the brother of Shaykh Aḥmad Rūḥī and belonged to the circle of Iranian exiles around Mīrzā Āqā Khān Kirmānī who were both executed – charged with being involved in the murder of Nāṣir ad-Dīn Shāh.[21] Afżal al-Mulk himself went into hiding for some time, probably in order to avoid meeting the same fate as his brother. He did the translation shortly before his death, when he was already back in Iran and used a Turkish version of the book. It is not clear though why Afẓal al-Mulk relied on that particular version, since it is said that he knew French; it may simply be for the reason that he had no French original to hand and the commentary of the Turkish translator might have been of importance for him as he translates it along with the main text. [22]

This translation – in contrast to the first translation – is written in fluent Persian and it is apparent that the author was well acquainted with Descartes' thinking. The text, however, sometimes reads rather like a paraphrase of the original French version, since it contains various explanations addressed to the Iranian reader that are not indicated as such in the text. In the preface Afżal al-Mulk, who was influenced by positivist thought, highlights the importance of philosophy and its complementary relationship with natural science. He argues that this work of Descartes' is a cornerstone of modern philosophy (*ḥikmat-i tāzih*) in Europe, which has influenced the course of European philosophy significantly and could hence have a similar effect on Iranian philosophy. All this information was missing in the introduction to the first translation. Yet even this translation was destined not to achieve its purpose: it was never published and we don't know whether it was ever circulated.

Afżal al-Mulk's translation is nonetheless an important source for modern Iranian intellectual history, since as a phenomenon it has at least two important

21 On Mīrzā Aqā Khān see below.

22 The text has a preface by the translator of about 12 pages and an appendix containing a commentary of 56 pages presumably compiled by the Turkish translator, the main text the *Discours* itself is about 81 pages long. See Mujtahidī, *Āšinā'ī-yi īrānīyān bā falsafahā-yi jadīd-i gharb*, p. 210. A manuscript of Afżal al-Mulk's translation can be found at Malik library in Tehran (ms. 6172/film 4677), contained in a volume with a manuscript of Mīrzā Āqā Khān's *Haftād o do Mellat,* an adaptation of Jacques-Henri Bernardin de Saint-Pierre's (1737–1814) story *Le Café de Surate* (1790). For this adaptation of de Saint-Pierre, see below. On Afżal al-Mulk's translation, see Mujtahidī, *Āšinā'ī-yi īrānīyān bā falsafahā-yi ǧadīd-e ġarb*, pp. 201–12, originally published in *Rānimā-i kitāb*, 18 (1354), pp. 4–6; Danishpazhūh, 'Nakhustīn kitābhā-yi falsafah wa ʿulūm-i jadīd dar Īrān', pp. 89–90.

and characteristic features. First: The fact that it was never published and perhaps not even widely circulated is a fate it shares with many other intellectual writings of that period. Yet despite the fact that these texts seem to have fallen into oblivion they still could provide important clues for a more comprehensive understanding of what narratives of the Enlightenment actually existed in the advent of the Constitutional Revolution. This of course also has some methodological implications with regard to the representation of intellectual history. It points to the very fact that one has to consider ways of integrating into the narrative these kind of sources that were always under the threat of being marginalised, banned or annihilated.[23] Afżal al-Mulk's translation was from one of the expatriate intellectuals who were the main protagonists of the early reception of European philosophy in Iran and at the same time permanently under threat. His translation therefore belongs to the type of (semi-) clandestine literature that formed an important part of the writings that influenced Enlightenment discourse around the Constitutional Revolution. Beyond that, a closer examination of this translation and a comparison with other writings by these intellectuals might also help elucidate the language, terminology and style that was developing amongst these intellectuals.

The second feature is the fact that this translation was done by proxy from a Turkish version which was not exceptional but rather a characteristic of a number of translations in Qajar times. The phenomenon of proxy translation in general needs to be researched in more detail as it is capable of elucidating alternative routes of knowledge transmission. The choice of the intermediary language has, of course, something to do with the language skills of the translator or availability of a particular copy of a piece of work. But the specific language and rendition of the translated original may also have an impact on the Persian version produced, not only because different languages may transfer key concepts and ideas differently (which is certainly the case but not necessarily significant in every instance) but particularly because behind a specific rendition in a certain language lays a specific history of interpretation and reception. Of particular importance for the Iranian reception of Enlightenment thought is therefore the Ottoman and the Russian context, as one can assume that the access to the archives of Enlightenment and modern European philosophy of a thinker such as Akhundzāda who lived in Tbilisi may have been differently filtered compared to that of an Iranian Exile such as Mirzā Āqā Khān who resided in Istanbul or Mirzā Malkum Khān who

23 For a highly valuable approach of considering this kind of 'precarious knowledge' for intellectual history see, Mulsow, M., *Prekäres Wissen: Eine andere Ideengeschichte der Frühen Neuzeit*, Berlin, 2012.

stayed in London. It is important to state that this does not mean that they will have a completely different account of the works they engaged with, at least they have largely been in contact via correspondences, but in order to examine the impact of the Turkish or Russian reception of European thought on Iranian intellectuals residing in Istanbul or the Russian territories respectively, one will also have to consider the phenomenon of proxy translations more carefully.

Paraphrases and Compilations

Besides Descartes' *Discours* it appears that no major philosophical works were translated into Persian during that period. However, we find various references in the scholarly literature to an alleged translation of John Stuart Mill's *On Liberty*, which is referred to both under the title *Manāfiʿ-i Ḥurriyyat*[24] and *Manāfiʿ-i Āzādī*.[25] It has been attributed to both Malkum Khān[26] and to Ākhundzāda.[27] The real authorship of this 'translation' has yet to be established. Both thinkers were at least influenced by the thoughts of John Stuart Mill.[28] If the alleged translation was Ākhundzāde's, it must have been done so from a Turkish or more likely a Russian version, since he didn't know any European language other than Russian. The evidence we have, however, suggests that no such translation did actually exist – at least we have no manuscript that could be an instance of a translation linked to either Ākhundzada or Malkum Khān. It seems that the respective text is actually only a short summary of Mill's treatise. Ākhundzāda had apparently written a brief essay on Mill's treatise, which, along with Ākhundzāda's translation or rather paraphrase of a speech by Mirabeau on the topic of freedom, circulated in handwritten copies in the early 1880s under the title *Guftār dar Āzādī*.[29]

24 See Afshar, I. 'Book Translations as a Cultural Activity in Iran 1806–1896', in *Iran,* vol. 41, 2003, pp. 279–289, here 284). He doesn't give any further references.

25 See Malkum Khān, M. 'Manāfi-yi Āzādī', in Malkum Khān, M., *Majmūʿa-yi Āthār* (ed. by Muḥammad Muḥīṭ Ṭabāṭabā'ī), Tehran, 1327 (1948), 177–178.

26 See Parsinejad, I., *A History of Literary Criticism in Iran (1866–1951): Literary Criticism in the Works of Enlightened Thinkers of Iran, Akhundzadeh, Kermani, Malkom Khan, Talebof, Maraghe'i, Kasravi and Hedayat,* Bethesda, MD, 2003, p. 97.

27 Algar, H., *Mirza Malkum Khan*, p. 18, n. 63.

28 See: Sanjabi, 'Rereading the Enlightenment'; Masroori, 'European Thought in Nineteenth-Century Iran'.

29 Cyrus Masroori is to be credited to drawing our attention to this. See Masroori, 'European Thought in Nineteenth-Century Iran', p. 668 – he refers to Pursafar A., *Kitābshināsī-yi inqilāb-i mashrūṭiyat-i Īrān*, Teheran, 1994, p. 224.

At least one manuscript that may be an instance of this text can be found in the National Library in Tehran. It is part of a *Majmūʿa* that primarily contains writings attributed to Malkum Khān and also one attributed to Ākhundzāda. The essay in question in the catalogue is attributed to Mill and Mirabeau, but no particular translator is mentioned.[30]

This example again points to literary phenomena which also need more scholarly attention on two fronts. First: The phenomenon of paraphrases and short summaries of philosophical doctrines. Although they are sometimes erroneously referred to as complete translations, they are nonetheless important and, because of their brevity, perhaps more influential than a full translation would have been. These paraphrases or short essays often inspired by particular texts or doctrines appeared in exile journals or circulated and were copied as leaflets and may have found a wide readership. As a first step, however, what is needed to estimate the significance of this particular form of adopting European philosophical doctrines would be an inventory of text that falls under this category and an evaluation of distribution.

Second: The phenomenon of the *Majmūʿa* is a specific type of source in which several texts are put together by some sort of an 'editor'. Sometimes the texts that are put together don't seem to have any thematic interrelation, in other instances though – like in the example mentioned above – the compiler obviously offers a kind of an anthology of writings he or she thinks to be relevant with regard to a particular discourse. An inventory of nineteenth- and early twentieth-century *Majmūʿa* compilations with regard to their representation of enlightenment thought would also be a fruitful task for further enquiries into the early circulation and appropriation of modern European philosophy in Qajar Iran.

Translation of Minor Philosophical Texts

Another category that shall be considered here is the translation of minor or secondary philosophical texts. The almost complete absence of major European philosophical works rendered into Persian in the period before and shortly after the Constitutional Revolution remains a striking contradiction to the general interest in European literature on the whole at the time. Particularly during the reign of Nāṣir ad-Dīn Shah (1848–1896) the number of translations of European writings

30 For further bibliographical information on this manuscript and the *majmūʿa* in which it is contained see the online catalogue *Agha Bozorg*: http://www.aghabozorg.ir/showbookdetail.aspx?bookid=66417, (last accessed 15 July, 2016).

– especially textbooks on technical subjects, medicine, geography and history, as well as travel literature and historical novels[31] – increased significantly, so that one may speak of a larger translation movement. As a means of educational and scientific reform this movement was also officially supported by governmental bodies such as the Bureau of Translation and Publication that commissioned a considerable number of translations with the help of hired translators. It was led by I'tiżād-al-Salṭana and later I'timād-al-Salṭana, who played a highly significant role in the official organisation of choosing and translating relevant European texts.[32] Despite this increasing interest in European literature of various genres, the translation of major philosophical works was obviously not the focus of this movement. Yet there is nonetheless some evidence of a number of secondary philosophical writings which were reportedly translated into Persian at that time.[33] Among them there are works that can be considered philosophical textbooks written by philosophers largely forgotten today but at least as local scholars quite influential in their times.[34] An interesting case in point is a translated work entitled *Mafātiḥ al-Funūn* in Persian. It seems to be a selective translation from one or several books by the Italian philosopher Pasquale Galluppi (1770–1846). Galluppi, in his later career professor of philosophy at the university of Napoli, had authored a number of philosophical works and textbooks among them *Elementi di filosofia* a textbook of 6 volumes that was enormously successful and saw 5 editions in his lifetime.[35] Another textbook that was apparently meant to be used for teaching philosophy at

31 Hāshimī, Sayyid Aḥmad. 'Tarjuma 4) Tarjuma-yi Fārsī dar Dawra-yi Mu'āṣir', in Dānishnāma-yi jahān-i Islām, (ed. by Ghulām-'Alī Ḥaddād 'Ādil), vol. 7, Tehran, 1382 Sh / 2003., pp. 50–57. See also: Afshar, I. 'Book Translations as a Cultural Activity in Iran 1806–1896'; Danishpazhūh, 'Nakhustīn kitābhā-yi falsafah wa 'ulūm-i jadīd dar Īrān'; Kīyānfar, J., 'Tarjuma dar 'ahd-i qājār', in *Nashr-i dānish*, no. 55, 1368(1989), pp. 23–8.

32 For the significance of I'timād-al-Salṭana see: Amanat, A., 'E'temād-al-Salṭana', in *Encyclopaedia Iranica,* vol. VIII, fasc. 6, 1998, pp. 662–666.

33 Among them there is a philosophical work by Jules Simon that was translated as *Zamān va Makān*, apparently by Khalīl Khān Thaqafī – See: Danishpazhūh, 'Nakhustīn kitābhā-yi falsafah wa 'ulūm-i jadīd dar Īrān', p. 92. Afshar gives a different Persian title, *Zamīn wa Zamān,* but does not provide bibliographical references, see: Afshar, I. 'Book Translations as a Cultural Activity in Iran 1806–1896', p. 284.

34 See: Danishpazhūh, 'Nakhustīn kitābhā-yi falsafah wa 'ulūm-i jadīd dar Īrān', pp. 90–92. Besides the translation of Descartes's *Discours*, he mentions four further translations of philosophical works.

35 Galluppi, Pasquale, *Elementi di filosofia del Barone Pasquale Galluppi da Tropea. professore di filosofia nella Regia Universita` di Napoli*, 6 Volumes, (5th Ed.), Naples, 1846.

the university level was his *Lezioni di logica e di metafisica*.[36] Galluppi belongs to the first Italian philosophers who highlighted the importance of Kantian epistemology; however, he does so without following him in every respect. For instance, he maintains that human cognition has the capacity to get access to reality and therefore holds the doctrine of the objective reality of human knowledge to be true. He nonetheless adopted aspects of Descartes and, more noticeably, Kant's subjectivist theory of knowledge into his own epistemology. Moreover, he also was inspired by Thomas Reid's doctrine of common sense.[37] The Persian translation of Galluppi's work seems to have been produced as a textbook introducing modern logic (*manṭiq-i nuwīn*), although it is not known whether, and indeed in what context, it was used as such. The translation, dedicated to Muẓaffar ad-Dīn Shah, was carried out by Mīrzā Maḥmūd Khān Afšār Kangāvarī, who belonged to the office of Ẓill al-Sulṭān the Governor of Isfahan (1874–1907), and published in 1309q/1892. Ẓill al-Sulṭān was among those state officials eagerly interested in gathering knowledge on European ideas and history.[38] Kangāvarī, one of the official translators charged with translating European texts from any field,[39] was specialised in translating from Turkish. For the translation of Galluppis work he used an Ottoman Turkish version, which was itself already a selective compilation.[40] The Turkish translator, the Armenian Sakızlı Ohannes (1830–1912), before he became known as an important voice of Ottoman economic liberalism, was – similar to his Persian colleague Kangāvarī – assigned to a governmental translation bureau, in his case in Istanbul.[41] Who commissioned the Turkish translation, for what purpose, and how

36 Galluppi, Pasquale, *Lezioni di logica e di metafisica: composte peruso della Regia Univ. degli studii di Napoli*, 4 Volumes. Naples, 1831. The book has had a number of reprints.

37 For Galluppi's *Elementi* and his significance in general see: Cane, L., 'Introduzione', in Galluppi, P., *Elementi di filosofia*, vol.1, 2001. For the significance of his adaptation on Thomas Reid in nineteenth-century Italy see: Copenhaver, B. P. and Copenhaver, R., 'The strange Italian voyage of Thomas Reid: 1800–60', in *British Journal for the History of Philosophy*, vol. 14, no. 4, 2006, pp. 601–626.

38 For Ẓill al-Sulṭān see: Walcher, H. A., *In the Shadow of the King: Zill Al-Sultan and Isfahan Under the Qajars*, London, 2008.

39 For a list of some of these translators see Afshar, I. 'Book Translations as a Cultural Activity in Iran 1806–1896' , 285–286.

40 A Turkish translation by Sakızlı Ohannes published under the title *Miftah ül-fünun / Paskuale Galluppi*, p. 164, can be found in various library catalogues. Danishpazhu assumes that it must be a selected translation of Gallupie's *Lezioni di Logica e Metafisica*. See Danishpazhūh, 'Nakhustīn kitābhā-yi falsafah wa ʿulūm-i jadīd dar Īrān', pp. 91–2.

41 On Sakızlı Ohannes see: Kilinçoğlu, D. T., *Economics and Capitalism in the Ottoman Empire,*

this particular translation found its way from Istanbul to the translation office in Isfahan has yet to be examined.

With this example we not only have another instance of a proxy-translation from an European language via Turkish into Persian but we also encounter a particular sort of text which may have been more significant to the reception and appropriation of modern Western philosophy and the European Enlightenment, than it was hitherto assumed. The issue of Persian textbook production and its importance for the dissemination of modern sciences, particularly in the context of the newly established European style institutions of learning in Iran such as the *Dār al-Funūn,* has already been recognised.[42] Yet we still lack a comprehensive overview of such textbooks, be they originally written in Persian or translated from other languages that specifically deal with philosophy. It is not unlikely that many Iranian intellectuals and official translators preferred secondary textbooks on specific currents of modern philosophy or compilations of various introductory texts over complex philosophical treatises for translation for at least two reasons: For one, it takes much more effort to comprehend and study (let alone to translate) a dense treatise than a text book that was particularly composed to introduce the reader to the foundations of a specific philosophical discourse, and as in the case of the summaries for that very reason they may have had a more immediate impact on intellectual debates of the time. For another, Qajar intellectuals may have been attracted by these sorts of writings because they represented up to date accounts of modern philosophy not only introducing eminent European thinkers such as Kant, Mill and Hume but also evaluating them from a contemporary perspective. We should therefore consider whether these genres of texts might have been underestimated so far in our evaluation of the ways, Enlightenment philosophy has been appropriated by Iranian intellectuals and instructors in modern style institutions of learning in Iran.

Intellectual Fiction and Hybrid Forms of Translation

Most of the translated intellectual writings, however, belong to the genres of intellectual fiction and historical literature that partly also dealt with philosophical

London, 2015.

42 See for instance Āriyanpūr, Y., *Az Ṣabā tā Mīnā*, 3 Volumes, 5th edition, Teheran, 1372 (1993–4), pp. 259–260; Gurney, J. and Nabavi, N., 'Dār al-Fonūn', in *Encyclopaedia Iranica*, vol. VI, fasc. 6, pp. 662–668, 1993, available online: http://www.iranicaonline.org/articles/dar-al-fonun-lit (last accessed 15 July, 2016).; Ringer, M. M., *Education, Religion, and the Discourse of Cultural Reform in Qajar Iran*, Costa Mesa, 2001, pp. 75–76.

questions, especially connected with the issue of good governance and ethics. Noteworthy here are for instance works by Voltaire.[43] A highly significant example for a translation of philosophical fiction is Mīrzā Āqā Khān Kīrmānī's rendition of François Fénelon's (1651–1715) *Les Aventures de Télémaque*, which is a didactic novel narrating the educational travels of Telemachus, son of Ulysses, accompanied by his tutor, Mentor, who at the end of the story is revealed to be the goddess of wisdom, Minerva, in disguise. This novel, which is said to have influenced Jean-Jacques Rousseau, reflects a number of political ideas in a philosophical vein. It advocates, for instance, a parliamentary governmental system and a kind of federation of nations intended to resolve disputes between nations in a peaceful way. Kermānī is reported to have produced an unfinished translation of this novel.[44]

Another translation of this kind – again by Mīrzā Āqā Khān – is his adaptation of two short stories by Jacques-Henri Bernardin de Saint-Pierre (1737–1814), who was a follower of the late Rousseau and whose novel *Paul et Virginie* criticised social class division turned into a bestseller at the end of the eighteenth century.[45] The two stories – *La Chaumière indienne*[46] and *Le Café de Surate* – appeared in 1790 and deal with questions such as the nature of wisdom, God and religion. Mīrzā Āqā Khān in his *Haftād o do mellat* merged both stories into one, which he then modified and extended. He does not mention Bernardin de Saint-Pierre as the author of the two stories. Although, in large parts, an accurate translation he uses the material to creatively reshape the story along his own convictions and goes so far as to change its final clue at the end. Whereas, for Bernardin, it was the romantic devotion to nature and a critique of natural science and rationalism, Mīrzā Āqā Khān in turn introduces a new character (that was absent in the original text)

43 Among the works by Voltaire translated into Persian in that period are for instance *Histoire de Charles XII* and *Histoire de l'Empire de Russie sous Pierre le Grand*. On these translations see: Kīyānfar, 'Tarjuma dar ʿahd-i qājār'.

44 On the significance of Fénelon's Télémaque see for instance: Kapp, V., *Télémaque de Fénelon: la signification d'une œuvre littéraire à la fin du siècle classique*, Tübingen/Paris, 1982. For an overview of Mīrzā Āqā Khāns works see, Ādamiyyat, *Andīšihā-yi Mīrzā Āqā Ḫān Kirmānī*; Bayat-Philipp, 'Mīrzā Āqā Khān Kirmānī: A Nineteenth-Century Persian Nationalist'.

45 This book was first meant to be an appendix to the 3rd edition of his *Études de la nature*. The book was translated into Persian by Ibrahim Neshat around the year 1906 (see, Muhammad R. F., 'Nehzat-e tarjome dar ahd-e Qajar', in *Negin*, vol. 9, no. 100, 1973, p. 55, cited in Masroori, 'French Romanticism and Persian Liberalism in Nineteenth-Century Iran, p. 548.)

46 Runte, R., '"La Chaumière indienne": Counterpart and Complement to "Paul et Virginie"', in *The Modern Language Review*, vol. 75, no. 4, 1980, pp. 774–780.

who advocates natural science and reason as the only way to truth and on these grounds highlights the ideas of religious pluralism.[47] This sort of experimental literary adaptation of European Sources belongs to the most intriguing instances of cultural knowledge transmission in Qajar times. It not only shows that one has to also look for translations of philosophical relevance in texts that, at first glance, neither seem to be translation nor philosophical works but it also hints to the fact that the translation process of European philosophy is often deeply entangled with an original intellectual engagement with the ideas of Enlightenment thought by the Iranian thinkers of the Qajar era.

Conclusion

The phenomenon of early translation of modern European philosophy is a multifaceted one. The expatriate intellectuals and dissidents of the Qajar era – the main protagonists of the early adaptation of Enlightenment thinking in Iran – were obviously less interested in producing accurate and complete translations of philosophy out of pure scholarly interest. They nevertheless engaged with texts and doctrines of Enlightenment thinkers and other strands of modern European philosophy as a means for political activism, critique of social circumstances and religious doctrinism. In doing so they produced a huge amount and variety of texts that can be regarded as translations of European philosophy in various understandings of the term. Besides short summaries of philosophical doctrines, we find hybrid forms of literature composed of translations and their own original writings. The significance of proxy-translations highlights the importance of transregional intellectual networks in the reception process of European thought. The issue of the translation of philosophical textbooks shows that one has to also search for seemingly secondary philosophical works translated into Persian. Hence, the fact that we don't find many major philosophical treatises of eminent European thinkers in Persian translation doesn't mean that there was no significant activity in the field. Quite to the contrary, the efforts of intellectuals and official translators paved the way for what form the late Qajar and early Pahlavi period onwards was to become and directly contribute to an ever increasing aspect of the intellectual discourse in Iran: the reception of modern Western philosophy by way of translation and appropriation of influential Western philosophical discourses, sometimes

47 Masroori, C., 'French Romanticism and Persian Liberalism in Nineteenth-Century Iran: Mirza Aqa Khan Kirmani and Jacques-Henri Bernardin de Saint-Pierre', *History of Political Thought*, 28/3, 2007, 542–56.

with and sometimes without their integration into the inherited Islamic philosophical tradition. One important figure who symbolises a transition into another phase is ʿAlī Forūghī (1877–1942). He combined the literary skills and political engagement of the earlier intellectuals with a greater care for systematic representation of modern European history of philosophy. His work *Sayr-i Ḥikmat dar Urūpā* was the first comprehensive Persian introduction to the topic, that also included an extensive glossary of philosophical terms. This three volume work was not only successful during his lifetime but is still popular today. Therefore it is not surprising that it was also Forūghī who succeeded to finally popularise Descartes' *Discours,* as he published the third Persian translation of the treatise as a part of *Sayr-i Ḥikmat.*[48] Yet, as this essay has shown, with regard to the period that preceded Forūghī many significant contributions to the modern history of philosophy in Iran that should be taken into account still remain largely unexplored.[49] A focussed scholarly effort that attempts to evaluate this rich material could be a fruitful task for future collaborative research projects and an important compliment to the Grand Narrative of the Enlightenment.

48 Furūġī, M., ʿAlī, Sayr-i ḥikmat dar urūpā, [Development of Philosophy in Europe], Teheran, 1318/1939. For the significance of Furūghī's *Sayr-i Ḥikmat dar Urūpā* see, Mujtahidī, *Āšinā'ī-yi īrānīyān bā falsafahā-yi ǧadīd-e ġarb*, pp. 309–40.

49 For an inventory of the relevant source material one may start with systematic evaluation of the extensive and highly valuable descriptive bibliographical works and catalogues related to the literature of the Qajar era compiled by scholars such as Iraj Afshār, Mujtabā Minuvī and Muḥammad Taqī Dānishpazhūh. Beyond that also the huge amount of private papers are to be considered. See: Gheissari, A., 'Khatt va Rabt. The Significance of Private Papers for Qajar Historiography' in *Gingko Library, Newsblog, August 8, 2015.* (Accessed www.gingkolibrary.com/news/khatt-va-rabt/).

Bibliography

Ādamiyyat, F., *Andīšihā-yi Mīrzā Āqā Khān Kirmānī* [The Thought of Mīrzā Āqā Khān Kirmānī], Tehran, 1357/1978.

Ādamiyyat, F., *Andīšihā-yi Ṭālibuf Tabrīzī* [The Thought of Ṭālibuf Tabrīzī], Tehran, 1363/1984

Ādamiyyat, F., *Amīr Kabīr va Īrān* [Amir Kabir and Iran], Teheran, 1969.

Ādamiyyat, F., *Andīšihā-yi Mīrzā Fatḥʿalī Ākhundzāda* [The Thought of Mīrzā Fatḥʿalī Ākhundzāda].1970.

Afshar, I. 'Book Translations as a Cultural Activity in Iran 1806–1896', in *Iran,* vol. 41, 2003, pp. 279–289.

Algar, H., *Mirza Malkum Khan: A Study in the History of Iranian Modernism*, Oakland, 1973.

Amanat, A., 'Eʿtemād-al-Salṭana', in *Encyclopaedia Iranica,* vol. VIII, fasc. 6, 1998, pp. 662–666.

Amanat, A., 'Mutahids and Missionaries: Shiʿi Responses to Christian Polemics in the Early Qajar Period', in Gleave, R. (ed.), *Religion and Society in Qajar Iran,* London, 2004.

Āriyanpūr, Y., *Az Ṣabā tā Mīnā*, 3 Volumes, 5th edition, Tehran, 1372 (1993–4).

Bayat-Philipp, M., 'Mīrzā Āqā Khān Kirmānī: A Nineteenth-Century Persian Nationalist', in *Middle Eastern Studies*, vol. 10, no. 1, 1974.

Bayat-Philipp, M., 'The Concepts of Religion and Government in the Thought of Mirza Aqa Khan Kirmani, a Nineteenth-Century Persian Revolutionary', in *International Journal of Middle East Studies*, vol. 5, no. 4, 1974.

Boroujerdi, Mehrzad, *Iranian Intellectuals and the West. The Tormented Triumph of Nativism*, Syracuse, NY, 1996.

Calmard, J. 'GOBINEAU, Joseph Arthur de', in *Encyclopeadia Iranica*, vol. XI, fasc. 1, 2001, pp. 20–24, available online: http://www.iranicaonline.org/articles/gobineau (last accessed: 15 July, 2016).

Cane, L., 'Introduzione', in Galluppi, P., *Elementi di filosofia*, vol.1, 2001.

Copenhaver, B. P. and Copenhaver, R., 'The strange Italian voyage of Thomas Reid: 1800–60', in *British Journal for the History of Philosophy*, vol. 14, no. 4, 2006, pp. 601–626.

Danishpazhūh, M. T., 'Nakhustīn kitābhā-yi falsafah wa ʿulūm-i jadīd dar Īrān', in *Nashr-i dānish,* no. 8, 1360 (1982), pp. 88–101.

Descates/Hamadānī(transl.)/Berney(transl.), *Ḥikmat-i Nāṣiriyya* (Kitāb-I Diyākart), Nakhustīn tarjuma-yi 'Guftār dar ravish'-i Dikārt dar ʿaṣr-i Qajar, (ed. by Muʿtamid Dizfūlī), Tehran 1393 (2014).

Furūġī, ʿA, Sayr-i ḥikmat dar urūpā, [Development of Philosophy in Europe], Teheran, 1318/1939.

Galluppi, P., *Elementi di filosofia del Barone Pasquale Galluppi da Tropea. professore di filosofia nella Regia Universita` di Napoli*, 6 Volumes, (5th Ed.), Naples, 1846.

Galluppi, P., *Lezioni di logica e di metafisica: composte peruso della Regia Univ. degli studii di Napoli*, 4 Volumes, Naples, 1831.

Gheissari, A., *Iranian Intellectuals in the 20th Century*, Austin, TX, 1998.

Gheissari, A., 'Khatt va Rabt. The Significance of Private Papers for Qajar Historiography' in *Gingko Library, Newsblog, August 8, 2015,* (Accessed www.gingkolibrary.com/news/khatt-va-rabt/).

de Goubineau, J. A. C., *Les religions et les philosophies dans l'Asie centrale*, Paris, 1865 (1928 edition used).

Gurney, J. and Nabavi, N., 'Dār al-Fonūn', in *Encyclopaedia Iranica*, vol. VI, fasc. 6, pp. 662–668, 1993, available online: http://www.iranicaonline.org/articles/dar-al-fonun-lit, (last accessed 15 July, 2016).

Hāshimī, Sayyid Aḥmad, 'Tarjuma 4) Tarjuma-yi Fārsī dar Dawra-yi Muʿāṣir', in *Dānishnāma-yi jahān-i Islām* (ed. by Ghulām-ʿAlī Ḥaddād ʿĀdil), vol. 7, Tehran, 1382 Sh / 2003., pp. 50–57.

Heydari, A. A., *Rezeption der westlichen Philosophie durch iranische Denker in der Kadscharenzeit*, unpublished Dissertation, Rheinische Friedrich-Wilhelms-Universität, Bonn, 2003.

Kadīvar, M. (ed.), 'Muqaddama-yi Maǧmūmʿa' [Introduction to the edited works], in *Majmūʿa-yi muṣannafāt*, vol. 1–3, Tehran 1378 Sh./1999.

Kapp, V., *Télémaque de Fénelon: la signification d'une œuvre littéraire à la fin du siècle classique*, Tübingen/Paris, 1982.

Kilinçoğlu, D. T., *Economics and Capitalism in the Ottoman Empire,* London, 2015.

Kirmānī, M. Ā. K., *Haftād wa du millat,* Berlin, 1964.

Kīyānfar, J., 'Tarjuma dar ʿahd-i Qajar',in *Nashr-i dānish*, no. 55, 1368(1989), pp. 23–8.

Malkum Khān, M., *Majmūʿa-yi Āthār*, (ed. by Muḥammad Muḥīṭ Ṭabāṭabā'ī), Tehran, 1327 (1948).

Manāf Zāda, ʿA. R., 'Nakhustīn matn-i falsafa-yi jadīd-i gharbī be zabān-i fārsī', in *Īrānnāma*, no. 33, 1369/1991, pp. 98–108.

Masroori, C., 'European Thought in Nineteenth-Century Iran: David Hume and Others', in *Journal of the History of Ideas,* vol. 61, no. 4, 2000.

Masroori, C., 'French Romanticism and Persian Liberalism in Nineteenth-Century Iran: Mirza Aqa Khan Kirmani and Jacques-Henri Bernardin de Saint-Pierre', *History of Political Thought*, 28/3, 2007, 542–56.

Mudarris Ṭihrānī, Ā.ʿA., 'Risāla-yi Tārīkh al-ḥukamāʾ', in Kadīvar, M. (ed.), *Majmūʿa-yi muṣannafāt*, vol. 3, 1999, pp. 125–142.

Mujtahidī, K., *Āšināʾī-yi īrānīyān bā falsafahā-yi ğadīd-e ġarb* [The acquaintance of the Iranians with Modern Western Philosophy], Teheran, 1384/2005–6.

Mulsow, M., *Prekäres Wissen: Eine andere Ideengeschichte der Frühen Neuzeit*. Berlin, 2012.

Ohannes, S., (transl.), *Miftah ül-fünun / Paskuale Galluppi*, Istanbul, 1277(1861).

Parsinejad, I., *A History of Literary Criticism in Iran (1866–1951): Literary Criticism in the Works of Enlightened Thinkers of Iran, Akhundzadeh, Kermani, Malkom Khan, Talebof, Maraghe'i, Kasravi and Hedayat,* Bethesda, MD, 2003.

Pistor-Hatam, A., *Nachrichtenblatt, Informationsbörse und Diskussionsforum: Aḫtar-e Estānbūl (1876–1896): Anstöße zur frühen persischen Moderne*, Münster, 1999.

Ringer, M. M., *Education, Religion, and the Discourse of Cultural Reform in Qajar Iran*, Costa Mesa, 2001.

Runte, R., '"La Chaumière indienne": Counterpart and Complement to "Paul et Virginie"', in *The Modern Language Review,* vol. 75, no. 4, 1980, pp. 774–780.

Sanjabi, M. B., 'Rereading the Enlightenment: Akhundzada and His Voltaire', in *Iranian Studies* vol. 28, no. 1–2, 1995, pp. 39–60.

Seidel, R., *Kant in Teheran. Anfänge, Ansätze und Kontexte der Kantrezeption in Iran*, Berlin, 2014.

Vahdat, F., *God and Juggernaut: Iran's Intellectual Encounter with Modernity*, Syracuse, NY, 2002.

Walcher, H. A., *In the Shadow of the King: Zill Al-Sultan and Isfahan Under the Qajars*, London, 2008.

10

Looking Back at Mashrutih: Late Pahlavi Narratives on the Constitutional Revolution

Siavush Randjbar-Daemi

The purpose of this article is that of providing an overview of the official discourse of the late Pahlavi era on the Constitutional Revolution. It will provide insight on how the Shah and the upper elite of the last years of the monarchy in Iran interpreted the aims and legacy of the Revolution, and how the same was subsumed and adopted as a legitimising factor within the state's own ideological construct of the period, with focus on the Rastakhiz period of 1975–78, when the discourse of the late Pahlavi era was consolidated under the bosom of the single party system. It will rely on speeches and articles made on key occasions, particularly the yearly Constitutional Revolution anniversary celebrations.

The Constitutional Revolution, or *Enqelab-e Mashrutih* of 1905–11 brought about a state system which formally existed until 11 February, 1979 – the day in which the Imperial Army announced its neutrality in the confrontation between the revolutionary movement and the last government to have been sworn in under the Mashrutih provisions – the one of Prime Minister Shapur Bakhtiar. One of the defining achievements of the Constitutional Revolution, the permanent *Majles*, or Parliament, ceased to exist under the old order on the same day, having held the last session of its 24th legislature five days earlier.

For the last two and a half decades of the Mashrutih state system, Iran was ruled by an autocratic monarch who eschewed much of the spirit and intended aims of the Revolution in order to consolidate his rule. Muhammad Riza Pahlavi effectively disregarded the lasting principle instilled by the Mashrutih process, that of instilling *shart,* or 'conditions', on the rule of the monarch,[1] and thereby replace monarchical arbitrary rule with what scholars have referred to as the rule of law.[2] Through a concerted and wide-ranging effort, which featured the Shah's progressive encroachment on the political sphere, the effort to create an all-encompassing political ideology known as 'Pahlavism', the adoption of frequent national celebrations, including his own belated coronation and the Persepolis celebrations which culminated with the establishment of the Rastakhiz single party, the Shah re-established the monarch as the driving and pivotal force in the Iranian state system. As noted by Prof. Ali Ansari, following the establishment of the Rastakhiz party, Muhammad Riza Pahlavi 'took to describing himself as the *farmandeh* [commander]' and did away with most of the constitutional limitations related to his post.[3]

While acting counter to much of the essence of the aspirations of the constitutional revolutionaries, the last shah did not dissolve the state structure which was encapsulated in the Constitution of 1906. Despite convening two Constituent Assemblies for modifying several elements of the Constitution to his own advantage,[4] the Shah did not suspend the institutions introduced by Mashrutih,

---

1 This view of the aims of the Constitutional Revolution follows Hairi, A., *Shiism and Constitutionalism in Iran*, Leiden, 1977, pp. 50–55.

2 See in this regard: Katouzian, H., 'The Revolution for Law: A Chronographic Analysis of the Constitutional Revolution of Iran', in *Middle Eastern Studies* vol. 47, no. 5, 2011, DOI: 10.1080/00263206.2011.588797, pp. 757–77.

3 Ansari, A. The Politics of Nationalism in Iran, Cambridge, 2014, pp. 183–184.

4 The Constituent Assembly was included in the provisions of the existing constitution and had been convened by Riza Khan in 1925 to constitutionally allow for dynasties other than the

preferring instead to superimpose bodies and political processes of his own creation, such as the White Revolution and the Rastakhiz single-party, to the Mashrutih arrangement his father had inherited from the previous Qajar dynasty. At the end of his reign, he saw Mashrutih as a useful foundation on which to bond together his own attempts at shaping and forming the state system. By doing so, he enabled a discourse to emerge from within the ranks of prominent inner-regime figures and the parastatal press, which collectively engaged in a selective celebration of the deeds of the constitutional revolutionaries, particularly in their struggle against foreign influence and colonialism.

This article will provide an analysis of the positioning of the ideals of the Constitutional Revolution in the discourse of the later Pahlavi era, which is here taken to mean the period between the Shah's announcement of the White Revolution, in 1962, and the end of the monarchy in 1979. It will seek to observe the pattern through which the essence of Mashrutih and the ideals championed during the Constitutional Revolution were re-interpreted and co-opted by the Shah during this timeframe. It will also argue, however, that Muhammad Riza Pahlavi's eventually incorporation of the Mashrutih state order also progressively left the political field devoid of an alternative which could have safeguarded the continuation of Mashrutih in the absence of himself, or the Pahlavi dynasty.

Muhammad Riza Pahlavi and the Mashrutih State Order

The attitude of Muhammad Riza Pahlavi towards the rest of the state system was subject to considerable change during his 37-year reign. At the time of his coronation, in September 1941, the young monarch did not possess the political experience or ability to assert himself over the political scene, which was then dominated by figures who had the ability of rising above the monarch and significantly subduing the influence and relevance of other state institutions, as his father had successfully done. During his swearing-in ceremony on 16 September, 1941 he went beyond the customary lip-service to the Mashrutih order contained in article 39 of the supplement to the Constitution of 1906, and claimed that himself, the executive and legislative branches of government and society as a whole should unite in order to safeguard the Mashrutih order, and that no

Qajar one to ascend to the throne. It also met in the aftermath of an attempt on Muhammad Riza Shah's life in 1949 to bestow him with more powers, including that of dissolving both houses of parliament. The modifications to the constitution brought about by these two assemblies are noted in the appendix to Rahimi, M., *Qanun-i Asasi-yi Iran va Usul-i Dimukrasi*, Tehran, 1978.

entity should rise beyond what had been stipulated by the legal framework. For most of the following 12 years, as the Shah was settling into the role of monarch and head of state, Iranian politics partially witnessed the essence of Mashrutih. The emergence of political parties separate from the state system, such as the Tudeh Party, the autonomy of veteran statesmen such as Muhammad Musaddiq or Ahmad Qavam from the royal court and the latter's inability to control, despite its frequent interference, the lively and chaotic parliamentary activities of those years provided opportunities for the lessening of the monarch's influence in realms beyond politics, such as the arts, literary production and the press. Such a process was not sufficient, however, to extinguish voices calling for the end to the monarchical state system. As this author has discussed at length in a forthcoming journal article, the hurried departure of the Shah to Baghdad and Rome in the aftermath of the first, failed coup attempt of 15 and 16 August, 1953 was the starting point of a brief, but spirited and concerted effort for the establishment of a republic, the last over one prior to 1979, which featured the separate support of key elements in the arc of supporters of Musaddiq, from the Tudeh Party, to the Third Force and elements of the youth movements aligned to the National Front.

Upon his return to Tehran in the aftermath of General Fazlullah Zahidi's seizure of power, the Shah had to contend with a critical juncture in the Mashrutih state order. For the first time since the Constitutional Revolution, a military manoeuvre, whether domestic or foreign-ordained, had been deployed by the monarch against a sitting prime minister, who in turn had acted on the boundaries of the constitutional provisions when calling for the dissolution of the *Majles* via referendum. The manifest calls for an end to the monarchical order and the establishment of a republic, meant that the Mashrutih state order was therefore subject to a significant rupture in both theory and practice by the end of August, 1953.

Rather than attempt a restoration of a political system which consigned the role of the monarch to heeding the constitutionally-mandated checks and balances, the Shah chose instead to increasingly assert his role into the political sphere. By doing so, he effectively resolved the underlying ambiguities regarding his role in the state framework to his advantage, progressively reducing the influence of figures who, like Musaddiq and Qavam in the past, were pressing him to engage in *saltanat*, or ceremonial reigning, rather than *hukumat*, or active governance.

The Shah asserted himself through a variety of processes. He adopted a discourse which was grounded on emphasising his paternal and indispensable role in relieving the country of political and ideological stagnation and assorted ailments, such as foreign meddling and domination. While maintaining a semblance of diversity through the creation of loyal parties, which eventually moulded into the Iran Nuvin-Mardum dual system and holding regular parliamentary elections, except for a hiatus in the early 1960s, the Shah presided over a state system in which the role and function of the other state institutions were effectively shrunken into irrelevance. In 1972, a CIA report on the structure and features of contemporary political power in Iran noted that the Shah saw himself at the centre of all political activity and specified: 'Although he frequently insists on the possibility of a true constitutional monarchy in Iran, his actions suggest that he does not foresee it in his time.'[5] One of the key deviations from the spirit of Mashrutih came in the form of the subjugation of the prime ministerial position to the royal court, a process which the Shah embarked upon after his return from the brief exile of 1953 and culminated with the long tenure of Amir Abbas Hoveyda (1965–77).

By the early Seventies, the Shah had gone through a decade in which he launched the deployment of an ambitious economic development plan, the White Revolution, which he couched in terms of the 'Revolution of the Shah and the People', performed a belated self-coronation in 1967 and organised the celebrations for the 2500th anniversary of the monarchy five years later. The latter two celebrations marked instances in which the Shah chose to buttress his role by assigning to himself an almost messianic mission, a circumstance which, as aptly noted by Rahnema, was brought about by the Shah's increasing belief in his predestination as a chosen leader by God, in the aftermath of events such as a miraculous cure from a severe childhood disease and the lack of success of various assassination attempts between the 1940s and 1960s.[6] Such a strand of thought is vividly encapsulated in the Shah's own writings and declarations and are also amply reflected in the courtier Asadullah Alam's celebrated personal diaries. In the entry for 16 February, 1971 he notes for example how the Shah told him, during a 'strange conversation', how he felt almost invincible (due to the rise in the price of oil), the extensive rainfall which had brought relief across the country and, above all, the vanquishing of regional adversaries, including regional opponents such as Nasser and the neutralisation of domestic opposition, due to the lack of figures such as Musaddiq or Qavam and Khomeini's exile.[7]

5 CIA Report, 'Centers of Power in Iran', 1972, (available online: http://2001–2009.state.gov/documents/organization/70712.pdf).

6 See in this regard: Rahnema, A., *Superstition as Ideology in Iranian Politics,* Cambridge, 2013, pp.122–125.

7 Alam, A., Yaddashtha-yi Alam, vol. 2, Tehran, 2008, pp.200–201.

Mashrutih: An Unfinished Revolution

Despite the hubris with which he conducted state affairs from the mid-sixties onwards, the Shah insisted on frequently bringing to the fore his interpretation of democracy and often equated it with the Mashrutih ideals. This was already apparent in *Mission for my Country,* the monograph through which he sought to instil the image of benign fatherly figure who was seeking the common good for his people. The Shah begins a lengthy analysis of the Constitutional Revolution with the following passage:

> While at the time of the revolution most of the people of Persia had little if any conception of the meaning of representative government, they were desirous of a change from the tired Qajar dynasty and clamoured for something new. The common people realized that the Qajars of that period were largely devoid of any feeling of moral responsibility for the Persian people or for the welfare of the country, which had been reduced to the status of a puppet of foreign powers, and especially of Russia. Many ordinary people had become the victims of arbitrariness and excess, and they welcomed the revolution of 1906 because it placed a check upon the autocracy of the Qajars.
>
> However, the leaders of our revolution, who were mostly educated men, had broader reasons for backing the revolt. They wanted to liberalize and Westernize our political system. They knew that only in this way could Persia maintain her independence and prosper economically and socially. Most of the Persian revolutionists believed that political Westernization could be harmonized with the principles of Islam. For instance, one of the greatest contributors to our revolution was Sayid Jamal Al-Din Assadabadi, a staunch pan-Islamist. He stressed the possibility of infusing the liberal, democratic, and nationalist concepts of the West into the philosophical framework of Islam without compromising such basic ideas of our religion as the unity of church and state. Some of the greatest pioneers among the constitutionalists were progressive Persian clergymen such as Sayid Behbehani and Sayid Tabatabai, who denounced tyranny from the pulpit.[8]

He then touched upon the factors which in his view led to the setbacks for the Mashrutih movement:

> 'I have already spoken of the unsuccessful Russian-supported attempts of

---

8 Pahlavi, M. R., *Mission for my Country*, New York, 1961, p.165.

> Mohammed Ali Shah, Muzaffar al-Din's son, to destroy the Constitution. Some of the ultra-conservative clergymen continued to oppose our democratic reforms, and the constitutionalists themselves split into quarrelling factions. Worst of all was the incompetence, slothfulness, extravagance, and lack of dedication of the Qajar rulers themselves, and their subservience to foreign influence.'[9]

Such themes were reprised in the following years, as shall be seen below, by the Shah's most trusted statesmen. In his message to the nation on the occasion of the annual Mashrutih Day of 14 Mordad, 1344/5 (August 1965), an occasion which the royal court never failed to celebrate, Muhammad Riza Pahlavi stated that the spirit of the Mashrutih principles introduced six decades prior were 'not enough' to bring about a full implementation of democracy, and that the achievement of 'social justice', which at that time he saw as having being brought forward by the White Revolution, was the necessary finishing step in the process: 'Mashrutiyat is only implemented when all people not just a small minority, can avail of it'.[10] In comments made on the occasion of the annual Constitutional Revolution celebrations in August 1971, the *Ittila'at* daily, whose editorials were usually an extension of the royal court's thinking on such matters, expanded further:

> 'The Constitutional Revolution provided the Iranian nation with the benefits [*mavaheb*] of freedom and a human identity, but it was not one which led the nation down the path of deep social and economic development. The social revolution of Iran [The White Revolution] delivered a final blow to the remnants of the period of despotism and feudalism, and completed the Constitution through yet another appendix. The first one [of 1906] provided political rights to Iran, while the newer one, the legacy of the 6th Bahman Revolution, effectively plays the role of guarantor of the social rights of this nation.'[11]

The Shah was therefore adopting Mashrutih as an ideal setting which was to be achieved through the implementation of social justice. Given his role at the helm of the latter process, the Shah implicitly cast himself as the sole figure capable of

9 Pahlavi, Mission for my Country, p.166.

10 Pahlavi, M. R., *Majmuah-yi Talifat, Nutq-ha, Payam-ha, Musahibih-ha va Bayanat-i Alahazat-i Humayun-i Muhammad Riza Shah Pahlavi*, Tehran, 1977, p.3904.

11 *Ittila'at,* 14 Murdad, 1350 [5 August, 1971].

bringing the Mashrutih ideals to fruition. In order to bring rhetorical support for such a mission, the Pahlavi state sought, not without logical acrobatics, to redress its reading of the Constitutional Revolution.

Another main pillar on which the Shah's vision of Mashrutih was based concerned his increasingly independent stance in foreign policy, a notion which is present in the demands of the political activists of the Constitutional Revolution era. By the mid-1960s, Muhammad Riza Pahlavi had become increasingly assertive in his attempts to distance the country from the two 'classic' foes, Great Britain and Russia/USSR. The Mashrutih ideals and objectives of relief from the tight grip of the two empires was to a great extent a theme that the Shah reprised in the 1960s, as he sought to lessen the real or imagined influence of both London and Moscow in Iran.

The Shah's casting of Mashrutih as an objective which had to be both achieved and nourished paved the way for the Constitutional Revolution to be remembered and revered, both within the political elite and the mainstream media. Throughout the late 1970s, the prominent newspaper *Ettelaat*, which always remained, at times in a docile way, within the shadow of officialdom, published a lengthy and popular supplement on modern Iranian and world history, which eventually came to be collected and known as *28000 Ruz-e Tarikh-e Iran va Jahan (28000 Days in the History of Iran and the World)*. It depicted Mashrutih as a struggle of virtue against tyranny, selectively focusing on themes such as: national independence, the connivance of Muhammad Ali Shah with the Russians to repeal the initial achievements of the Constitutional Revolution, slogans such as 'Ya Marg Ya Esteghlal' (Either Death or Independence), and less on themes intrinsic to political development, the rule of law, or social democracy.[12] The *Rastakhiz* newspaper, which was launched shortly after the party was founded, also engaged in an extensive special series dedicated to Mashrutih and provided, on almost every anniversary, a thorough descriptive narrative of events. While refraining from focusing on fringe elements, social democratic movements, or the conspiratorial activities of the *faramushkhaneh*, the daily chose to concentrate on politically safer themes, such as emphasis on the roots of the revolt, which it summarised in 2536 (1977) as being 'pressure of *zulm* (injustice) and *zur* (heavy-handedness), the dark shadow of despotism, poverty, hunger, deep class divides, the limitless colonial pretensions of Russia and England – all these factors contributed to the awakening of the people.'[13]

---

12 See in particular: 28000 Ruz dar Tarikh-i Iran va Jahan, Tehran, 1976.

13 *Rastakhiz,* 14 Murdad, 2536 [5 August, 1977].

The link between the White Revolution and the Constitutional Revolution also comes to the forefront in the second volume of Pahlavism, a set which is considered to be the foundation stone for the official state ideology of the late Pahlavi period.[14] Its author, Manuchihr Hunarmand, casts the whole of the millenarian monarchical era as one distinguished by a Mashrutih monarchical rule, and compares the political system in place at the time of the book's publication to the one of antiquity, and notes:

> 'After the Constitutional Revolution, a government conditional upon ethical principles and strong and certain human rights preferred by the lawmakers and its founders, was not established. The main reason for this was the existence of feudal overlords, who were not allowing genuine elections to take place. Secondly, they were approving laws solely to the benefit of their own social class. This condition placed the peasant and worker class under great injustice.
>
> The Shah, from the start of White Revolution, and the execution of the land reform law, removed this great obstacle from the execution of true Mashrutih. And by granting the right of vote to women, he ensured that half of the citizens of this country would exit subaltern status and achieve legal rights and therefore established an effective legal and social equivalence between men and women.'[15]

The Pahlavist ideology therefore decisively shifted the effective fulcrum of the Mashrutih ideals from the concept of the rule of law to that of societal participation within the economic and political frameworks within the bosom of the paternal monarchical supervision. This view was reinforced after the formation of the Rastakhiz Party.

The Rastakhiz Party: The Intended Missing Link between the White Revolution and Mashrutih

In early March 1975, the Shah surprised the political scene by suddenly announcing the formation of a single party, the Rastakhiz-e Mellat (Resurgence of the

---

14 See: Shakibi,Z., 'Pahlavīsm: The Ideologization of Monarchy in Iran', Politics, Religion and Ideology, vol.13, no.1, 2013, DOI: 10.1080/21567689.2012.751911, pp.114–135, and Ansari, A., Nationalism, pp.169–172 for studies of the political significance of this set.

15 Hunarmand, M., Shahanshahi-ye Mashrutih-ye Dow Hezar va Pansad Saleh-ye Iran, Tehran, 1968, p.121.

Nation), which was to incorporate the previous two inner-regime ones: Mardum and Iran-i Nuvin.[16] The development had the effect of ushering in a new era for the post-Mashrutih state. Overnight, Iran entered into the peculiar realm of the single-party monarchies, a distinction it shared with virtually no other contemporary state system.

The creation of Rastakhiz, which the Shah envisaged as the single clearing house for politically-minded and active Iranians of all persuasions, was justified by the Shah as a necessary step towards the fulfilment of the Mashrutih ideals during a press conference on 2 March, 1975 when he delivered a brief overview of the 'principles of Mashrutiyat', before focusing on the realisation that 'playing the role of a loyal minority' is very 'arduous' in Iran, and is effectively a role which is 'not possible to play'.[17] He then urged all Iranians loyal to the 'Constitution, the Monarchical system of Iran and the 6th Bahman Revolution' to join forces and enter the new party and termed the same as a natural step in the coming together of these disparate processes and, crucially, for the fulfilment of the principles of *mashrutiyat*. One of the early Rastakhiz theoreticians, Daryush Humayun, expanded further on the rationale for its creation by noting that how

> 'A loyal opposition party in Iran has an unrealistic role in Iran. [...] All political organisations need to be grouped under the ruling party. [...] Those [within society] opposed [to Rastakhiz] have to be either in jail or abroad.'[18]

Humayun, who was effectively tasked with devising the first elements of the ideological bedrock of the nascent party, expanded on the bonds between the White Revolution and Mashrutih further:

> 'There is no historical precedent in Iran for such a public movement. We have experienced revolutions which have drawn a strong societal backing, but we never had a political party imbued with the participation of the majority of the men and women of this country.'[19]

16 See Afkhami, G. R., *The Life and Times of the Shah,* Berkeley, 2007, pp.430–435, for a brief and cogent explanation of the creation of the Rastakhiz Party.

17 Pahlavi, M. R., Majmuah-yi Talifat, p. 7847.

18 *Ayandigan*, 12 Isfand, 1353 [3 March 1975].

19 *Ayandigan,* 15 Isfand, 1353 [6 March 1975].

He also attempted to carve out of a role for the constitution, which had not been subject to modification as a consequence of the creation of Rastakhiz:

> 'The Constitution, which is the legacy of the Constitutional Revolution – the first socio-political revolution of Iran, which is also the oldest document of its kind in Asia and Africa, still maintains, after 70 years, the capacity to bring together all the disparate political forces within Iranian society. [...] The essence [*manshur*] of the 6 Bahman Revolution, which completed the Constitutional Revolution and removed the last fundamental obstacle from the development of Iranian society, is a programme for a practical revolution'.[20]

The Rastakhiz Party was therefore seen, by the Shah and his associates, as the necessary step for the forging of a strong *trait d'union* between pre and post-Pahlavi Iran, between the admirable portions of the Qajar era's legacy, such as the enlightened vizier Amir Kabir, the Tobacco Rebellion of 1891, and Mashrutih itself on the one hand, and the rapid and ambitious developments of the latter part of Muhammad Riza Pahlavi's rule, which culminated in the White Revolution and his paternal and all-encompassing vision for the monarchy on the other. In order to reach this aim, the distinction between the discredited Qajar dynasty and the constitutional revolutionaries was effected in a more elaborate way. On the one hand, popular heroes such as Sattar Khan and Baqir Khan were anointed as exemplary figures, with their military initiatives to rescue the early Mashrutih movement linked, with thinly veiled references and verbiage, to the similarly 'salutary' march of Riza Khan on Tehran.[21] The party organ chose to deliver a clear but limited narrative of the driving forces behind the constitutional drive, choosing to focus upon the role and agency of Ayatollah Tabatabai and Sayyid Abdullah Bihbahani, who are presented in no uncertain terms as 'the great clerics who laid the foundation stones of Mashrutih'.[22] This interpretation, which effectively omits the role of secret societies, social democratic organisations of Caucasian inspiration, and religious sects, is centred on the two clerics' quest for the rule of law as a bulwark against the excesses of Qajar monarchs, and can be related to the Pahlavi state's policies with regards to the political successors of each of the various groups which collectively took part in the Revolution. In the last but typical example

20 *Ayandigan,* 15 Isfand, 1353 [6 March, 1975].

21 See for example: the first *Rastakhiz* special insert on the Constitutional Revolution, which appeared on 5 August, 1975.

22 *Rastakhiz,* 11 Murdad, 2536 [2 August, 1977].

of the extensive yearly special reports on Mashrutih to appear on *Rastakhiz,* the official daily of the party, a junior historian who would gain prominence in the post-1979 period, Khusraw Mutazid, would amply decry the lasciviousness of the Qajar dynasty, highlighting the extensive expenses of Nasir al-Din Shah's famous travels to Europe. He then focuses on Muzaffar al-Din Shah, who is depicted as a 'superstitious simpleton' who thought that such trips, which included the purchase of toys and other frivolities, were an 'essential element' of his monarchy.[23] As late as the summer of 1978, when the fervour against the Shah was moving towards its apex, the Party still therefore felt the need to buttress the Pahlavi dynasty through a selective reading of the roots of Mashrutih and the inadequacy of the Qajar monarchs, and the implication of a more salubrious relationship between the West and Muhammad Riza Shah.

Besides driving a wedge between the two dynasties of twentieth-century Iran, the Rastakhiz era discourse sought to augment the aforementioned bonds between the Constitutional Revolution and the developments of the latter half of the century. In the words of Abdollah Riazi, the late-Pahlavi grandee who served as cabinet minister, long-time parliamentary speaker and head of the University of Tehran, the latter processes brought about the 'emancipation' of the lower tiers of Iranian society:

> 'The White Revolution was the completing element of Mashrutih. This revolution, on 6 Bahman 1341, was precisely along the lines of the requests and aspirations of the fighters and the senior clerics of the Constitutional Revolution.'[24]

A common thread in this discourse was the identification of land reform with political development, the former being praised due to its role in decreasing the influence and role of major landowners in the electoral process. According to Riazi's comments on the occasion of the Mashrutih anniversary in 1976, the then-present legislature – the last one prior to the Revolution of 1979 – included 70 teachers, 40 simple peasants, 16 workers, and 20 women and therefore created an institutional setting which vindicated the claim that *mashrutiyat* was brought to completion by the creation of the Rastakhiz party.

A more elaborate account of the bonds between the Mashrutih and the purported achievements of the late Pahlavi era was provided during the same period by

23 *Rastakhiz,* 11 Murdad, 2537 [2 August, 1978].

24 Riazi comments in Rastakhiz special dossier on Mashrutih, 14 Mordad, 2535 [5 August, 1976].

Mahmoud Sajjadi, who became Senate speaker in the waning years of the Pahlavi dynasty. While praising Amir Kabir as a patriot who would have hastened the arrival of Mashrutih had he been allowed to govern longer, Behbahani was once again eulogised as a martyr in the *rah-e mashruteh*, or pathway towards Mashrutih. Sajjadi then praised Riza Shah as being the harbinger of the 'first real phase' of Mashrutih, for it was during his reign that the Parliament actively approved laws which led to the 'rapid progress' of the country and added:

> Everyone who is interested in democratic principles knows how in the bosom of this revolution, *mashrutiyat* succeeded in putting forward fundamental steps in towards attaining such principles. We are all aware of the essence of the Revolution and are aware of how, with the granting of freedom to peasants, a large segment of the population succeeded, without any political or financial interference by the big landowners, in electing their own representatives, and today, the National Parliament is the locus for the authentic representatives of workers and peasants, and ultimately women, who are themselves half of the national population. Mashrutiyat has finally assumed its real essence, every Iranian individual can today represent, and be represented, whether he is a worker, a peasant, a teacher, or of any other social and professional extraction.[25]

Conclusion

This article has sought to provide examples of how the official discourse in the late Pahlavi era sought to benefit from the legacy of the Constitutional Revolution, an event which occurred outside the time of Pahlavi rule but which maintained a lasting, albeit redressed, effect during the reigns of Riza and Muhammad Riza Shah. By the end of the 1970s, the various stages in the development of the Shah's worldview had brought about an important role for Mashrutih, that of featuring as a significant element in the ideological construct of the Pahlavi state. The high societal esteem for Mashrutih, the rich array of revered heroes as well as the lack of a direct involvement by the Pahlavi monarchs, meant that Mashrutih could be utilised, through the selective adaption of some its themes and objectives and part of its characters, as a legitimising factor in the Shah's attempt to shape the state system through his own, highly individualised trajectory. By providing a connection between the White Revolution and Mashrutih, and treating the former

25 Rastakhiz, 14 Mordad, 2535 [5 August, 1976].

as a corrective and completing step for the latter, the Shah, however, effectively reduced the Mashrutih legacy to a supporting act of his regime, a circumstance which eventually led to the identification of the Mashrutih framework with the late Pahlavi state, so much so that the lasting public holiday of 14 Murdad was discontinued in August 1979, thereby handing over the annual remembrance to the realm of occasionally sympathetic but sporadic messages by statesmen and media coverage. Subsumed as it was by the Pahlavi regime, there was little that the few, meek voices which pressed for the continuation of Mashrutih until early 1979 could do to preserve the central legacy and praxis of the Constitutional Revolution, which came to an end as the other major societal upheaval of twentieth-century Iran brought about the Islamic Republic.

Bibliography

28000 Ruz dar Tarikh-i Iran va Jahan, Tehran, 1976.

Afkhami, G. R., *The Life and Times of the Shah,* Berkeley, 2007.

Alam, A., Yaddashtha-yi Alam, vol. 2, Tehran, 2008.

Ansari, A. The Politics of Nationalism in Iran, Cambridge, 2014.

Ayandigan daily, Tehran, 1975.

CIA Report, 'Centers of Power in Iran', 1972, (available online: http://2001–2009.state.gov/documents/organization/70712.pdf).

Hairi, A., *Shiism and Constitutionalism in Iran*, Leiden, 1977.

Hunarmand, M., Shahanshahi-ye Mashrutih-ye Dow Hezar va Pansad Saleh-ye Iran, Tehran, 1968.

Katouzian, H., 'The Revolution for Law: A Chronographic Analysis of the Constitutional Revolution of Iran', in *Middle Eastern Studies* vol. 47, no. 5, 2011, DOI: 10.1080/00263206.2011.588797, pp.757–77.

Pahlavi, M. R., Mission for my Country, New York, 1961.

Pahlavi, M. R., *Majmuah-yi Talifat, Nutq-ha, Payam-ha, Musahibih-ha va Bayanat-i Alahazat-i Humayun-i Muhammad Riza Shah Pahlavi*, Tehran, 1977.

Rahimi, M., *Qanun-i Asasi-yi Iran va Usul-i Dimukrasi*, Tehran, 1978.

Rahnema, A., *Superstition as Ideology in Iranian Politics,* Cambridge, 2013.

Rastakhiz daily, Tehran, 1975–78.

Shakibi,Z., 'Pahlavīsm: The Ideologization of Monarchy in Iran', Politics, Religion and Ideology, vol.13, no.1, 2013, DOI: 10.1080/21567689.2012.751911, pp.114–135.

Contributors

Ali M Ansari is Professor of Iranian History & Founding Director of the Institute for Iranian Studies at the University of St Andrews. He is Senior Associate Fellow, Royal United Services Institute and currently serves as President of the British Institute of Persian Studies. He was elected a Fellow of the Royal Society of Edinburgh in 2016. Among his publications are: *Iran: A Very Short Introduction* (OUP, 2014) and *The Politics of Nationalism in Modern Iran* (CUP, 2012). A third updated edition of his *Iran, Islam & Democracy – The Politics of Managing Change*, will be published by Gingko in 2017.

Ali Gheissari is professor of history at the University of San Diego and has research interest in the intellectual history of modern Iran. He studied law and political science at Tehran University and history with concentration on Iranian Studies at St. Antony's College, Oxford. He has written extensively in both Persian and English on modern Iranian history and on modern philosophy and social theory. His books include *Contemporary Iran: Economy, Society, Politics* (ed., Oxford University Press, 2009); *Tabriz and Rasht in the Iranian Constitutional Revolution* (ed., Tehran, 2008); *Democracy in Iran: History and the Quest for Liberty* (co-author, Oxford University Press, 2006, 2009); *Iranian Intellectuals in the Twentieth Century* (University of Texas Press, 1998, 2008); Persian translation of Immanuel Kant's *Groundwork of the Metaphysic of Ethics* (with Hamid Enayat, Tehran, 1991, 2015); Manfred Frings *et al*, *Max Scheler and Phenomenology* (tr., Tehran, 2015). Dr. Gheissari serves on the Editorial Board of Iran Studies book series published by Brill (Leiden) and is also the Editor-in-Chief of the journal *Iranian Studies*.

Elahe Helbig graduated from the University of Bonn in 2008 with a major in Media Studies, focusing on aesthetic communication, and minors in Art History and Iranian Studies. Between 2006 and 2012, she was curator and associated researcher for various exhibition projects in museums and exhibition halls in Germany. For her work on nineteenth-century Iranian photography Elahe had been awarded several fellowships, amongst them for extensive research at the Photo Archive of the Golestan Palace in Tehran, at the Freer Gallery of Art and the Arthur M. Sackler Gallery in Washington DC, at the Middle Eastern Centre Archive in Oxford, and at the Kunsthistorische Institut in Florenz – Max-Planck-Institut. Currently, she is working as an academic assistant at the University of Geneva.

Kamran Matin is a senior lecturer in International Relations at Sussex University, UK. His research focuses on international historical sociology, state-formation, nationalism, Marxism, and postcolonial critique with special reference to the Middle East. He is the author of *Recasting Iranian Modernity: International Relations and Social Change* (London: Rutledge, 2013) and coeditor of *Historical Sociology and World History: Uneven and Combined Development over the Longue Durée* (Lanham: Rowman & Littlefield, 2016). He is the co-convener of Historical Sociology in International Relations (HSIR) working group of British International Studies Association (BISA), and management committee member of Centre for Advanced International Theory (CAIT).

Milad Odabaei is a PhD Candidate in the Department of Anthropology and the Program in Critical Theory at University of California, Berkeley. His dissertation, 'Giving Words: Translation, History, and the Modern Iran', offers an anthropological and ethnographic investigation of practices of reading, translation, and history-writing in modern Iran.

Pejman Abdolmohammadi is Resident Visiting Research Fellow at the London School of Economics – Middle East Centre and Assistant Professor in Middle Eastern Studies at the University of Genoa. He also teaches History and Politics of the Middle East at John Cabot University in Rome. His research and teaching activities focus on the politics and history of modern Iran, the intellectual history of Iran, geopolitics of the Persian Gulf, and international relations of the Middle East. His newest book *Modern Iran: Between Domestic Affairs and International Relations* was published by Mondadori, Italy's leading publisher, in October 2015.

Salour Evaz Malayeri graduated with an MA in Persian literature and language from Azad University of Tehran in 2011. He did his thesis on the relationship between Ideology and Literature in Persian Medieval poetry through analysing the odes of Nasir-e Khusraw and Sa'edi's first chapter of *Boustan*, which earned him a first-class grade. He has attended numerous series of masterclasses about modern literary theory and criticism in Tehran and published a number of essays on cultural production in Iran, as well as film and book reviews in Iranian journals.

Salour's PhD thesis focuses on Persian classical Literature between the eleventh and thirteenth centuries. By analysing texts from different discursive contexts, his research shows how literary texts as a reflection of social life and power relations, represents different forms of cultural resistance. This article is part of his post-doctoral research which is about the birth of Persian literature as a discourse in contemporary Iran.

Dr. Urs Goesken studied Near Eastern Science and Greek and Latin Literature and Philology at the University of Zurich and is currently assistent professor for Iranian Studies at the University of Bern/Switzerland. He graduated with the paper 'Kritik der westlichen Philosophie in Iran: Zum geistesgeschichtlichen Selbstverständnis von Muhammad Husayn Tabâtabâ'î und Murtazâ Mutahharî' (Munich 2014). His present research focus is on twentieth/twenty-first century Iranian intellectual history, Islamic philosophy and hermeneutic approaches of modern Qur'ân exegesis.

Evan Siegel is a life-long student of Iranian history. For more information, please visit his site at http://iran.qlineorientalist.com/.

Roman Seidel is a postdoctoral fellow at the Berlin Graduate School Muslim Cultures and Societies, Freie Universität Berlin. His primary research interest is the study of contemporary philosophy in the Middle East. He earned a PhD in Islamic Studies in 2011 from the University of Zurich, where he was Lecturer for Islamic Studies focussing on Persian and Modern Iran at the Institute for Asian and Oriental Studies from 2011 to 2014. He is involved in the Ueberweg-History of Philosophy project (Philosophy in the Islamic World, nineteenth- and twentieth- century) and serves on the editorial board of the *Philosophie in der nahöstlichen Moderne / Philosophy in the Modern Middle East* book series published by Klaus-Schwarz Verlag (Berlin) and on the advisory board of the *World Philosophies* book series published by Mimesis International. His doctoral dissertation, *Kant in Teheran: Anfänge, Ansätze und Kontexte der Kantrezeption in Iran*, was published by De Gruyter (Berlin) in 2014.

Siavush Randjbar-Daemi is Lecturer in Iranian History at the School of Arts, Languages and Cultures, University of Manchester. His main research interests are the evolution of the state structures, state-society relations and political parties in modern and contemporary Iran. He is currently working on the early Islamic Republic period, as well as the last decade of Pahlavi rule.

Index

A

ʿAbd al-Raḥīm Ṭalibūf *see* Mirzā ʿAbd al-Rahim Tālebof Tabrizi
Abdulhosein Azerang 103
Abu al-Qāsem Nāser al-Molk 23fn15
Afżal al-Mulk Kirmānī 209–11
Aḥmad Fardīd 155–7, 161
Aḥmad Kasravī 7fn17, 55–6, 65, 172, 192
Aḥmad Shah 53
al-Afghāni, *see* Sayyed Jamāl al-Din
ʿAlī Forūghī 219
ʿAlī Monsieur 173–180, 182–3, 189–96
Amir Kabir 88, 109, 120, 233, 235
Āqā ʿAlī Mudarris Ṭihrānī az-Zunūzī 206
Ayatollah Khorāsāni 35,112
Āyatollāh Sayyed Mohammad Tabātabāʾi 23fn15
Ayn al-Saltaneh 99, 103

B

Babi faith 118–19, 120–2
Bahāʾi 24
Baku 27, 28, 31–3, 173, 177, 193, 194
Bāqer Khan 63–5
bast 60–2, 66–7

C

College of Dār al-Fonūn, College of 54, 216
Corbin, Henry 155–7, 161, 164, 166
Critika 133–4, 140–3
Cyrus the Great 118, 120–1, 127fn21

D

Dāryūš Šāyigān 156

E

Estepān Estepāniān 64–5

F

Foucault, Michel 16, 100–2, 108
Freemasonry 4, 7–8, 18, 21fn10, 171

G

Ǧalāl Āl-i Aḥmad 156
Ganjīnayi Funūn 172, 176–8, 180
Gulistan, Treaty of 88, 119

H

Ḥājī ʿAlī Davāfurush 173, 176, 179, 189
Ḥājī Mīrzā Naṣr-Allāh Eṣfahāni *see* Malek- al-Motakallemīn
Ḥājī Rasūl Sidqīyānī 173, 176, 180

Ḥājī Zayn al-ʿĀbidīn Marāghaʾī *see* Hājj Zain al-ʿĀbedin Marāghaʾi
Hājj Zain al-ʿĀbedin Marāghaʾi 27, 172
Hegel, G. W. F. 17, 77, 135fn8, 136, 138, 144–5, 207
Hegelism *see* Hegel

I
Iʿtimād-al-Salṭana 214

J
Jamaleddin Afghani *see* Sayyed Jamāl al-Din
Javad Tabatabaei 109, 112fn27

K
Kant, Immanuel 16, 77, 209, 215–6
Kantian, *see* Kant
Karbalāʾī ʿAlī *see* ʿAlī Monsieur
Karīm Ṭāhirzāda-Bihzād 174, 177, 178fn44, 179, 180–2, 183–5, 193–7

M
Malek- al-Motakallemīn 67
Marx, Karl 10, 16, 31, 76, 78–80, 83, 93, 152
Marxism *see* Marx
Māshāllāh Khan 57
Mashhadī Yūsuf Khazdūz 194–5
Mashrutih ideals 228–32
Masons *see* Freemason
Mirzā ʿAbbās Nuri 24
Mirzā ʿAbd al-Rahim Tālebof Tabrizi 32, 157, 166, 172, 203
Mirza Abdolhossein Bardsiri *see* Mirzā Aqā Khān Kermāni
Mirzā Aqā Khān Kermāni 24, 32, ch. 5, 132, 141, 144, 150–1, 202fn3, 203, 210, 211, 217
Mirza Fathali Akhundzadeh 119–21, 124–27
Mirzā Fath-ʿAli Ākhundzādeh 11, 119, 120–1, 124–5, 127, ch 6, 134, 142–3, 151, 203–4, 211–3
Mirza Fathali Akhundzadeh *see* Mirzā Fath-ʿAli Ākhundzādeh
Mirzā Hasan Shirazi 34, 98, 104–5
Mīrzā Jahāngīr Khan 67
Mīrzā Maḥmūd Khān Afšār Kangāvarī 215
Mirzā Malkam Khān 24–5, 32, 132, 140, 144
Mirza Saleh Shirazi 104–8, 110
Mirzā Yusof Khān Mostashār al-Dowleh 32, 25
Mirza, Abbas 88, 109
Moʾayyed al-Islam Kāshāni 18
Moḥammad Ali Mīrzā 53, 69, 117, 120
Moḥammad- Walī Khan 55
Mohammad-Hosayn Nāʾini 35–6, 112
Mohammad-Kāzem Khorāsāni 35, 112
Moʿir-al-Mamālek 55, 66
Mojāhedīn (revolutionary militia) 54, 56, 63–5
Montesquieu 119, 122–3
Mozaffar al-Din Shah 37, 60, 92
Muḥammad ʿAlī Furūġī 152
Muḥammad ʿAlī Tarbīyyat 176, 180
Muḥammad Ḥusayn Ṭabāṭabāʾī 151–3, 166
Muhammad Riza Pahlavi 224–5, 229–30, 233

Mulla Ahmad Naraqi 91
Mullā Ṣadrā 151–2, 155, 165, 260fn10
Murtażā Muṭahharī 151–2, 166

N
Naghmeh Sohrabi 103
Naīeb Hossein-e Kāshī 57
Nāser al-Din Shah 34–5, 89, 103, 120, 171, 208, 210, 213, 234
Nāṣir ad-Dīn Shah, *see* Nāser al-Din Shah
Naus, Joseph 67
Nāzem al-Dowleh, *see* Mirzā Malkam Khān

P
Poesy 138, 143, 145

Q
Qajar dynasty, the 17, 31, 53, 58–9, 67, 79, 86–9, 92–4, 103, 104, 107, 118, 120, 130, 140, 144, 200–1, 203, 205, 213, 225, 228, 233–4
Qajar Pact, the 35
Qara Chaman affair, the 187–8

R
Rasht 31–2, 117, 179, 188
Rastakhiz party, the 224–5, 231–5
Renan, Ernest 52, 142
Reza Shah Pahlavi 127
Rižā Dāvarī Ardakānī 156
Rousseau, Jean-Jacques 17, 122–3, 202, 204, 217
Russia 108–9, 119, 141, 144

S
Ṣadr al-Dīn Šīrāzī 155
Said, Edward 2, 3, 77, 101fn6,
Satār Khan *see* Sattār Khan
Sattār Khan 63–5, 69, 177, 181, 191, 233
Sayyed Jamāl al-Din 1, 2, 4, 8–9, 18–19, 24, 28, 37, 121–2, 125, 203
Sayyid Ḥasan Sharīfzāda 176, 180
Sayyid Ḥasan Taqīzāda 172, 175–6, 176fn33, 177, 180–1, 183, 196
Sayyid Muḥammad Ṭabaṭabā'ī 171–2, 228
Secret Center ch. 8
Seqat al-Islam Tabrīzi 70
Seyyed Ali Mohammad Bab 118
Shaykh Ahmad Ruhi 24, 210
Shaykh Fazlollāh Nuri 35, 90–1, 111–2
Shiʿa/Shiʿi 15, 19–20, 22, 24, 30–1, 33, 35–6, 39, 55, 79, 107, 112fn27, 117, 120, 151, 175
Shiʿism, *see* Shiʿa/Shiʿi
Shiʿite, *see* Shiʿa/Shiʿi
Shuturbān 190–3
Šihāb al-Dīn Suhrawardī 155, 165
Sunni/Sunniism 30

T
Tabriz resistance 55, 60, 62–65, 69, 70
Tabriz 7, 11, 31, 32, 33, 35, 55, 60, 62, 63, 64, 65, 66, 69, 70, 100, 105, 109, 117, 120, ch 8
Taqī Arānī 152
Tbilisi 28, 31, 141, 144, 211
Tehran 8, 23fn15, 55, 60, 62–5, 69, 70, 92–3, 108–9, 111, 117, 143, 206, 208, 213, 226, 233–4
Tobacco Protests 1, 26, 34, 92, 233
Treaty of Gulestan 108

Trotsky, Leon 83–4, 85, 86, 87
Turkmenchay Treaty 108

Y
Yahyā Dowlatābādi 54

Z
Ẓill al-Sulṭān 215